IRIS: I remember when Dad died we stayed up all night. About one in the morning Mum made some scones. Crazy the things you do –

TED: Like singing round a coffin?

IRIS: Hang around Ted – that's just the start.

—*Wednesday To Come*

Renée

THESE TWO HANDS
new edition

m

First published in 2017
This edition published 2020

Cover design by Mary McCallum
Typesetting and book design by Paul Stewart
Edited by Mary McCallum
Editorial assistance: Sucheta Raj (2017 edition) and
Madison Hamill (2020 edition)

Cover image © Doug Lilly
Back flap image © John Miller
Back cover image: *She Counts Kāhu – Tahi* © Penny Howard
Penny exhibits at **www.whitespace.co.nz**

This book is copyright apart from any fair dealing as
permitted under the Copyright Act, and no part may
be reproduced without permission from the publisher.

© Renée 2017, 2020

ISBN 978-0-9951110-4-2

A catalogue record for this book is available from
the National Library of New Zealand.
Kei te pātengi raraunga o Te Puna Mātauranga o Aotearoa
te whakarārangi o tēnei pukapuka.

Printed in Aotearoa New Zealand by Ligare, Auckland

Published with the assistance of Creative New Zealand

ARTS COUNCIL OF NEW ZEALAND TOI AOTEAROA

m

MĀKARO PRESS
PO BOX 9321, WELLINGTON, AOTEAROA NEW ZEALAND
WWW.MAKAROPRESS.CO.NZ

CONTENTS

PATCH 1 • I was born in Napier, 1929 — 11

PATCH 2 • The dance (poem) — 21

PATCH 3 • When my oldest son, Chris — 22

PATCH 4 • From *Pass It On* (play) — 25

PATCH 5 • Drama as a meant-and-planned activity — 30

PATCH 6 • This is a letter from my uncle Mick — 37

PATCH 7 • From *Daisy and Lily* (novel) — 40

PATCH 8 • When I turned eighty — 43

PATCH 9 • From *Touch of the Sun* (play) — 49

PATCH 10 • There is a photo of me — 55

PATCH 11 • From *Wednesday To Come* (play) — 60

PATCH 12 • One day, must have been around 1942 — 62

PATCH 13 • I made a decision in 2016 — 71

PATCH 14 • Anzac Day (poem) — 78

PATCH 15 • It was in the early 1970s — 80

PATCH 16 • When I was a kid — 88

PATCH 17 • Once upon a time (poem) — 96

PATCH 18 • From *Finding Ruth* (novel) — 97

PATCH 19 • It was a yearly event — 100

PATCH 20 • I was twenty-nine — 104

PATCH 21 • From *Setting the Table* (play) — 109

PATCH 22 • Saturday, 30 May 1981 — 115

PATCH 23 •	When I applied for the Robert Burns	117
PATCH 24 •	After you walk on water (poem)	124
PATCH 25 •	Sunday, 1 January 1984	125
PATCH 26 •	My political views were formed very early	132
PATCH 27 •	Tall woman in a frame (poem)	139
PATCH 28 •	On Friday, 13 November 2015	140
PATCH 29 •	And as we gather (poem)	151
PATCH 30 •	The garden looks amazing	152
PATCH 31 •	What led me to try te reo	155
PATCH 32 •	Someone asked me a question recently	160
PATCH 33 •	Wairoa Hotel, Marine Parade	162
PATCH 34 •	Porohiwi	166
PATCH 35 •	From *Does This Make Sense To You?* (novel)	171
PATCH 36 •	Rain (poem)	174
PATCH 37 •	From *The Snowball Waltz* (novel)	176
PATCH 38 •	The first time on Waipoapoa Station	179
PATCH 39 •	Whatever gave me the idea I could write	187
PATCH 40 •	Leafy greens: a fairy tale (story)	191
PATCH 41 •	From *The Skeleton Woman* (novel)	195
PATCH 42 •	Being old. What's it like? How does it feel?	199
PATCH 43 •	From *Willy Nilly* (novel)	204
PATCH 44 •	In the early 1980s	211
PATCH 45 •	On 29 May 1988	216
PATCH 46 •	I fell in love with Dunedin	224

PATCH 47 •	In London, in 1903	231
PATCH 48 •	Late October 1988 we left for New York	234
PATCH 49 •	It's 2015, and I've been asked to write a play	244
PATCH 50 •	The year 1992 didn't start off that well	248
PATCH 51 •	From *Secrets* (play)	256
PATCH 52 •	I have always liked visiting cemeteries	258
PATCH 53 •	February 2003, and for some while after	262
PATCH 54 •	Tiger Country (poem)	265
PATCH 55 •	On 19 April 2008	266
PATCH 56 •	I must have made a million meat loaves	273
PATCH 57 •	Dowsing (poem)	279
PATCH 58 •	It has come to this	280
PATCH 59 •	Mum and the bull (poem)	285
PATCH 60 •	I went to a wonderful theatrical event	287
PATCH 61 •	When we first arrived in Dunedin	292
PATCH 62 •	From *Tiggy Tiggy Touch Wood* (play)	297
PATCH 63 •	I was told about an old pop song	308
PATCH 64 •	More from *Wednesday To Come* (play)	312
PATCH 65 •	My first weeks as the Robert Burns fellow	314
PATCH 66 •	June 2016, Orlando	318
PATCH 67 •	From *Yin & Tonic* (anthology)	321
PATCH 68 •	Old people are (poem)	324
PATCH 69 •	I haven't included much about the 1990s	327
PATCH 70 •	Old songs (poem)	333

PATCH 71 • *A House To Let* was performed	334
PATCH 72 • I first became interested in Asbestos Cottage	338
PATCH 73 • Open home (poem)	344
PATCH 74 • I'm fascinated to read the me of 2004	345
PATCH 75 • I wrote a poem to Grace Josephine	351
PATCH 76 • Red moon time (story)	354
PATCH 77 • From *Kissing Shadows* (novel)	355
PATCH 78 • I was invited to speak	360
PATCH 79 • On 11 January 1993 Bernadette got a call	365
PATCH 80 • We got into gear	369
PATCH 81 • I hadn't watched TV for a year	376
PATCH 82 • Teaching is	379
PATCH 83 • My brother died on 23 June 2016	383
PATCH 84 • Massey and Auckland universities	387
PATCH 85 • From *Jeannie Once* (play)	392
PATCH 86 • Presents (poem)	399
PATCH 87 • In February 2008 I'd arrived back home	400
PATCH 88 • I was diagnosed with macular degeneration	406
PATCH 89 • From *The Wild Card* (novel)	409
PATCH 90 • At ninety, I went into social isolation early	415
PATCH 91 • Naomi comes to cook (poem)	418
'Tonight' (poem)	420
ACKNOWLEDGEMENTS	421
INDEX	425

> *Quilt (n)*
> Thick bed-covering made of patches.
> Batt, bedspread, blanket, comforter, counterpane, cover, covelet, down, duvet, eiderdown, pad, patchwork, pouf, puff.

Purpose? To warm, to comfort, to read under or to read like a book, to shelter, to wear when there's a flood, to grab when there's an earthquake, to say this is how it was and these are the stitches that sewed opposing ends together, to marvel at, to be quiet under, to think of the hands that made it and the brain that chose some patches and the heart that chose the others.

A reminder of certain stitches, some even, some lively, some hard, a few in really neat blanket stitch, the good old 'drawing everything together' stitch and of course you can make lazy daisies, roses or little love knots. All of these seem hard at first but the more you do them the easier they get, and then after they're done you think *what on earth was I worried about.*

Some patches are small, some large, some oblong, square or round, but they all fit together. All the patches are sewn onto a backing, an old blanket, say, or a sheet, an old tablecloth, a life.

Crazy patchwork quilts were invented by women who had bundles of rags, old clothes, some cotton, a needle, a pair of scissors and nimble fingers. They weren't meant to be a work of art. They were a practical solution to an eternal problem – how to keep warm at night.

For Rose

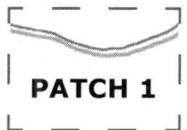

PATCH 1

I was born in Napier on Friday, 19 July 1929, and the world went into a deep depression. Then Napier fell down. Two years after that my father shot himself. He was from Gore. Drama didn't just follow me, it came out and met me with a big *tah-dah*.

There were four of us and we had four chairs. Each chair was wooden but each was different. Unless we were trying to pick a fight, no kid ever sat on another kid's chair. And no kid ever dared to sit on Rose's chair. Our mother's name was Rose. One way to make her angry was to call her Rosie. She said it made her sound like a barmaid. Once, Cliff banged his empty glass on the table and said, 'Who shot the barman, Rosie?' and had to wait a long time before his glass was filled. He never did it again. Rose's ability to hold a grudge was like an ember dropped in a green forest. It smouldered steadily until one day – *whoosh* – the whole forest went up in flames and everyone in the vicinity ran like hell.

The chairs were placed in the same positions around the oblong wooden table. Rose's was at one end, Val's and Jimmy's on each side of her and mine was down from Val's. We had meals called breakfast, dinner and tea. Dinner was what we called lunch, tea was what we later learned to call dinner. I often slip back, though, and call it tea.

Rose was a stickler for manners. You had to say please and thank you. You had to wait to start eating until she sat down and took up her knife and fork. Beside her on the table sat the breadboard and on it the bread and the bread knife, which was actually called a bread saw I found out some years later. Rose cut a slice from the bread and, balancing it on the knife, held it out to the one whose slice it was. I got the first slice because I was the oldest. She always served herself last.

Jim and Val accepted my position without question because I'd always been the boss. Ever since I was three, I'd been delegated to look after the kids. I took them to the lav, made sure they wiped themselves properly, made them wash their hands before meals, commanded them to blow their noses when they needed to. I growled and nagged – in fact I was a miniature Rose, except I didn't swear. Rose was a great swearer. 'Jesus bloody Christ,' she'd call out, 'if I have to come out to you kids, you'll be *sorry*.' Now I'm a far worse swearer than Rose. For example, she never said 'fuck', not in my hearing anyway.

Down the end of the room, we had a couch with a wooden-railed back and side and a wire-wove bottom covered with a lumpy mattress, a blanket tucked round it. Rose called it a colonial couch. That couch was hers. She sat on it, lounged on it, rested on it. She read and smoked on it every night. Sometimes we'd sneak a sit on the couch, but one look from Rose and we'd be off. She saved butts and when it was getting near pension day she'd sit on the couch, lay some paper over her knees to catch any bits she dropped, unroll the butts and make cigarettes from the remains. On pension day she'd shout herself a packet of ten Capstan tailormades along with a new tin of Melrose tobacco, a couple of packets of yellow Zig-Zag papers and a box of Beehive matches. She often twisted a piece of paper into a barley-sugar twist, shoved one end of it in the range and then lit her smoke that way.

Rose was born in Wairoa to Grace and William 'Bill' Brown. Grace was a Harmer – daughter of Charles Harmer and Puti Mary Harmer née Lewis. Puti Mary was the granddaughter of Kokotui and Porohiwi. Grace and Bill had a large family – I'm not quite sure how many children, but six or seven – then she had three to Walter 'Scottie' Martin, her second husband. There was a whisper that young Grace was Scottie's, which, if true, means the affair with Scottie began before Bill died.

Rose attended St Joseph's School in Wairoa along with her brothers and her sister, Mary. Mary was often sick (she was to die of TB) and Rose, though younger, was in the same class. She did the exercises and hissed the answers to Mary. One day Sister caught them and Mary got three cuts from the leather strap for cheating and Rose got six cuts for helping her. Rose told this story to one of my uncles and I've never forgotten it. I could hear the old anger burn when she spoke about this injustice. There must have been a few other experiences like that, or worse, that she didn't talk about because when she was taken into hospital one Saturday, very ill, she reacted badly when I put her religion down as Roman Catholic. What did I know? I was nineteen and never had to fill in a hospital form before. A priest came into her room the next day. She saw him enter and, although she was a very sick woman, she reared up off her pillow, eyes burning with outrage and shouted, 'Get out, *get out.*'

The Rose I knew was a good-looking woman. She had big brown eyes, dark olive skin, a mouth that was meant to smile but was often set with a grim endurance. She was small and short, but a formidable expression made up for that. She was highly intelligent, always angry, and her greatest joys were her son and reading. Her wavy black hair only ever grew three strands of white, and that was in the weeks when she was dying.

Rose had some strange reservations about things. When I was working and Val was at high school it took us months to persuade her to buy a bra. Woolworths had them cheap, we said. We offered to measure her, gauge the size, go and buy it. No. She didn't want one. Bras were *fast* – in other words, only women out to draw attention to themselves wore them. Anyway, what was wrong with the way she looked? As if Val and I would tell her.

Rose had breastfed each of us for nine months, believing I suppose that as long as you were breastfeeding you couldn't get pregnant. I guess it worked because first there was me (the reason she married Stan), then a year and two weeks later, Jimmy, and a year and two months later, Val. Stan shot himself in April 1934, when I was four, Jimmy was three and Val was two. Anyway, Rose's breasts were like Maya Angelou's – how that writer described them to an interviewer anyway: they were having a race to see which one could get to her waist first.

After months of intermittent nagging, pleading and hinting from us, Rose finally bought a bra. It was a close-run thing because she saw the price, and if Val hadn't been standing there she would have turned and walked away. '*Sixpence?* They want *sixpence* for that? You can buy a skein of wool for sixpence.' She bought one but would only wear it on pension day.

Rose was a great knitter. She could knit and read at the same time, and one day I would do that too. If you want to knit jerseys for your kids – in this case, red for Renée (because she was dark), blue for Valerie (because she wasn't), dark green or brown for Jimmy (because he was a boy) – and you still want to read, then you have to do both at the same time.

Jimmy. My brother only found out that Jimmy wasn't his real name on his first day at school. His first name was Russell. So he got called Russell by the teachers and Jimmy by the kids, and eventually Jimmy by everyone. When he got older and wanted to be called Russell, we obliged. I still slip back, though, if I'm not thinking. And the older we got, the more I did it. He told me he learned that 'jimmy' was a Scottish term for a little boy. Someone might say, 'Saw a bunch of jimmies on their way to school.' Stan was of Scottish descent so maybe using Jimmy as a name for his little boy instead of his given name, Russell, was a term of endearment, which is exactly how I use it.

I had a lot of irritations with my name too. *Renée? Who does she think she is? Reeny will do her.* And my second name was Gertrude. Every goat in the district was called Gerty.

In the last house we shared together, there was a long room where the couch and the table and chairs were. On the floor in front of the wood and coal range was a balding deerskin. It lay on the old lino that covered the floor, its pattern fading, holes in it where the wooden floor showed through. When I was deemed old enough – ten – I had to clean and wash the floor ('down on your knees' stuff). This meant I had to perch all the chairs upside down on the table and throw the deerskin outside, giving it some vigorous shakes, which really only shifted the dust. How we got it and where it went I have no idea.

The deerskin and the other bits and pieces of the furniture we owned had come with us every time we'd moved, and we'd moved often because landlords were always selling the house. No one wanted to rent to Rose because she didn't have much money, she was 'dark' (they meant Māori) and had three kids, so the kind of houses she managed to rent got progressively worse. Those were the days when houses had *To Rent* notices staked in the lawn, and underneath one of them I remember someone had printed: *No Dogs, No Maoris*.

Rose taught me to read, so I was in the happy position of being able to read before I started school. She taught me in the hope that it would shut me up. This is the best gift, the best thing anyone has ever done for me in my entire life. It's the kind of gift that not only lasts forever but also gets better and better.

I zipped through the four primer classes in no time simply because I could read. It meant that I was always the youngest in any class after that, which led to some bewildering experiences. 'Got your monthly yet?' asked one of the girls in standard six. 'No,' I said, 'we just get the *New Idea*.' The day I started school was no less bewildering. I stood at the bottom of the steps and two teachers stood at the top and looked down at me. 'Pretty little thing,' one said to the other, 'pity she's so dark.'

In 1937 a great thing happened. I read *Emily of New Moon* by LM Montgomery. This was the first time I'd understood the magic of a book that went on and on. Here was Emily – a girl with ideas, resentments, observations, judgements – who spoke to me. She was on her own in the middle of others and I felt I was too. I must have known that books were not just collections of short stories, because I had the example of Rose losing herself in a book every night, but now I understood the enchantment. Reading was a drug, and a spell under which I fell willingly – fact or fiction, it was my escape from the real world. Then and now.

In 1938 we got a radio. A Zenith. I heard my first blues. I can't remember the title of the song but I can still feel the way it made me stop and listen. The words and music sank right into me unlike any music before and the effect has lasted. At 7pm the radio played 'God Save the King' and Rose made us stand up 'to show respect'. Then we went to bed.

At the table, no one sat on Rose's chair but Rose. Ever. When visitors came for a meal it was the same, but the three of us had the unpleasant experience of watching other people sitting on *our* chairs and not being able to say a word. We knew Rose would kill us if we said anything, so I'd go and fling myself on my bed, one of two on the sleeping porch, grab my book from under the pillow and read till they'd gone and I was called to do my turn at either washing, wiping or putting away the dishes.

As I got older I dreaded being called back to sing to the visitors, but I never refused. That would have been rude. There was one day when I did protest. Not about singing, though, or my stolen chair.

My young aunties and uncles had called unexpectedly, and to my horror Rose went and got the meat from the safe and put it into a meat dish with some dripping and salt and pepper and then into the oven of the wood and coal range. She told me to peel potatoes and Val to wash the cabbage. Jimmy, of course, being a boy, didn't have to do anything. I said, 'But, Mum, that meat's for our Sunday dinner.' I'd been looking forward to it. We hadn't had roast meat for so long. She grabbed me and pushed me out on the porch, shutting the door behind us. 'Shut up,' she said, her face very fierce. 'Just you *shut up*. They're visitors. Visitors always come first.' Rose gave me a good shake, left me on the porch, went inside and shut the door. I stayed there and refused to cry.

When Val turned ten, she was deemed old enough to cook on our wood and coal range. She cooked on Sundays and continued for as long as we were at home. This meant that the first time I got to cook, as opposed to just preparing the veges, I was nineteen and Rose was in hospital. I cooked the potatoes and was so ignorant that I put them on the stove at 2pm for the 5.30pm dinner. That day we ate potato mush. You can't waste food.

Each of us had our own cutlery and we were as possessive of them as we were of our chairs. God help anyone who touched my knife, fork or spoon. Retribution was swift. I was the oldest so I could think up more fiendish paybacks than the other two. I'd chuck Val's teddy bear, Edward Jones, up on the roof, or hide the Nugget shoe polish and smile as Jimmy looked everywhere, until finally I'd say, 'What's that on the roof?'

Rose had a dog collar on a hook on the wall, which she used to strap us if we did something wrong. If we threw the porridge pot at each other when we got angry and bits of porridge went all over the wall or if we caused a big fight just as she'd settled down to roll a smoke and have a read, if we behaved badly outside the house or if we put three oranges on her bill at the dairy and she only found out about it on pension day when she went to pay the bill and felt a fool in front of the shopkeeper – down came the strap.

I must have known I'd be found out and figured the oranges were worth it. Or maybe I thought I'd get away with it this once. Not only was I sore, I was outraged because she didn't strap Val who had eaten one whole orange. She deserved a strapping too. But when Rose asked her if she'd eaten any orange, Val shook her head. I don't blame her now, but then I was angry, vengeful, unforgiving. I refused to speak to her for days. I wanted to chop Edward Jones into pieces with the little tomahawk we used for kindling but she hid him under the cushion on Rose's couch. He might have got a bit squashed but he survived.

This kind of punishment from Rose didn't happen often. Being shamed publicly was something she endured a gutsful of and she wasn't going to have her kids adding to it. This makes her sound like a bad mother but she wasn't. She was a young woman driven to extremes because that's where she'd been pushed. She was twenty-seven with three kids when her husband shot himself, and forty-two when she died. In those fifteen years after Stan's death, Rose never had a moment when she wasn't worried about money or about where she and three kids would go if the landlord sold the house. It simmered underneath the reading of an Agatha Christie or when she'd had a couple of beers. She couldn't buy beer herself because Māori weren't allowed to. She had to ask a Pākehā to buy her a beer, and if they agreed, she'd give them the money and they would go up to the bar and buy it. This law was changed in 1949, the year she died.

Rose died twice. The first time she stopped breathing, the nurse said, 'She's gone,' and put the sheet over her face. My sister screamed, 'Mum, Mum,' and fell on the floor in a faint. Rose started breathing again. The nurse nearly passed out and then rushed out into the corridor crying, 'Oh *Holy Mother* – Sister, Sister?' Rose died again after fifteen more hours of laboured breathing.

The day after my mother died, the landlord sent a letter to say we had to vacate the house, but our next-door neighbour told me to just keep on paying the rent to the office in Napier and he couldn't legally do anything. So I did. And he didn't. She was right.

My relationship with Rose was never easy. She found it hard to show me warmth, but she did teach me to read. She wasn't always pleased about that because I read every spare minute. I walked along the footpath reading. I read when I was peeling potatoes and when I should have been making my bed. Rose said, 'If you don't get your head out of a book, you'll end up on Queer Street.'

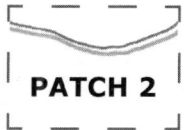

PATCH 2

The dance

O how we dance, O how we dance
round and round and round and round

we dance by the lectern dripping with fire
past the camps, the ghosts, the hands on the wire
we skirt past the thorns and sidestep the stones
our ears turn away from the chorus of bones

the dry cliffs hiss warnings, a cyclonic chime
the black ice moves closer, the maestro is Time
we stop and see clearly the chains on our hands
we stumble on iron waves, collapse over sand

our song is salt seaweed, the dead fruit, the bells
measure our footsteps and muffle our calls
we fall and we stagger we cling to the sea
and there are the crossroads and there is the tree

but O how we dance, O how we dance
round and round and round and round
O how we dance, O how we dance
round and round and round

PATCH 3

When my oldest son, Christopher, read on my blog that I was going to do eighty-six patches for my memoir (I was eighty-six at the time, and two years on I am doing eighty-eight), he sent me this ...

> Eighty-six, eighty-sixed, 86, 86ed, 86'd, were slang terms for getting rid of someone, refusing them service, shoving them out the door. It is said that in the prohibition era the cops would call ahead and tell the publican they were on the way so better *eighty-six their patrons*.

So eighty-six had a lot more going for it than I'd realised.

My father's brother Les and Les's two mates used to have a still somewhere in the wilds outside of Gore, perhaps more towards Invercargill way. They made Hokonui moonshine and did very well in the prohibition era. They had some close calls with the police, though, and had to keep moving the still and changing their tracks into and out of the bush.

Neighbours, strangers and travellers made bets with local bookies on the date and time when Les would get done. If he'd been a little less smart-mouthed he might have lasted uncaught forever, but he couldn't resist teasing the police. He'd walk out of the bush and come up behind the local cop: 'Evening, Bert, caught any bad boys lately?' It became a point of honour with the local cops to catch him because he was so cheeky, so damn sure of himself.

Les and his mates knew every move the police made. They must have had a deep throat somewhere in the ranks. The cops knew they knew. They tried every trick in the book to catch them, but Les and co were gold-medal eighty-sixers and always one bound ahead of them.

The local temperance union was outraged at this blatant eighty-sixing and marched to the police station, demanding action. It wasn't so much the demand as the singing that drove the cops crazy. 'Won't you sign the pledge, dear friends, today?' on the one hand and on the other the local publicans declaring 'no more free booze' if the cops didn't stir themselves and catch the buggers. The only ones smiling were Les and the bookies.

Finally they got caught. It wasn't dramatic. One of them needed a toilet break, couldn't wait, so took a few steps away from the track, sat under a bush, all good.

No, mate. All bad.

They were caught because a cop did what cops are supposed to do – he sifted the evidence. He came across the little mound and glimpsed a scrap of paper in it. Aha? Could this be a clue? Visions of a police medal perhaps? The commissioner saying a few kind words? He held his nose with one hand, grabbed the piece of paper with the other … and lo, it was a sales docket from a local shop, and it had the guy's name on it. Done and dusted, you might say.

So here's Les and his two mates enjoying a quiet home-made snort, laughing about how they'd put it over the cops again, and there's a knock on the door. The kind of knock they know very well. This time when they try to eighty-six, there's a cop stationed at the back door too. Les and his mates are charged, convicted and fined in the Invercargill court.

Les gave up his Hokonui enterprise. Decided there was more fun in doing what he was really good at: smooching women. Les was married four times, and had numerous affairs from Cape Rēinga to Bluff. He might not have been a successful entrepreneur in the alcohol trade but he became a star at eighty-sixing when things got too hot in the bedroom.

That's another story.

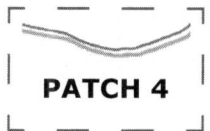

PATCH 4

The 1951 waterfront lockout in New Zealand was an industrial dispute involving the country's wharfies and allied workers that lasted 151 days. The National Government of the day brought in emergency regulations (kept on the books till the 1980s), which meant that if you were caught giving food or assistance to a wharfie or his family, you would be arrested, and newspapers were forbidden to publish anything on the wharfies' side of the story. The wharfies had their own illegal bulletin and although the police did night searches of houses, looked under kids' mattresses and in kitchen cupboards, they never found the typewriter. Those who disagreed with the wharfies called it a strike; wharfies and their supporters called it a lockout, which it was. Even now I'll correct anyone who, in my hearing, calls it a strike.

From *Pass It On* (Victoria University Press 1986), first performed at Theatre Corporate, Auckland, 1 March 1986, with the following cast:

Nell … Jennifer Ward-Lealand
Jeannie … Judith Gibson
Cliff … John Watson
Gus … Michael Hurst

Other parts played by Caroline Hutchison, Alison Wall, Marion Parry, Simon Prast, Michael Morrissey, Miles Taylor and Peter McIntyre.

Directed by Roger McGill
Designed by Donald Grant-Sutherland
Lighting by Andrew Mayo

NELL appears at the Relief Depot, where people are weighing out sugar and flour into smaller bags and sorting clothes, shoes, vegetables and meat.

SUE: Hello.

JEANNIE: Nell.

NELL: Had a couple of hours to spare, so I thought …

MARIE: You're an angel. Most of the regulars are off asking for donations.

JEANNIE: Didn't want a known commie with them so I got left behind.

MARIE: You said you understood.

JEANNIE: Oh, I do.

Pause while they work

SUE: Want to clean some shoes?

NELL: Might as well make myself useful.

JEANNIE: Nell's my sister-in-law. Nell, this is Marie, and the one with polish on her face is Sue.

SUE: Have I?

MARIE: On your chin.

SUE: *(wipes it)* I've seen your girls, I think, Christine and …

NELL: Di.

SUE: That's right. Christine's in the same class as my Aileen.

NELL: Has she had any trouble at school?

SUE: 'Red, Red, you'll never get fed?'

NELL: Christine's upset and I couldn't get much out of Di.

SUE: Aileen was like that so I taught her a rhyme to say back. 'Gab, Gab, don't be a scab.'

NELL: Did it work?

SUE: Shut them up for the moment.

MARIE: I should try that.

JEANNIE: When do you go?

MARIE: In a couple of days. I'm told the police have got the town sewn up.

SUE: What'll you do?

MARIE: I'll be 'visiting my sister'.

JEANNIE: No wonder your husband's shirty. He's not a wharfie is he?

MARIE: My sister needs help. He's caught up in it whether he likes it or not.

SUE: *(offering help)* If there's any trouble …

MARIE: Trouble's my middle name.

NELL: What say you get caught? What about your kids?

MARIE: They're old enough. Oh don't worry, I'm no Joan of Arc. I'm just going to see how the land lies, that's all.

SUE: See that it stays that way.

MARIE: Huh, who was it sneaking round the back streets with some coal in a pram?

NELL: I've got some clothes my girls have grown out of. Maybe your sister?

MARIE: Already got two cases full. Bring them here. Someone'll use them.

JEANNIE: Are you all right, Nell?

NELL shrugs

MARIE: Having rows at home?

NELL: How did you know?

SUE: We all are dear. Fight the good fight, unity's the word and all the rest of it, but at home it's a different matter.

NELL: We don't usually argue.

MARIE: It's a big strain being a threat to the country.

PATCH 5

Drama as a meant-and-planned activity – reading a play, learning a character, learning lines and presenting a public performance – didn't happen for me until I was eleven-going-on-twelve.

I was useless at sport. I simply wasn't interested. This meant I was made to run, based on the assumption that everyone could walk, so everyone could walk just a little quicker. You didn't need to be taught. You just lined up with the star runners and the other no-hopers in your age group and when the teacher yelled go, you moved. Some shot out like they were being fuelled by a secret force. I started at a quick amble that almost immediately slowed to a walk, then a slow walk, then just one foot in front of the other till the torture was over for that day. I came in last every time but it pacified the teachers. They could tick a hundred per cent for class involvement. If there'd been a sport called reading I would have won by a country mile.

However, I did have the honour of having been a member of one of the first marching teams in the country, the Taradale Girls Marching Team. I was persuaded by Val. She said, 'You just have to walk and remember signals … and there's a big dance at the Foresters' Hall on the night of the competitions.' I was in.

When I was six, the Labour Party was elected to govern. Rose thought Michael Joseph Savage, the new prime minister, was a saint. I was more interested in the fact that I was now in the standards and most of the kids who'd started with me were still in the primers. I frowned even more. I don't remember making any special friends in the primers so it wasn't that. I think it was an indication of my life-long aversion to being in a situation where I don't know anyone. Especially in a crowd of someones. Even though some of the faces in standard one were familiar, I still felt the odd one out.

As an adult I – unknowingly – solved this by becoming an actor, then a director, then a teacher. The faces in front of me might be strangers but I'm safe in a world of my own. I'm playing a part, I'm someone else, I'm acting like I know what I'm doing.

I moved from Greenmeadows School (standards one to four) to Taradale School (standards five and six), and my uncle Orm went to war. There was a small farewell party and we were sent off to bed, but I crept back for a little sneaky look before Rose caught me. It was like watching a play. The lights were on, the fire was going, Frankie (Rose's cousin) was sitting on my chair playing the guitar and singing, and Cliff, Rose and Orm (in uniform), were sitting on the other chairs, drinking beer and singing along with Frankie. They sang about girls as sweet as red roses in June and how they'd come back some sunny day, and they laughed and drank and I wanted to cry because Orm was my Absolute Favourite Person in the Entire

World and he was going away. I didn't understand what war meant. I had no idea what he'd be facing. I only knew that the most benign influence in my life was going away. I didn't even really understand what 'away' meant.

I'd read about war or at least stories about war, but it didn't feel like something that actually happened. This war was just a *story* and I knew that stories weren't true. Stories were another name for lies. You told stories? You were a liar.

I wasn't so keen on fairies or the Red Queen or Wonderland and I thought Alice was stupid. I didn't like boarding school stories about girls having midnight feasts. I thought they were mad getting up to eat in the middle of the night. I liked books by Charles Dickens because he was real. He didn't witter on about fairies or midnight feasts, he took me straight into the guts of worlds I didn't know, but where the borders and signposts were the same as the ones I did know. So did LM Montgomery, and although she was unduly concerned with God, her heroines, Anne and Emily, knew hardship and misunderstanding and had dreams that were often squashed.

At Taradale School I was appointed library monitor, and I loved that. I also loved being taught dancing. We learned the lancers and a dance that went to a song about the Duke of York.

> *The grand old Duke of York*
> *He had ten thousand men*
> *He marched them up to the top of the hill*
> *And he marched them down again ...*

But it was the annual concert that really won me over. The first half was 'items': singing solos, piano solos and duets, solo and class recitations. Once our class did 'The Highwayman' by Alfred Noyes, all seventeen verses.

> *The wind was a torrent of darkness among the gusty trees*
> *The moon was a ghostly galleon tossed upon cloudy seas ...*

The second half was a play. A play? My first thought was that this was yet another thing where I'd be made to walk while everyone else jumped and marched and yelled, but no. I don't remember the first play, perhaps I wasn't in it, but I remember the second one where I was the princess stolen away as a baby by an evil tinker and finally found and identified as the lost princess, whereupon I flung off the long dark cloak I'd been wearing and *tah-dah*, there I was in my auntie Olive's pink taffeta evening dress, pinned at the back with a safety pin so it would fit. This meant I could only face the front but who would complain about that? I had a solo (probably why I was given the part) in which I sang, 'An orphan, I, without a name ...' and the chorus sang, 'Poor orphan child.' Bliss.

Well it was until the evil tinker started grinning fiendishly and beating on the pot with her spoon. Attention immediately moved from me to her. That was the moment I learned the meaning of 'scene-stealer'. I didn't know the word then, I just knew I wanted to jump on her, grab the spoon and hit her with the pot. So my moment of glory was over very quickly. Not quickly enough in Rose's opinion. She thought the whole thing gave kids ideas. 'Prancing around the stage,' she said, 'where's that going to get you?'

The experience went to my head a bit. When spring came I began organising concerts up at the river. I was the organiser, so I said who had to be in it. Three of us – me and my sister, Val, and her friend Joy – were keen; but the boys – Bobby, Lenny, Ian, Graham and Jimmy – were not. They had to be in it because otherwise they wouldn't be allowed to go to the river. I was the oldest and in charge of this mob and, by God, they could 'do' an item or stay home. I needed items because I needed an audience. If you were in the concert you had to watch the others. That was the basic unspoken etiquette. It is also the underlying rule of all school concerts, then and now. You put as many of the kids onstage as you possibly can. The standard will be uneven but the hall will be full.

I turned twelve and Rose said, 'At the end of the year, you'll have to get a job.'

'What about high school?'

'If you get a job and bring some money in then Val and Jim can go to high school.'

I don't know what it was like for her saying these words, I only know what it was like hearing them. I had looked forward to being a high school girl. I'd gone into the primers, then I'd gone into the standards, now I was nearing the end of the standards and I expected to go to high school. With my head in a book all the time maybe I'd missed the signs. Maybe Rose didn't have the heart to say anything until she had to. Lots of other oldest kids I knew had gone off to work. Joan, who'd told me I was lucky not to have a father, had gone off to work. I saw Rose's point. While I rebelled inside, I did as I was told.

Jimmy had an absolute bitch of a teacher in standard five who got him into such a state he forgot all his carefully learned spelling. Perfect when he left home, it vanished the instant he entered her classroom. He fumbled over the words and she made him stand behind the stove for hours. This happened every school day of that year. He was a mess. He started to be terrified of even going in the school gates. Rose decided to take him away and send him to Napier Intermediate. He would have to repeat the year, but he would be free from the punitive authoritarianism of that cow's classroom. Jimmy went to work weeding carrots for Mr Hetherington, who had a market garden and paid him sixpence an hour. Rose weeded carrots for Mr Hetherington too. Between them they got enough money for the bus and the intermediate school uniform.

If I worked, and he and Rose weeded carrots, there would be enough for school clothes, shoes, books and bus fares for both Jimmy and Val. I didn't argue. I didn't know how angry I was for a long time. At the end of the year I applied for two jobs. One at the woollen mills around Pandora Point in Ahuriri and one at a printing factory on Dickens Street, Napier.

I went to the interviews on my own. I said I was fifteen, and both men doing the interviews pretended to believe me. I got a week's trial at the woollen mills and started the week after. If I did the work okay for a week, I'd get the job. The only clothes I had were my school gym tunic and black stockings, black shoes with holes in the soles, and a coat that had been given to Rose. The only underwear was what I was wearing. On Saturdays I put my togs on underneath my old clothes and washed every article in the tub, then boiled them in the copper. If it was fine I'd hang the washing on the line, if not it hung on wire over the stove. I didn't feel sorry for myself. I just did it.

The women at the woollen mills were kind. They taught me to handle the machines. They showed me how to watch the bobbins and how to make sure they were kept fed with the different coloured wools. Smooth and easy, smooth and easy. I didn't realise it then but now I think that sort of challenge, where I had to use my brain as well as my fingers, was right down my alley. I liked to do well. I liked to conquer new skills. I loved it when one of the women said, 'Good girl, good girl.' They didn't ask any questions but they knew I wasn't fifteen. Their goodwill was extraordinary.

For a forty-hour week I got twenty-two shillings. I caught the workers' bus at 7.30am for four shillings a week, I paid Rose ten shillings a week and I had eight to go mad with.

I look at twelve-year-olds now and wonder how they'd go working for forty hours a week. I didn't have time to be depressed or to repine over missing out on high school – that came later. I ran for the bus, ran around the road from the bus stop to the mill, ran back after five to catch the bus. What I didn't know was that although I would always regret not going to high school, a whole new world of reading was waiting just round the corner for me.

PATCH 6

This is a letter from my uncle Mick, Rose's brother, to their sister Grace. They share an aunt Rose, and the 'Granny' he refers to is Puti Mary.

Dear Gracie,

Received your letter today and was very pleased to find you had not forgotten me altogether. I'm in practically the same predicament as you for finding enough news, anyway, news that would interest a young girl who has just celebrated her eighteenth birthday, who, although I'm late, I wish a happy birthday. I would like to send you something, but my money, though it isn't much, is all tied up.

I had a funny experience the other night. I was induced by Mrs Scurr senior to go with her to a clairvoyant and the first thing she said was that she could see a lot of water, and in it a man, not very big, fairish in complexion. It seemed as though financial worries had beset him and he had taken this way out. She asked me if I knew to whom she was referring and I was almost too surprised to speak. Naturally I thought of Rosie's departed. Why she should bring that up to me has got me beat. Rather strange.

This lady also got a message from Granny for me, which told me to go straight and keep honest in all my dealings.

Anyway that's what I made out of it as it was spoken in Māori but it's a funny thing – it was Granny's voice and the actions this lady did were Granny's mannerisms. You know how Granny always used to have her hand to her mouth every now and again when she was speaking. It is rather strange, don't you think?

This lady can tell you all sorts of funny things, and whether one believes them all depends on the person. For instance if I had something personal of yours and gave it to her she could tell me what you were thinking of me and how you were going to get on in life and all the rest of it. Your letter would do but you needn't fear. I won't try to find out anything of your past and future.

I lost a pound note the other day and for the fun of it, I asked her where it was and that very near got her bluffed. She said in the end it wasn't lost but that I had put it away safe and have completely forgot where I put it, and I would remember one of these days. So far I haven't remembered. If I find it I'll give it to you for your birthday present. I've got so used to the idea that it is lost that if it does turn up and I send it to you I won't miss it. But I'm afraid it will not.

I've just got a tailor-made suit £4.2s.6d. Everybody here reckons I'll look nice in it. It's a brown, a sort of herring-bone design and the cloth seems to be good material.

I'm thinking of going to Auckland at Christmas. I might look Auntie Rose up. I suppose they won't be very pleased to see me. I'll write to them a couple of days before, and they won't be able to refuse to see me if they do happen to. Uncle Bert gave me sixpence last time I seen him and if he's still as generous as he was then, I'm liable to come back with a lot of chips. Ha. Ha.

I'm still in the pink of condition. I seem to thrive on love somehow. The weather isn't so bad now, wasn't a week back.

Just got the result from Melbourne of the Centenary Race. We got a good short wave wireless here and I often listen to London. Heard the start of race from Maldenhall aerodrome in London. Gee it was good. It's a great thing wireless, isn't it? It's a wonder Scottie hasn't had one by now. We get Russia, Germany and a swag of European stations. We used to listen to all the cricket test matches, used to sit up – all night.

Tons of love to all and don't be so long-winded about answering next time. I'll go crook if you are.

Your loving brother,
Mick

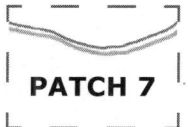

PATCH 7

From *Daisy and Lily* (Penguin 1993).

On the Friday before the last march, Uncle Auntie and I went to Farmers to buy two of the raincoats advertised on special. They were bright yellow and we joked that maybe the cops would think we were meter maids. It was safer to wear dark clothing but we weren't out to do anything that'd get us photographed and onto some cop's list.

My stomach clenched as I looked at the rack of coats. I moved in a daze of fear, my mind never free of batons and shields, of barbed wire, of big bins, of angry eyes, of beer crates carried high on the shoulders of rugby supporters, of newspapers and TV interviews with sincere quiet-voiced cops talking about professional protesters, or Muldoon with a balloon coming out of his mouth with law and order written on it.

That Saturday march, the last one, we wore our new yellow plastics. Uncle Auntie had on a black wig under a red chiffon scarf and a pair of bright yellow gloves. We waved to a group of the girls. Uncle Auntie had confessed her fears about marching. 'Gives me the shits,' she said. 'Every Saturday night half of Auckland is boozed out of its collective mind.'

'And the other half is stoned.' I said.

'And,' said Uncle Auntie, 'the goss is that most of the cops are flakoes too, except for the poor unfortunates on duty. And then they come into Titty Titty Bang Bang crying for their mothers.'

Today people seemed subdued. The jokes about good exercise, the shouted greetings to friends, the jaunty waves to people on the footpath were gone. There were still people with children in pushchairs, and on shoulders. All sorts. Old, young, long hair, short hair, blond, dark, some well known, some not. Uncle Auntie pointed out some theatre people. I saw someone I thought stole a book from Worms; a dark-haired woman took photographs.

Does she, I wondered, have bad dreams, stiff legs, get irritable all week before the next march? Did that woman there, the one with the grey hair, the one we've seen every Saturday, does she go home to a house where she can scream or shout or stay in the bath all night if she wants to? Would that young boy holding his father's hand remember the adults towering over him shouting, *One two three four – we don't want your racist tour*? What problems had that old woman set aside to come on the march? Did she lose her one true love years ago because she lacked spine? Does she booze too much and wonder if she's following in her mother's footsteps?

Fear of the police never left me. It increased or decreased but was never not there. I almost fainted with terror once when Uncle Auntie yelled out something to the cops, something about us paying their wages. My mind whipped through various scenarios. They would take a photograph, grab her at the end of the march, belt her with those long batons. The cops did that a lot at first until marchers got canny and left for home in groups. That was only a partially successful ploy because if a cop had a bad day it was easy enough to pick out someone, teach them a lesson, give them a going-over down an alleyway or behind a shop, make their day better.

I became excessively efficient at home and at Worms. My half-house was cleaned within an inch of its life, the windows shone, the garden was free of weeds. At Worms, Wilf grumbled that he could hardly put his cup down before it was whisked away and washed. 'We're throwing out perfectly good pots of tea,' he moaned, and I promised to watch it.

We saw the Artists Against Apartheid troupe, with huge flags and batons of French bread, bags of sweets, some clowns, a bumble bee and a rabbit. Gang members, huge, intimidating. *You call us mongrels, judge, and that's what we'll be.* Marshalls, advising, sorting out volunteers for something more direct, handing out slips of paper with instructions and songs to sing.

Uncle Auntie and I walked down the steep slope and became two of these hundreds making our way to Fowlds Park. We saw the space travellers with their helmets, cardboard and newspaper padding, shin pads, cricket gloves, ice hockey masks, and the groin protectors you couldn't see. Not one left in Auckland according to Uncle Auntie.

The day had a desperate feeling. This is it. The last chance. This is where the jokes stop.

PATCH 8

When I turned eighty I wanted to do something to mark the occasion. So on 3 April 2010, I went to China.

My son Chris and his wife, Zuzu, lived and worked in Guangzhou then. Their first child, Freddie Renée, had been born a few months before and I wanted to say *ni hao* to her. My oldest granddaughter, Naomi, happily for me, wanted to come too. My first granddaughter would meet my youngest granddaughter. Very satisfying.

I took Irish breakfast tea and demerara sugar for Chris, and earplugs, lots of earplugs. Two tins of milk powder for Freddie as requested. I was in charge of first-aid requirements, so I had Panadol, plasters, tablets for diarrhoea, tablets for constipation, lotions, antiseptic ointment, a bandage, some hay fever pills and my blood pressure pills. I took a gift for Zuzu of a pounamu necklace, and one each for Freddie and Nanxi (Zuzu's daughter by her first marriage). For Zuzu's parents, I took pounamu and two kete.

Everyone at Wellington Airport looked like they'd got up too soon, but not Naomi. Whatever time of day or night, whatever she's wearing, Naomi has something about her that makes people turn and look.

I checked in my suitcase, picked up the small backpack and my red canvas bag and followed my granddaughter's shiny dark curls through the security checks.

When we arrived in Guangzhou everyone was wearing infection masks – they looked very sinister – but getting through customs was easy, and soon we were walking out and there was Chris waiting for us. I ran over and hugged him and then ran back and joined Naomi in the queue to get our luggage. We headed out into the pink smog that hangs over the city.

Guangzhou was once Canton – the spider spinning the web of business for the Silk Road. Commerce and money still ruled. It was cosmopolitan, so we saw many countries represented – dark business suits on the British, wonderfully colourful clothes with turbans to match from Africa or Iran or Istanbul, yarmulke from New York. Whatever people wore, they had phones clamped to their ears and talked rapidly in their own language.

Hundreds of cars sped flat out along the streets. Chris speaks Mandarin and when he'd given the driver instructions, the driver congratulated him on his pronunciation, then indicated me and said, 'Mamma?' He smiled and chuckled at me when Chris said yes. The lights went red and pedestrians crossed, and the cars panted and growled like frustrated tigers.

Zuzu greeted us with happy smiles, but beautiful four-month-old Freddie cried loudly at the sight of these two strange faces. We ate together, then Chris took us to the hotel. I fell asleep almost straight away.

Guangzhou was loud and friendly. When you went to the markets the vendors shouted, 'Hello, hello,' and beckoned you into their space. People on the streets smiled at these 'white ghosts', nodded when we smiled back, and some pointed or tapped their companions on the shoulder to alert them that we were passing. All seemed to like the fact that I was old and Naomi was young, recognising us as grandmother and granddaughter.

Chris took a fortnight off work and we walked miles. I needed help up and down steps but managed to wander around old burial sites, markets, temples and shops. The number of parks surprised me. Perhaps with the smog and the frantic busyness of a city of over fourteen million, the need for green spaces is high. People in parks did t'ai chi, rode bikes, sang in groups; old men took their caged birds for a walk and held them up so they could see the children in little boats on the lake.

The food was cheap and delicious, and at night we either had dinner with Chris and Zuzu at their apartment or we all went out to a restaurant. I had made up my mind before we left that I would eat everything that was offered me and I did. I wouldn't try chicken feet again but I'm glad I tasted them.

One of the most exciting things we did was visit Zuzu's parents in Xiayukou in the north of Hunan Province in South China. We caught a fast train to Changsha where Zuzu's brother, Wu Qiao, was waiting. He took us to meet his wife, Hong Xia, and daughter, Cai Lei, and we drove around the city where Mao rose to prominence and where the revolution began.

At the foot of the Yuelu Mountain there is an ancient academy. We moved through the entrance gate looking at stone tablets and inscriptions and then into a large room, where there were paintings and stories of all the famous men who had taught there. A covered walkway took us through vegetation to a park, where there were statues and stories engraved on them. On the way back we went to the souvenir shop, where I bought two little framed pictures of the comedy and tragedy masks. Then we attended a concert, partly music, partly dance. Naomi and I marvelled at the beautiful reds, blues and golds of the costumes. A young woman in flowing red and blue robes walked up and down behind the musicians as they played, and once or twice tapped a chime hanging on a frame at the back. Bright yellow, red and gold costumes hung on a rack to one side, and I wondered if I could steal one without being noticed.

The day we went to visit Zuzu's family was misty, threatening rain. It was warm in the vehicle, though, as we drove under a lush green canopy of spring growth. The car-ferry trip across the Lishui took us to a muddy track and onto a road, where we stopped for lunch at a café.

From 9 May to 12 May 1943, the Japanese army moved east from Shanghai, up the Yangtze River and its watery tributaries, killing all those they came across until they were eventually forced to retreat. In three days they killed thirty thousand people. We approached a memorial to the Changjiao massacre, and Wu Qiao stopped the car. Zuzu said this was the place where ten thousand of the thirty thousand people were killed. She and her family always stopped there to remember.

Zuzu's father, Cai Ju Hai (aka elder brother or *da ge*), then aged twelve, was lucky. He was captured by the Japanese and made to work in the kitchen. He got on well with his captors but always looked for an opportunity to escape. This came six weeks later in the middle of winter. The twelve-year-old boy walked barefoot from Changde to his home in Xiayukou – a two-hour drive today, but much longer back then on older roads with black ice and the threat of capture. No surprise that he has severe foot problems now.

At the house we walked into a kind of courtyard, where Cai Ju Hai and his wife, Liu Yu Zhen, were waiting, along with Zuzu's brothers (first uncle, second uncle and so on), their sons and wives, and a neighbour or two. It was just like walking onto a marae. We approached, they smiled, and as we shook hands, fireworks *shooshed* and shimmered into stars. I felt like royalty. We all smiled and nodded and then went inside. I knew Liu Yu Zhen had very bad arthritis and that she'd made a huge effort to stand and greet this 'travelling momma'.

When I gave them the pounamu pendants, they put them on immediately but it was the kete that the family exclaimed and wowed over. Everyone had to have a close look at the weaving and express their amazement and delight in the work. We couldn't speak each other's language but the messages were loud and clear. They were making us very welcome and we were pleased to be there.

The greeting rituals were the same as the greet, meet and eat rituals of many, perhaps all, cultures. Zuzu's family had presents for us too, little red envelopes of money to bring good luck to both the giver and the receiver. I made a mental note to pass on that good luck to Freddie.

There was a large poster of Mao on the wall and second uncle was wearing a Mao cap that I instantly coveted.

When I told him, Chris laughed and said, 'Dream on.'

We sat around a heating box called a kaoxiang and snuggled under the quilt that covered everyone's knees to keep the heat in. This effect could have been marred by the fact that they left the doors to the outside wide open, but as we ate the delicious food and exchanged smiles of admiration and pleasure, the room became warm and cosy and I felt very happy.

I thought about Zuzu's father, Cai Ju Hai, as a child, and about myself at twelve, and how that boy and this girl, from such different backgrounds and experiences, both in our own particular ways, learned the hard lessons of endurance. The odds against us ever meeting were pretty high, and yet here we were, aged eighty, sitting across from each other, smiling, part of the same family now.

PATCH 9

From *Touch of the Sun*, first performed at the Globe Theatre, Dunedin, 1992, with the following cast:

Mugro … Bernadette Doolan
Lillibet … Hilary Norris
Director … Renée

MUGRO and LILLIBET are clearing out their mother's clothes.

LILLIBET: Get out of this room. Get out, *get out*.

MUGRO: I've never sold bits of myself, Lill. Given away lots of free samples but I've never sold them.

LILLIBET: *Bitch.*

MUGRO: How do you think she got all this?

LILLIBET: *Dirty mouthed lying bitch.*

MUGRO: She got them because while Father was away ministering to the other small parishes, she conducted her own personal mission right here.

LILLIBET: You always hated her.

MUGRO: So she sold what she could to get what she wanted. So what?

LILLIBET: She was a good manager and she could sew and all the filth you send sliding off your tongue won't alter that.

MUGRO: (*starts packing clothes again*) You're angry because your illusions are being shattered.

LILLIBET: I am not the type to harbour illusions. I'm a practical, down-to-earth, responsible woman. I'm a member of several service organisations and I drive for Meals on Wheels. I attend church regularly. I do not have illusions.

MUGRO: You had one about Motherdear. Damn name. Why did she insist on it? Motherdear. Motherdear. Makes me sick.

LILLIBET: You didn't know her. She was beautiful.

MUGRO: I suppose we always think that those who gave us warmth and light are beautiful.

LILLIBET: Motherdear was kind and compassionate. Whatever she did, you drove her to it.

MUGRO: You don't take to your husband with a poker just because he upsets you.

LILLIBET: She wanted money for new shoes. Black and white court. The finishing touches to her ensemble.

MUGRO: He tried to stop her breaking open the collection box, so she hit him.

LILLIBET: I didn't say she was right. I said she was upset.

MUGRO: When he got back from having the stitches she locked him out. So he went into the little bach and stayed there till he died. A little more than upset wouldn't you say?

LILLIBET: You and Father were always wanting something from her. Never let her be. Always interrupting. She hated to be interrupted. If she locked you in the cupboard, it was because it was the only way she could get some peace.

MUGRO: All right, Lill, all right.

LILLIBET: You were a trial to her, a daily trial. And you were ugly and nasty, she couldn't bear to look at you.

MUGRO: She couldn't bear to look at anyone but herself.

LILLIBET: She was a bright, shining star. There was nothing ordinary about her. She created her own setting and she *shone*.

MUGRO: Why didn't you visit her then?

LILLIBET: What?

MUGRO: Why didn't you visit her?

LILLIBET: This wasn't a good idea.

MUGRO: She always asked for you.

LILLIBET: I thought we might be able to do this sad essential task, the clearing out of our mother's life and maybe come a little closer together. I should have known better.

MUGRO: Why, Lill? In the two years you didn't have time to visit her once?

LILLIBET: I wrote notes.

MUGRO: She asked all the time. You wouldn't answer my calls.

LILLIBET: I told you. I was flat out.

MUGRO: Or my letters.

LILLIBET: She was paralysed.

MUGRO: She could say your name.

LILLIBET: She was ugly.

MUGRO: She had a bad stroke.

LILLIBET: I couldn't.

MUGRO: She didn't look so bad.

LILLIBET: I wanted to remember her as she was.

MUGRO: She never stopped asking.

LILLIBET: She hated ugliness. And so do I.

MUGRO: Just once, Lill, you could have come just once.

LILLIBET: It's all right for you. You live over a little tinpot shop in a squalid neighbourhood, you're the widow of an habitual criminal, everyone knows you sleep with anyone who looks sideways at you, you're used to ugliness – you *chose* it.

MUGRO: I see the leaves when they're there and I also see the bare branches. I see the little mites ripping and tearing but I also see the blossoms.

LILLIBET: (*gets more and more upset*) And you're always spouting rubbish. And you don't know what you're talking about (*slight pause*). I wanted to go. I really wanted to. Would get all dressed up. Hat, bag, gloves, the lot, just like she wanted. A properly thought-out ensemble. But – I *couldn't go in*. I'd get to the hospital, park the car, go and stand at the doors but I couldn't go in. People going in and out stared at me but I couldn't go in. I said things like 'Now then, Lillibet, this is your mother, this is Motherdear, lying sick and sorry and wanting you, you have to go in.' But it was no use.

LILLIBET is crying

MUGRO: (*watches her for a moment or two, then goes to her*) Never mind, Lill, never mind (*she puts her arms around Lill who leans into her*).

'There's no more to be done or feared, or hoped; None now need watch, speak low, and list, and tire; No irksome crease

	out smoothed, no pillow sloped does she require.'
LILLIBET:	You and your poetry.
MUGRO:	Had to do something. And who slid the sweeties under the door, then?
LILLIBET:	I never agreed with that cupboard business.
MUGRO:	I used to hear the little scratchy sound of the paper around the lolly and I'd think, that's Lill. Lill hasn't forgotten me.
LILLIBET:	She might have been an ordinary star but she was a star. A *star*.
MUGRO:	We're all stars, Lill.

PATCH 10

There is a photo of me taken when I was nineteen. I'm holding a large black cat. The cat's name was George. We had four cats during my childhood and they were all called George. It never occurred to me that this was odd. You had a cat. You called it George. A bit like the royals I suppose. You have a baby, you call it George.

This particular George was found at the river. He was wandering through the lupins, mewing piercingly. He was about six weeks old, we estimated. An old story. Someone had put George and his siblings in a sugar bag and thrown them in the Tūtaekurī River. Somehow George had escaped. Somehow he attached himself to us and somehow we worked up enough courage to take him home.

'That cat's not staying,' Rose said. But George knew better. He avoided her eye while lapping furiously at the porridge and milk one of us had left out for him. George had learned very early in life that, where food was concerned, it was no good being picky. Unlike most cats I've known since, he ate what was put in front of him.

It was this sterling virtue that finally won Rose over. Eating what was put in front of you was one of the key planks of her platform as Mother. While the rest of us might pull faces at stringy corned beef served in its own very salty and greasy juice, George swallowed it as though it were the finest smoked salmon. While her children turned pale green at the sight of sloppy junket, George downed it ecstatically as though it was thick cream fresh from the cow. He was living proof of Rose's dictum that if you ate what was put in front of you, you survived. Or what was even more important, if you ate what was put in front of you, you earned her approval.

My mother's approval was handed out like a rare honour. You didn't get it by coming top in class. You didn't get it by doing your jobs properly. In Rose's opinion these kinds of things were done automatically. Of course you came as near to the top of your class as you could. Of course you did the jobs allotted to you. No child of hers would do any less. Nothing to make a song and dance about. You could see a glimmer of approval if someone said you were a very polite little girl, but I think that was really more for herself. It meant she was winning in her one-woman campaign to eradicate any answering back, pig-headedness or laziness she observed in her children.

The only time she ever told me I'd done well was one hot Hawke's Bay summer's day, when Gerry Wells set fire to our front lawn then had a heart attack and fell over on the path. I ran. I turned the hose on, dragged it from the back of the house right round the front, and snaked it over poor Gerry to the lawn. I was sorry for him but I had my priorities. Gradually, with the help of some wet sacks as well as the hose, I won. Gerry crawled to the letterbox and dragged himself upright. He had no stomach for facing Rose when she saw the remains of the lawn, and in any case he needed to get home to the drops that he was supposed to carry with him at all times. So off he staggered to his little bach, hanging on to people's front fences to keep himself upright.

'Well done,' Rose said later, when she returned from checking on Gerry – to see how he was, she said, but really to see if the story I'd told her was true. Rose did not go along with the concept of childish purity and innocence. All children were born devils, hers were no exception, and only the most stringent work on her part would change that. *Well done.* I glowed for weeks. So for a cat called George to win her approval said a lot for feline resolution.

By the time I was nineteen Rose had died and George the cat was eight. I was the head of our household and the worst had happened. My sister had fallen in love. She had fallen in love with a young man from the South Island. When I was young Rose never mentioned my dead father except to say he was 'from the South Island'. I always thought he'd died of pneumonia, and it wasn't until I was twelve that she told me he'd shot himself when I was four. 'He was from Gore,' she said, as if that explained it.

My mother had fallen in love with a man from the South Island and look what happened to her. So it wasn't surprising that I was far from pleased with my sister's news. What was even worse was that his name was George.

'If you had to fall in love with a man from the South Island why did you have to fall in love with one called George?' I was irritable.

'It's not my fault,' she said, 'by the time I found out what his name was, it was too late.'

I didn't enquire exactly what she meant by 'too late'. These were the good old days when nobody had sex until they'd gone out together for ten years and been married for three.

My sister brought George home for me to vet. This was a difficult meeting. It was made even more difficult because George the cat took a liking to George the man and kept trying to get up on the couch to sit on George's knee. By the time George the man had leaped up and down half a dozen times and I'd snarled over and over, 'George, *get off that couch*,' he and I were pale with suppressed rage and my sister was hysterical with laughter.

George the man wasn't just from the South Island. He was right from the very south of it. He'd been brought up properly. He knew you couldn't haul off and strangle your hostess's cat on the first visit to her house. Especially if said hostess was the sister of the woman you'd fallen in love with. Especially if your loved one had said she wasn't getting engaged unless her big sister said it was okay. Gradually George the man, having the nerves of steel all men from the South are born with, got used to being roared at. What he felt for my sister must have been love. Only love would have got him through those months, where every time he entered our house he got screamed at to get his black hide out to the shed or he'd be sorry.

One day George the cat didn't appear. We called and called. We went up and down the street calling, knocked on doors, and on the third day, after one such fruitless quest, I saw a black shape under the big clump of red-hot pokers. Yes, it was George. And yes, he was dead. 'Must have got cat flu,' our neighbour said. 'That's what cats do,' she added, 'they go away on their own to die.'

I missed him terribly. We all missed him. Even George

the man confessed it wasn't the same sitting in our kitchen and not being told to bugger off outside.

I knew he was working up to ask me if he could marry my sister and I did not want to have to say no. But of course I would. No South Island man for her. But if I could stop him asking that would be even better.

Every time he came inside I would suddenly be very busy, or on my way out to get some meat for tea, or popping over to see a sick neighbour. My sister moped, George looked worried, but still I kept as far away from him as possible.

One night George arrived as usual, and my sister and he sat on the couch in the kitchen, whispering and giggling. Then, 'See you for a minute?' George had appeared beside me at the bench, where I was peeling small onions to pickle. I was crying hot, oniony tears.

'What do you want?' I blew my nose loudly, 'This is not a good time.'

George looked at my sister. She jerked her head as if to say 'get on with it'. He reached into his pocket and pulled out a small black bundle. A small black bundle with fur and bright yellow eyes.

'George the fifth,' George said, grinning.

As I automatically reached out to take the kitten he, a Southern man to his fingertips, knowing the moment was exactly right, moved in for the kill. 'I was – wondering – ah – how you felt about – ah – me and your sister getting engaged,' he said.

George the fifth was snuggling into my neck and purring happily. I knew when I was outsmarted. 'On one condition,' I said, trying not to sniff, and hoping to sound like a woman of forty instead of only nineteen.

'You are never, *ever*, under any circumstances, to shoot yourself. Is that clear?'

'As crystal,' yelled George, grabbing my sister and swinging her off her feet.

I'm happy to say he kept his word.

My brother-in-law, George West, died 20 May 2016.

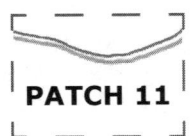

PATCH 11

From *Wednesday To Come* (Victoria University Press 1985), first performed at Downstage Theatre, Wellington, on 17 August 1984, with the following cast:

Granna … Davina Whitehouse
Mary … Kate Harcourt
Iris … Jane Waddell
Cliff … Tim Homewood
Jeannie … Lucy Sheehan
Ted … Cliff Wood
Molly … Michelle Leuthart
Dot … Ruth Dudding

1934. MARY'S kitchen. TED has returned from bringing his brother's body home in a coffin. The coffin has been placed in an alcove to one side.

MARY: *(to TED)* You must be tired.

TED: Had better days.

MARY gives him his tea.

MARY: Like an egg? Some toast?

TED: No thanks. (*Mary goes to the pantry*) I'll just have a drink …

MARY: No need for that.

TED: ... and be on my way.

MARY: No argument.

She returns to the table with bread on a board, butter, jam and a plate. She takes a bread knife and another knife from the drawer.

TED: *(as MARY slices the bread)* I'm buggered, Mary. Couldn't raise an argument if I tried.

MARY: Did you find out anything?

TED: Nothing much. The chaps in his tent said he got more and more depressed (*he takes a piece of bread and butters it*). One day he just went out and hung himself. There was no note – nothing.

MARY: Any trouble about bringing him home?

TED: There'll be an inquest but the police said they had no objection.

MARY: Must've been hard.

TED: Wouldn't do it again for a thousand quid.

PATCH 12

One day, must have been around 1942, I was thirteen and walking to the bus stop to catch the 7.30am workers' bus, when out of the gate from the house down the end of Moeller Street, came a man. He was old, maybe thirty, and wore a tweed coat, grey trousers, a grey felt hat, and carried a leather satchel. He said, 'Good morning,' and I nodded. Must be the new neighbours who'd just shifted in. Poms. I walked faster so I wouldn't have to talk to him.

We did this for a week or so, and then either I was slower and thinking about something else, or he was faster and better mannered, because we ended up walking together for an uncomfortable moment. Then he said, 'Nice day,' and I said, 'Yes,' and he strode on past.

I didn't have much of a repertoire for talking to older people. He didn't have much to offer in the way of conversation with kids either. We continued to walk to the bus stop every day in a kind of walking tandem, he briskly and me at my usual fast clip.

We might have carried on like this forever, but one morning instead of saying something about the weather, he asked, 'Do you like reading?'

'Yes,' I said. I'd learned what it meant to be polite but I hadn't learned how to talk. Why was he asking anyway?

I was on my way to work at Venables Willis, the

printers. I'd been at Napier Woollen Mills some weeks when I received a letter from Venables Willis to say that the person they'd given the job to had not proved suitable, so if I was still interested would I come and see them. I did. They offered me the job and I accepted. It was a step up from the woollen mills. I'd start on Monday.

This meant I couldn't give the manager at the woollen mills a week's notice and I was worried I'd miss out on my week's pay, so I looked in the telephone book, found the address of the manager (Nelson Crescent) and walked there from the Clive Square bus stop. Probably the one time in living history I have ended up where I meant to end up.

I knocked on the front door but no one answered. I went round the back and there was the manager weeding his vege garden. He looked very surprised to see me walking towards him. I didn't bother saying hello or good afternoon, I dived straight into the reason for being there.

'I've come to give you my notice,' I said, 'from today.'
'I see,' he said.
'But I still want my pay for last week.'
'You know you're supposed to give a week's notice?'
'Yes, but I did the work.'

He looked at me. I don't know what he saw. He thought for a moment, then said, 'Fair enough. You can collect your pay from the office any time from Thursday.'

On Friday I caught the bus round to the port, got off at the corner, ran like hell to the woollen mills' office, collected the envelope then ran like hell back to the bus stop on the other side so I could catch the bus making its return trip. I got back to work, unfed, but on time. I couldn't eat lunch on the way. One of the things frowned on, not just by Rose, was eating in public. It was okay to eat in public at the Labour Day Sports at Clive, our one outing of the year as a family, but that was a picnic so it was acceptable.

At Venables Willis I learned how to sprinkle silver dust on just-printed wedding invitations while the ink was still wet, and eventually to bind books. I was the youngest and probably the brightest junior assistant they'd ever had, but definitely the dumbest when it came to adult jokes. I was also the only female. I was taught to hold a ream of paper and jump it up and down onto the table so all the 'anyhow' pages were miraculously restored to the neat oblong ream they'd been before they went in the printer. They called this 'knocking up'. When I said, 'I've knocked up the paper,' they'd laugh. Knocking up paper sounds easy but it's harder than you'd think. I got very good at it, in spite of my small hands, and I can still do it. Ivo Venables (shortish, thin and quiet) and Norman Willis (big and hearty), both very hardworking, showed me things once and expected me to pick them up instantly. Neither Ivo nor Norman ever asked me if I liked reading.

The guy at the chippie where I went to get the men's fish and chips asked me to marry him. When I said a blunt no – my only conversational alternative to yes – he said, 'I'll bring you breakfast in bed every day.' Even at thirteen I knew this was a lie so I repeated my no. I took the free packet of chips he slid across the counter though. I might not have much in the way of conversation but I knew a free lunch when I saw it.

My blunt yes to the neighbour who'd asked me if I liked reading didn't put him off, because the next day he asked, 'What do you like reading best?'

Bugger. I should never have answered him the first time. Perhaps he was going to ask me something different every day?

In any case this wasn't an easy question to answer because at that time I had no discrimination at all, I read anything with words on it. I made no judgements about the story or the writing. It wouldn't have entered my head to do so. They were what they were. I read the library books I borrowed for myself and I read the ones I borrowed for Rose. I'd been allowed to borrow from the adult section from the time I was eleven. The librarian kept an eye on my selection, however, and *Her Gypsy Lover* was taken out of the pile I slid across her desk. She said it needed repairs.

I fell into books like Alice fell into that hole in the ground and I didn't really think much about why I liked them or not, I simply read. I read Agatha Christie, Dorothy L Sayers, Ngaio Marsh, Charlotte Brontë, John Buchan, Vicki Baum, Leslie Charteris, Somerset Maugham, J B Priestley, Evelyn Waugh, Jane Austen, Charles Dickens and a hundred others I've forgotten. Some of them I read twice. As soon as I read the last page, I'd start at the beginning again. This has become a life-long habit when I enjoy a book. It's like I know I haven't got all that book has to offer the first time round so I need to go back for another helping. Maybe the first read is to find out what happens and the second read is to begin enjoying the journey.

I read fast, gulping the story down, just like I ate meals at the table, eager to get the food down my throat, get the dishes done and go back to my book. I wasn't allowed to read at the table, although Rose did sometimes. She propped her book up against the sugar bowl and read. It didn't stop her noticing us pinch a bit of bread from another plate, or try and put a spoonful of pale and watery cabbage from one plate onto someone else's. Without lifting her eyes from the book, quick as a lick her hand grabbed the bread saw and faster than light it slapped across the back of whichever of our hands had attempted this bit of evil put and take. Rose actually did have eyes in the back of her head.

There was an endless supply of books at the library and I wanted to read them all. I was avid for good stories – stories that would take me away from the here of the present to the there between the covers. I read non-fiction too. And I didn't pay any attention to the how of the writing, instead judging a book on whether it held my attention or whether it didn't. Great wodges of description or exposition were skipped, and if I got too frightened by a character I only read the book once. I've only read *Nicholas Nickleby* once. At eleven, Mr Squeers terrified me. Forever. I couldn't watch the TV series either. Not all Dickens did that. *Great Expectations* has frightening scenes in it, too, but I've read it a number of times.

I always took a book to work to read while I ate my lunch – maybe the neighbour had noticed me reading on the bus – although this was unsatisfactory because

I couldn't allow myself to drown in the book in case I missed my stop. So what did I like reading best? He was waiting for an answer.

'Books,' I said eventually, 'books.'

He reached into his satchel and pulled out what looked like a newspaper. '*John O'London's Weekly*,' he said. 'It's sent to me every week by my mother and once read, it goes on the fire. It's all about books. Have a read and if you like it, I'll pass them on.'

So, sitting on that workers' bus in 1942, I began reading *John O'London's Weekly* and was immediately entranced. I must have known the writers on the covers of the books I read were real human beings but I'd never thought about them as people. They were names on a cover. I had no idea or interest in where they came from – I was only interested in the words between the covers. Charles Dickens could have been living around the corner in Greenmeadows for all I knew. Or cared.

In *John O'London's*, though, people did care. They not only wrote about books but also about the people who wrote books. They wrote about plays and playwrights. They published short stories, theatrical news, interviews. Sometimes they didn't like a book – and I thought they were very rude. Did they not realise the writer might read what they wrote? Did they not care about being polite? Kind? Obviously not.

The only other newspapers I knew were the *Daily Telegraph*, published six days a week in Napier, and *Truth*, a weekly paper. I had no idea where that was published. The *Daily Telegraph* published stories about local councillors, national and local crimes, political news, social affairs like debutante balls, and had a crossword and a racing column. My eyes crossed with boredom when I read it at the library. I knew *Truth* because Rose bought that newspaper every week and hid it under the cushion on her couch. We all read it though. We sneaked it out when she wasn't around, hastily read a few bits we didn't really understand and then shoved it back under the cushion in case she came in and caught us. My only motive for sneaking a read was that I wasn't allowed to. It seems amazing to me now that Rose would even have it in the house after the way they'd covered Stan's suicide, but perhaps she liked reading what they said about other people.

With *John O'London's*, I could hardly wait for lunchtime to carry on reading, and when midday arrived I sat at the table where we had our lunch and read, every now and then darting a glance up at the big clock on the wall just to make sure I wasn't late back to work.

I began to look at the names of people who wrote these articles. I knew the name Winston Churchill but I didn't know he wrote. I didn't know Arnold Bennett, but I knew Rebecca West and Somerset Maugham. I didn't know any of the playwrights or the poets. *John O'London's Weekly* introduced me to this world and although I only understood half of what was written, if that, it showed me that there were people who talked and wrote about books and plays, who got excited and argued about them, who wrote letters to the editor about them, who thought books were worth something. Here was a world that, if I just kept reading, I would somehow be able to enter and I would have all the answers to everything I'd ever wondered about. No one would care that I hadn't been to high school because there was a different kind of expectation here, which had nothing to do with school or age or money. I was half right.

Over the next few months, like magic, some of the things I'd read in books began to make sense. Like *Gaudy Night* by Dorothy L Sayers. Set in Oxford, it has a love affair between Harriet Vane and Sir Peter Wimsey as the main thread, and this is worked out as they solve a mystery. It has quotations, not only at the tops of chapters but also in conversations between the characters in the book. They talk about books and poetry and ideas and relationships and the right for a woman to work after marriage. The book makes the assumption that the reader is intelligent, and it does this under the guise of a crime novel. Sayers wrote patronising caricatures of working-class people, but this was how they were portrayed in most novels then, and they passed my uncritical eye because the world she opened to me was like looking in on another planet. Not the real world at all. I loved the female dons, their conversations and their disagreements. I was a little Gulliver peering into a strange new world.

I read *John O'London's Weekly* for as long as the neighbour passed them on. I think Rose glanced through them too. I marvel that at that time, an adult, a man, would even think to pass on such a thing to an uncommunicative girl, just on the basis of her saying she liked reading. The only reason I can think of is that he saw I carried a library book each day and the titles must have shown him I was already a precocious reader for my age, so he'd guessed I'd be able to tackle the *Weekly* without too much trouble.

Our walks to the bus were silent. He never asked me what I thought about the weekly, just handed over the next issue each Wednesday. We never sat next to each other on the bus, and he said nothing about himself. I don't know what work he did or if he liked gardening. I don't know why he came to New Zealand. Obviously he liked reading. Perhaps he gave me *John O'London's* because he didn't like waste – better to pass it on rather than burn it after just one reading. Two years later he and his wife moved away. I don't even remember his name. Maybe I didn't know it.

So, Dear Mr Someone in a Grey Tweed Coat, this is to say thanks and that I remember your act of random kindness with huge gratitude and pleasure.

PATCH 13

I made a decision in 2016 that I would wait to plant tomato plants until a bit later on, say mid-September. The previous year I'd planted in late August and that was a mistake, and not just because of the planting time. I'd read about some new plants that had tomatoes on the top half and potatoes down below – Potato Toms – and I challenged my brother to a competition. He had a bit of a search before he finally found one in Palmerston North, while I put my name on a list and waited before I got mine. Then it was all on.

You know the old saying if it sounds too good to be true it probably is? Although Jimmy won the tomatoes (fourteen) and I had more potatoes (nine), the plants were a waste of time and space and a reminder not to get carried away. Potato Tom sounded good, but either we did the wrong things or it just didn't deliver on its promise.

I came to gardening when I was nearly forty – the vegetable weeding I did for Rose could not be called gardening. I'm not sure what drove me to it but one day something came to life when I stood in the back and looked at what my kids and dogs had left of the large lawn. I looked over at the nondescript straggle that passed for a flower garden inside the fence on the right. There was a sad-looking lemon tree (or was it an orange?)

halfway down the lawn, and a tree tomato, which had become a tamarillo, in the corner by the gate. Perhaps it was simply that my gardening ancestors said it was time. While the Otago/Gore/Invercargill ones would have grown swedes and parsnips, and the Wairoa ones marrows, kūmara and greens, there would, I'm sure, also have been some flowers somewhere. I couldn't have been the only one who liked roses, irises and whichever other flowers I happened to be looking at.

My husband, Laurie, kept a vegetable garden down the back. He wasn't keen on gardening but it was what men did, so he did it. He grew wonderful tomatoes, lettuces, peas and beans. Also pumpkins and the inevitable marrows. No flowers. If I wanted flowers it was up to me.

Whatever the reason, something stirred, and I began what has become a sometimes frustrating, sometimes disappointing, but mainly happy experience. I've grown a few gardens since then, all different, and with each one I've learned. At first I turned as always to books for information, but it has been the actual day-to-day gardening, the thinking, the mistakes, the impulses that have taught me. I found out what kind of garden I wanted by doing it. I've had large gardens and small gardens. I had a garden that I divided into various parts according to the terrain, and I called these parts after the places I'd lived in or loved. So there was a Wairoa, Dunedin, Waikaremoana, Māhia and Auckland.

I garden for my own pleasure. I garden according to what I want to see when I look out the window. If other people like it that's a bonus. I like a feeling of space so my gardens are all very open, and when I moved here to this little square section with a little square unit on it, I had no doubt that I could make it into something I enjoyed looking at. I was seventy-nine and fairly fit.

There were no worms though. Or if there were, they chose to hide. Chris, with a borrowed shovel, did the first dig in the front. I indicated the shape I wanted with a sweep of the hand. A new garden needs at least three digs but the first one's the hardest. In one day he dug a wide area round the front lawn. He got huge blisters on his hands because he wouldn't wear gloves, and because he wouldn't stop till he'd done the whole thing. So it was done in one day. When I expressed concern about his hands, he said, 'No worries.'

His brothers got involved too. Tim pulled up tiles along the side of the house and dug the first dig there. He wore gloves. When he left, he said, 'Good luck, Mum.' David, the other gardener in the family, rang from Wairoa to see how it was going and said, 'Gypsum.'

I was very happy as I looked at the clods of earth. It wasn't going to be easy but what was? It's not a big garden but my hands soon got very sore, and I got very sick of picking up clods of earth and breaking them up. But it was the quickest (although in action very slow) way I knew of making it crumbly. I suppose I could have used my little 'lady's spade' and belted the clods, but I'd have got just as tired. I needed to look after my back for the second dig. I took a day off then I scattered lime and sheep pellets and began digging. This took me a week, and only determination – or, if you like, pig-headedness – got it finished.

I had decided that for this first year I wouldn't be social. I would work in the garden, teach and write.

People going past were interested but only a few

commented. Most contented themselves with a 'Good Morning' or a 'Mōrena' and quick reccie of the work so far. Some asked what I was doing. I curbed my desire to say, 'What does it look like?' and said, 'Making a garden.'

I needed to do something to keep up my energy so I went to the garden centre. These places don't sell plants, they sell dreams. In no time I had a head full of dreams and a car full of shrubs and seedlings too. To hell with the third dig, I would start planting. The rose place down the road was having a sale so I went in, walked among the ones marked down to ten dollars and chose some on the basis of colour.

A vegetable gardening tutor once said to me that we get the kind of garden that suits our personality, and she's right. Mine's a bit of that, a bit of this. If something doesn't work I take it out and either give it away or chuck it. My rule of thumb is – does what I see when I look out the window give me pleasure? If so, it stays. If not, it goes. If there's a chance that cutting it back might liven it up, then that's what happens. It's either shape up or ship out around here. My main vegetable garden is the bit down the side that Tim dug for me. I grow enough greens, probably more, to keep me supplied all year.

Every Anzac Day I plant broad beans and think how this day has changed since I was young. For years it was a day many of us dreaded. We stayed home to avoid seeing the drunks, the men spewing in the gutters, some lying on the ground snoring or, worse, shouting at everyone. A student once told me that her mother always made Anzac biscuits and took a plateful round to each neighbour as a kind of apology in advance for the inevitable drunken shouting and roaring that would come from her house later that day. I knew lots of women and kids nerved themselves up for their husband/father's return home and the rows and/or blows that followed. I've just read Greg McGee's *The Antipodeans*, which gives a powerful picture of why men who returned from the war were like they were. Some men are at their best in war but at their worst in the peace when they return home. And there are some – this is me speaking, not Greg – who belt their wives, partners or kids and are at their worst whatever their situation.

So the broad beans get planted and the world gets sorted. The strawberry plants were new last year so they'll do another year. They grow in bins in the backyard. It's odd but the birds don't seem as interested as they were when I grew them in the garden. As late as June 2016, I was still getting four or five strawberries every few days.

There are seasons where plants surprise me. Last year I grew basil outside for the first time. I'd always grown it on the kitchen windowsill, but I saw the seedlings and thought why not? So I bought two extra punnets and planted them where I had space. It was a situation that got the morning sun and was shady for the rest of the day. I suspected that when the first rain and wind came they'd turn up their toes, but I was wrong. They thrived. I made lots of pesto and gave lots of basil away. I'll try it again this year.

I choose plants because I like the look of them, or they're a colour I like, or have a growing pattern that suits the spot where I plan to plant them.

I went into Mitre 10 in Paraparaumu one day and said to the woman who asked if she could help me, 'I want a climbing vine that'll grow like hell in poor soil and need no special treatment, because I haven't got time.'

'Right,' she said, and walked briskly to the back of the shop, grabbed a pot and brought it to me. 'Honeysuckle,' she said, 'that'll do it.' She was right. It's a pretty hard corner, but the plant triumphed and now it's away.

I've bought most of my roses either by colour or because I've seen them somewhere else or just because. When I saw Ingrid Bergman on the label of an expensive standard rose, I knew I would have to have it. I knew it would be gorgeous. I was right. I bought two and the flowers are a deep, voluptuous red. They stand alongside the path in front of my kitchen window. They flower for a very long time. Of all the gardens in all the world, I'm really happy she walked into mine.

I've got lots of irises and, except for the mini ones I bought out of curiosity, they've all been given to me. They come from as far south as Dunedin and as far north as Napier. One mini has blossomed and today a grown-up one is out. Soon there'll be clumps everywhere. And I have loads of plants in pots. You can grow almost anything in pots. Maybe I'll grow an orange tree in a pot? I think of the gardeners who grew orange trees in pots for the Sun King, knowing if there were no oranges their heads would be on the block. Yes, I'll grow an orange tree in a pot.

Two of my granddaughters, Naomi and Abbie Marie, gave me an apple tree that has bloomed and provided cooking apples from its second year. I was given a crabapple columnar tree, which started off its first season with about five apples and this year had five cups – my best harvest – and I made crabapple jelly.

Last year Kim came on Fridays and helped with the harder jobs. I don't get up on a ladder anymore and some digging is too hard. She still comes now and then. This week she'll find I've planted silver beet, pansies, stock and there's a perennial wallflower waiting. I've been picking celery, lettuce, spinach, rocket, parsley, coriander and other herbs all winter. I sound smug. I don't care.

By the time I made the garden here, I knew that a garden was a mixture of romantic notions and ruthless decisions, and that above all else the soil had to be looked after. The trouble is you can't always see the value of compost, you just see the cost. If you have a small section you can't make enough of it for a garden, but if you want the garden to thrive, buying or making enough compost is an investment. I buy it. The guy delivers, and once here he places the bags where I point. Last year I bought fourteen bags. I split them with a knife to let all the nasties out, then a little later spread it on. Kim did ten bags to my four but I tripped on my spade, which I'd carelessly left on the lawn, so that took some of my enthusiasm away from the job. I have to keep reminding myself to take it easy. Like the doctor says when I get a bit sour about not being able to do all I used to, 'You're eighty-eight, Renée, just accept it.' 'Why should I?' I mutter, but not in her presence.

Now in its eighth year, the garden looks established, like it's always been here. The same people, new people, out-of-town people all pass by and it makes them smile. My granddaughter Freddie smiles every time she sees the flowers, and every time I look out the windows I smile too. Which is the whole purpose. Long may it last.

Anzac Day

The band packs up her troubles

She remembers him waving.
He fixed the lemon tree with salt,
carved his name on the wooden spoon
she used for mixing pikelets. She said
she'd wait. This was before.

in her old kitbag

The club went south to tramp.
One day the boys played bullrush.
She made scones and apple shortcake.
He whipped the cream, sneaked a lick
from the beater. This was before.

and smile, smile, smile.

The lieutenant colonel sings,
the minister prays, reads a poem,
talks about sacrifice. She smells
mint, remembers the tomato sauce.
She'd sterilised the bottles.

Now there's a Lucifer to light your fag

It all got spilt, the spoon was broken,
the bottles, her arm. He got a warning
from the constable after he chopped down
the lemon tree, the frame on the photo
of him smiling. This was after ...

smile boys, that's the style.

PATCH 15

It was in the early 1970s when someone knocked on my door in Wairoa and asked me to teach two classes at the college while their teacher was on sick leave, a fifth form English class and a seventh form history class with only one student. I was asked to do this on the strength of the history papers in the extramural degree I was studying through Massey. At that time you had to do the third year of a degree as an internal student, which was why I went to Auckland a bit later.

I became fascinated by the way the lone girl in the seventh form and the students in the fifth form responded (or didn't) to the lessons I prepared. I over-studied, over-read, over-prepared for these classes, because I was nervous that I wouldn't do it 'right'. At that stage I thought there must be one right way. It was only later I realised there are many ways of teaching, but all of them have to start with preparation and be transmitted to a class by performance.

I hadn't been to high school or teachers' college and I was conscious of that, but I soon realised that my years working in all aspects of theatre had probably been just as good as anything at preparing me to face a room of fifth form girls who didn't want to be there. I couldn't blame them. The curriculum was fairly uninteresting to kids who had to get up at 5am to help with the milking and the younger kids, then have breakfast, walk to the bus stop and endure an hour's drive to the college. When they got home around 4.30, they'd throw their bags on their bed, get changed, and go and help with the cows or whatever, return around 6.30 for dinner, then slump down on a chair and watch TV, going to bed later than was conducive to a readiness to work at school. That was on the good days. Of those that lived in town, many of them would have dawdled around the main street, shoplifting or simply sloping around here and there, often where they weren't supposed to be, not caring about that.

Factor in bad weather, parents' upsets, bad temper, the bus driver's changing moods, their own adolescent ups and downs, and it's not hard to understand why Katherine Mansfield, or a British novelist or poet, bored them stupid. Janet Frame didn't strike a chord and neither did poems that talked about larks ascending. On some days these writers bored me stupid too. I understood how far away from the lives of students this sort of literature was, because a lot of the time it was aeons away from mine.

I understood why they read Mills & Boon romance novels. They weren't like real life either, but they had pace, adventure, a handsome hero and a beautiful young heroine, who after some ups and downs lived happily ever after. They were short, the language wasn't testing, they were just there to fill in time and take reality a little bit further away. These girls didn't want impenetrable and discursive passages, and they didn't want to delve into the dark areas of life. They wanted the quick fix. I didn't blame them.

They were cheeky and rough-tongued at first. They slumped around and giggled among themselves. They eyed me like 'What're you gonna do about it, miss?' I had two things in my favour. My sons David and Tim. All the girls liked one or the other. But that wasn't enough to guarantee a willingness to learn, or an investment in behaving well. I had to deal with what was in front of me in the here and now.

I thought about it a bit. I had to establish myself as someone they at least respected and I had to get them to want to work. So I needed to present a persona that would achieve this. Oh, great. I had to work out what this would be and I had to prepare lessons that would make the girls, if not mad about learning, at least interested enough to have a go. There had to be consequences for rude behaviour. I had to show them I had limits. That I meant what I said.

I abandoned the books the previous teacher had left and made up my own teaching plan, which was focused on what they already knew, stuff that had never been seen as important or relevant to their education. I had to make them want to work and they were not going to do that if they were asked to consider stories, poems, topics that had no relevance. I didn't think all this through all at once of course. At the time I worked on experience and instinct.

I decided my persona should be as much like myself as possible (easier to keep up) but exaggerated a bit. I needed to be quick and a step ahead all the time, be inventive, ready to change course if the first one wasn't working, and I had to do what I said I would do if they played up. I'm short so my personality and voice had to do what more centimetres might have achieved without any effort. I have a deep voice, which was a plus. I was used to the changing nature of adolescents. I didn't like it but I was used to it. I had to think of a project.

And that was the problem. I could do all these things but if I couldn't think of something to do that motivated them as a group – like a cast has with a play, or a netball team with a trophy it wants to win – I might as well give up. The project had to come out of individual effort bolstered by group support, it had to result in a series of projects all focused on the same topic. I thought of various topics but nothing appealed. Whatever I thought of had to appeal to me as well.

Then Witi Ihimaera's *Tangi* came out and I had the answer. Death. Death was the topic. It was a subject they knew quite a lot about. They knew it from observation, from events, from stories and from history. There were all sorts of ways to approach it. There could be photographs, drawings, as well as words. There could be fiction and non-fiction, poetry and plays. It could take any number of shapes. Perfect.

To prepare the way, we read *Tangi* – I read it out loud chapter by chapter and we discussed it. I didn't have to jump up and down. Then I put the book away and announced the project. Tangi. I held my breath and waited. 'Choice,' they said. '*Choice*.'

Some of the other teachers were a bit alarmed at the subject. They felt uncomfortable. I didn't blame them. I didn't know how comfortable I was either. But I did know one thing – for the first time these girls were interested and enthusiastic about a work topic. They knew about tangi. They'd been attending them before they could walk. We spent a bit of time talking about it, about how it might be done.

That afternoon I took them down to the river, and we mucked around for thirty minutes then went back to the classroom. I said, 'Okay. Grab your exercise books and pens and write about what has just happened, write about the river, what you said, what you thought, what you saw.'

These were not kids who were keen on writing. But this seemed okay. They *had* been down to the river. They *had* seen things. Ms Taylor *had* said the writing didn't have to be fancy, and not to worry about the spelling, they could fix that later. They didn't have to worry about their language either. *Choice*.

They were right. For these kinds of exercises they couldn't fail. That was the plan. Or the first part of it. And, if you ignored the spelling and the language and the grammar, the results were definitely better than anything they'd done before. Death in some form had found its way into every piece of writing but that was okay too. They'd done exactly what I'd asked. They had met the criteria. So they all got an A. The first they'd ever had.

'Why'd did she get an A, miss? My story was better than hers.'

'Because,' I said.

The next day we started on the projects. The overall title was 'Tangi' but they had to think of a title for their projects and a plan. They didn't have to tell me what their titles were but I wanted to see the plan. I made a list of things the projects should include and half of every class time was spent on writing and on subjects that contributed to more lively and interesting writing. The students worked in groups on their individual projects, like they were all weaving the same kete.

I crammed in some spelling competitions – old-fashioned perhaps but it had worked for me – and some ways to start paragraphs, and I made a list of suggestions their pieces of writing might include. They could choose which ones, but they had to have at least half of the items from the list. I introduced them to the radical notion of rewriting, that first drafts were never as good as the next one. I said their written pieces could be short(ish) but correct spelling could get them extra marks. Punctuation remained idiosyncratic. Their attitude was that if there was an 's' you stuck an apostrophe in front of it.

It wasn't all smooth. I yelled at times. They sulked at times. I laid down the law. At first I tried a walk round the rugby field for the deliberately intransigent, but found I had to walk with them or risk them vanishing from school altogether. And if I walked, the rest of the class had to walk with us because I couldn't leave them on their own in the classroom. I soon gave that up.

I smiled and coaxed. I discovered my nickname was Rocky. There was a series on TV at the time about a group of women, one of whom was called Rocky. She was tough and cynical and not always likeable. To see it, they had to have been up very late but there was nothing I could do about that. In any case, I agreed with them. I could be a bit rocky at times especially when they forgot my strictures on yes please, thank you and good morning.

Why, miss? They wanted to know. Because, I said. I had lost patience over the apostrophes and couldn't be bothered explaining yet again that while good manners can be seen as frills, they help to make a group of people gel and, more importantly, they keep this teacher happy.

But they did it. The projects got completed. Writing, drawing, fiction, non-fiction, even a couple of poems, some history. We invited visitors to come and have a look. Some of them liked what they saw, some were a bit off-hand, but the parents who came were very proud although they tried not to show it. Perhaps the material was confronting for some? Mostly the exhibition on the walls got a thumbs up. There was astonishment from some staff that these kids had actually done anything at all, let alone started and finished a project.

I was over the moon with satisfaction. I was so pleased I could have danced. I had a permanent smile on my face for days. We all did.

As a reliever with no teachers' college training, I was on the A list, which meant I wasn't a proper teacher but was good enough to babysit classes while their real teacher was away. Then the inspectors called.

The first I knew was when a couple of men in suits knocked on the door one afternoon, introduced themselves and asked if they could look at this project they'd heard about. Shit, I thought, shit, shit, shit. All the forebodings and doubts expressed to me by others, their cautionary speeches about the wisdom of such a topic, their hints that only someone who wasn't a proper teacher would think of such a thing echoed in my ears. My smile became fixed as I watched them look through the projects. They remained stony-faced. I was able to pull myself together and answer their questions coherently, but it took willpower. Performance, I told myself. Act as though you know what you're doing. They thanked me and left.

I heard nothing until one day I was handed a note. The inspectors had been really pleased, so pleased they'd put me onto the B list. This didn't mean, as I first thought, that I didn't deserve to be on the A list, but that my teaching skills were good enough to apply for other jobs. I was now considered a teacher. I still had the feeling that I'd sneaked in the back door while everyone else marched through the front door, and some of those who'd been to teachers' college made sure I knew my place. Did I care? Nah.

The class invited me to watch them play netball one Saturday. I got there, tin of biscuits in hand, cursing myself for saying yes. The day was windy, cold and raining. They ran and found me a blanket from somewhere, possibly stolen from someone's car, and I sat huddled on the sideline like those old nannies I was scared of, who used to sit on the footpath outside the butcher's shop in Taradale when I was a kid.

Then I started yelling encouragement, and jumped up and down and screamed myself hoarse when they got a goal. Didn't feel the cold at all. The team didn't win but came close.

'We call you Cookie now,' said one of them after the game, as she bit into one of my peanut brownies.

'Why?' I was angling for a compliment on my baking.

'Because.'

We all grinned.

PATCH 16

When I was a kid the Labour Party ran all sorts of community gatherings. The ones I knew best were the learners' dances and the Labour Day Sports & Picnic, which was a Hawke's Bay-wide event held at Clive.

The learners' dances were smaller than the picnic and run by a group of Taradale Labour Party supporters who organised the hall, the music and the teachers. They made sure there were enough adults present who could dance because the first thing that happened was we were paired up with an oldie (all of twenty-five to forty-five years old) who taught us the basic steps. The atmosphere was very friendly and welcoming but this wasn't a social event. There were plenty of smiles and good humour, but we were there to learn and they were there to teach, so there was little mucking around with social niceties apart from the welcoming words.

One thing they taught girls was that the boy could be a useless dancer or have bad breath, and he could be – and sometimes was – drunk, but it didn't matter. Girls had to smile, accept the invitation to dance, stand up immediately and keep on smiling. Whatever the standard of dancing skills the boy had, however many times he tripped over your feet or stood on your toes, if he insisted on talking or remained stolidly silent, if he grabbed you and held you in a vice-like grip or his arms worked up and down like the lever on a water-pump, whether he stank of perspiration or Lifebuoy soap, you maintained a fixed smile. And when you were taken back to your seat after the dance, you said thank you.

For a shy good-looking boy like my brother, it really was agony. He hadn't quite struck his growing taller time, so he was shorter and skinnier than a lot of the other boys, and he didn't have a way with words. He shot up and became tall around sixteen although he stayed skinny. Bravely he went through the motions but still remembers the terror.

Val and I were naturally good dancers and although we moaned to each other about some of the boys we had to dance with, thanks to our teachers we'd learned the steps to the Maxina, the Gay Gordons, the fast and slow foxtrots and the waltz, so we had no worries about sitting out the dances.

By the time we were finally allowed to go to 'outside dances' we were very good dancers. I only ever turned down one invitation to dance, and that was from a guy who wove out of the crowd of boys huddled together at the end of the hall and lurched towards me, leering drunkenly. I made up my mind. 'I'm not going to dance with him,' I hissed at Val.

'You have to,' she said, 'you have to say yes.'

'No,' I said, 'he was caught drunk in charge of a bike – it was in the paper – and he's drunk now. Everyone will laugh.'

'I'll get someone to say excuse me,' she said. 'Just say yes and do a few steps and I'll get Lenny or Jimmy to tap him on the shoulder.'

When you were dancing with someone and another

boy (never a girl) wanted to cut in, he came onto the dance floor, tapped the boy you were dancing with on the shoulder and said, 'Excuse me,' and the boy you were dancing with had to immediately relinquish you to this burglar and walk off. Sometimes, if you were the girl, having to change partners was bliss but other times it was a damn nuisance. It didn't matter anyway. You had to smile. Some of the dances were nominated as 'excuse me' dances, but if you had the nerve you could do it any time.

I looked at this shambling guy standing before me and thought, No, I'm not saying yes. The politeness instilled in us by Rose and our Labour Party teachers was forgotten. He loomed over me. I smelt the booze, and when he said, 'Fancy a dance?' I said, 'No thanks.' He looked absolutely astounded and so did everyone around us. No worries about anyone laughing. They didn't think this was funny at all. Val was mortified but I stared ahead and ignored the boy until he finally lurched off. I didn't have the guts to get up and dance that dance, though, in spite of the fact that I was asked by three other boys one after the other. I sat it out because I knew any boy I danced with would be beaten up by that guy and there'd been enough drama for one night.

The Labour Day Sports & Picnic was quite different. It was a day we kids really looked forward to. We had no transport so outings were always a treat. We went with the Hamiltons. Bill Hamilton had a truck. His wife, Carol, and my mother, Rose, sat in the front with Bill driving and the kids, eight of us, sat in the back. As usual I was in charge. This meant nothing when we were all crammed in the back of the little truck. We hung on to anything we could grab that appeared solid. The kids in the middle were the unlucky ones. I always sat with my back up against the cabin and my right hand gripping the side of the tray. I held on to Val's jersey with my left hand, and she in turn gripped Joy Hamilton's jersey with her left and hung onto my arm with her right, so it would be a trio that went over the side together if anything happened.

We were three girls and five boys and as always the boys spent most of the time showing off to each other. One of them would stand up, attempt a few jumps or wave his arms around, wave to people in their gardens, shove his bum out and pretend to fart then crash down against another boy, who would shout and punch him as the truck sped along the rough shingle roads, bumping and jiggling its way to Clive. Bill Hamilton was a relatively good driver when he was sober, so the trip to Clive, while bumpy, was okay.

I hated being in cars or trucks because I always got carsick. Rose had no sympathy for such 'carry-on'. 'Don't watch the road, just concentrate, look straight ahead and you'll be fine.' I never was. So by the time we got to Clive, I was pale and heaving, just managing to keep from actually being sick.

'Just run around,' she said, looking at my white face. 'You talk yourself into these things, my girl, and the sooner you talk yourself out of them, the better.' This made absolutely no sense to me but I got off the truck and stood still while the earth moved. Not exactly a Hemingway moment though.

There were sports for all ages: egg-and-spoon races, running races, sugar-bag races, piggy-back races for the kids, and more competitive running events for the adults. I started feeling better, not great, but we all had to at least run. So I ran. I never won but it was easier to enter and lose than put up with Rose's nagging. She never entered any of the adult things herself but I knew better than to ask why.

The day was usually cloudy with rain. It always rained on Labour Day. Nevertheless we spread rugs or blankets, put out the food – hard-boiled eggs, cold roast mutton, tomato relish sandwiches – and sat around eating in the pouring rain like it was fun. In a way it was. We were 'out at a picnic', and there were things we could do. There were kids you remembered from last year, kids who remembered you.

The atmosphere was good-humoured and happy, lots of greetings and handshakes between those who only saw each other once a year, or those who met regularly at union or Labour Party meetings. The DRINKS tent began to do a brisk trade as the afternoon wore on and men wanted to drink as much as they could before setting off home. There was a speech or two from local Labour dignitaries and everyone clapped, some cheered.

We kids got noisier or we got tired and scratchy. If you were little you went to sleep. The women enjoyed the chance to talk to each other. Little knots and huddles of them sat all round the grounds knitting or crocheting, catching up on the news, enjoying the one day of the year they saw each other and had time to talk. Every now and then one of them would get up, rinse out the teapot at the nearest tap, stick some tea leaves in and get it filled with boiling water from the TEA tent, come back to the group and pour fresh tea all round.

Finally the races were all run and the DRINKS tent closed but not before the men had grabbed three glassfuls so they could stand outside and talk, making the drinks last as long as possible. It was time to go home, but not for the men. Carol and Rose packed things up, chivvied the kids, got us all onto the back, spread a couple of blankets over our legs, got into the front and waited. It was a long wait because Bill had to finish his last drink, shake hands with everyone again, agree this was the best day out ever, before weaving his way back to the truck. He was always in a good humour.

He got himself into the driver's seat, sat for a minute, then said, 'Better go and have a leak,' got out again and made for the tent that had MEN painted on a placard nailed to a stake outside it. He did this every time, and every time it made Carol wild. When he got back Carol would say, 'You've got a Woolworth's bladder, Bill. I've told you before – why can't you remember?' He always answered, 'I did remember.'

'Earlier,' she'd stress, 'you should remember earlier.'

'Shut your moaning, woman,' he'd say, beer-brave.

Finally we'd start off. The truck would join the line of cars and trucks with drivers in a similar condition of drunkenness. When Bill had had a few beers he liked to go fast. The roads weren't made for this and neither was the truck. There was no showing off from the boys on the way home, we were all too busy hanging on. We ripped and roared around the back way home, hitting potholes, large rocks, possums, pūkeko, anything that got in the way.

Carol's voice got so loud we could hear it at the back. 'Watch what you're doing, Bill,' she'd yell.

'Just pipe down, Carol,' he'd say.

Or he might say, 'Roll us a cig?'

Carol would feel around in his trouser pocket for his tin of tobacco and papers and he'd yell, 'Careful there, girl, dangerous ground,' and laugh uproariously at his own wit. After a second or two Carol couldn't help it, she'd start giggling and tell him to stop it, 'Mind your tongue, Bill, there are kids in the back.' Bill just pressed his foot down harder, laughing when Carol commanded him to slow down. 'Not what you said last night,' he yelled.

'He's drunk,' Carol shouted at Rose. Like this was news?

We raced and revved through Pākōwhai, Waiohiki, Taradale, around corners, up and down rises, flat out along the straight bits. The road became a blur. Finally, with a screech of brakes, we got to our gate where the truck sat trembling while we got off. We said, 'Thanks Mr Hamilton,' and Val and Jimmy ran to be first to the dunny. I was too relieved to feel sick. My legs trembled in time with the truck. Rose got out, stood still and looked at me. She nodded to herself. She might as well have said the words out loud. I had proved her thesis. I'd had something other than myself to think about so I hadn't got sick.

'Thanks, Bill,' she said. Another Labour Day Sports & Picnic survived.

The organisation behind these events was amazing. At the time I took it for granted, now I wonder how the Labour Party did it. I don't know who contributed the tents, the stalls, the prizes, who persuaded the organisers of the sports events to stand around all day in the pouring rain and referee races for over-excited kids and adults. And it doesn't matter, because every year on Labour Day it's not the organisation I think of but the goodwill, the generosity, the putting into practice the good old (but alas not so obvious these days) Labour principles of looking after working-class people and their families, not only seeing to their working and living conditions but also giving them some time out. No doubt there were political reasons for reminding us of their presence – but these dances and picnics, even the ride home afterwards, remain in my memory as happy family times.

PATCH 17

Once upon a time

Once upon a time when the earth was blue
and the cross turned over and the grey stars sighed
I played Etta James and I thought of you.

How we dived for love and for wreckage too
how we stamped and sang and waited for lies
Once upon a time when the earth was blue.

Why do the songs always come on cue?
Why do the words slither and sigh?
I played Etta James and I thought of you.

I was told that a garden only grows rue
when the memory of laughter lies fallow and dry
Once upon a time when the earth was blue.

There's a track on a hill where a cross stands true
it's a place that the flesh and the fires deny
I played Etta James and I thought of you.

Here where the songs and the heart balance true
here where the blood and the body cry
Once upon a time when the earth was blue
I played Etta James and I thought of you.

PATCH 18

From *Finding Ruth* (Heinemann 1987).

Now there was a point to practices. We were going to sing for other people, strangers. I was to sing a solo. I practised it in my bedroom, on the way home from school, in the lavatory, in the bath.

Rescue the perishing
Care for the dying
Snatch them in pity
From sin and the grave.

'For God's sake,' Mum said, 'can't you sing something else?'

There was a popular song at the time called 'Blue Hawaii'. So I would switch to that, carefully rounding out my vowels and sounding my consonants like Mr Stone wanted. Mum buried her head deeper in her library book.

The Junior Choir presented their programme in Sunday school as a sort of trial run.

'I am the Way, the Truth and the Light. No man cometh to the Father but by me.'

The superintendent's voice rang out very confidently

and very earnestly. What about me, I thought. I was a child, and a girl at that. What *was* the Way? I knew about *Truth*, that was a weekly newspaper I wasn't allowed to read. And truth with a small 't' was what I had to tell at all times. If it was *Truth* I couldn't see Mum letting me take that way because she always hid the paper, and if you found the way by a little 't' then I already knew about that because Mum told me to, nothing to do with Jesus.

I was there at half-past five. My dress was freshly ironed, my socks as white as scrubbing could make them. My sand shoes were stiff with chalky cleaner and I walked straight-footed so I wouldn't get creases in them. I had a hanky in my pocket and Joe had given me a penny for the collection.

I had sung my solo for him out in the woodshed and then I'd sung 'Blue Hawaii' as an encore. Joe had clapped and said that when I grew up I'd be much better than a lot of the rubbish they put on the radio.

We were welcomed by a smiling woman who gave us a biscuit and a glass of orange. Then some of us went to the lavatory and we marched into church. The choir sang 'What a Friend We Have in Jesus', Mr Stone led a prayer and then it was my turn. I stepped forward.

'As it's our Missionary Week,' said Mr Stone, 'Ruth has a song specially suited to this time.' He smiled at me, Miss Dyer played the introduction to 'Rescue the Perishing', I took a deep breath and out came my beautifully rounded vowels singing about heavenly nights and a blue Hawaii …

The piano crashed, faltered, then gamely followed me as I sang right through to the end. I knew I was singing the wrong song but I couldn't have stopped if Jesus himself had commanded me ... all those dreams coming true ... the magic night of nights with you ...

I walked back to my place in an electric silence. Mr Stone rapped with his baton and the choir launched into 'Shall We Gather at the River'. I didn't sing again that night.

Mum was putting on the kettle when I got inside. She listened to the shameful story with an impassive face.

'Serves them right,' she said, 'and you, my girl. Kids singing about rescuing the perishing? What would you know? Or that lot if it comes to that. Now get the cups out. You can have some cocoa and then off to bed. One good thing, at least I'll be spared hearing that mournful dirge, day in, day out.'

I sipped my cocoa very slowly. It was obvious that as far as Jesus was concerned I just didn't measure up. Not for me the Way, the Truth and the Light. But it was a fair exchange, I decided, to bask for once in Mum's approval.

PATCH 19

It was a yearly event. The appointment with Dr Rose was in my diary: 22 January 1998. When we'd gone to live in Lower Hutt I'd looked through the hospital/medical practitioner pages, scrolled down the lists, saw there was one called Rose and made an appointment. It turned out to be an inspired method of choosing a doctor.

This particular day when she was doing the breast exam she found a lump. A lump? 'I'll organise some tests,' said Dr Rose. 'You need cleverer fingers than mine.' After the lump had been investigated and found to be cancerous, I decided it couldn't be true. I was fit, how could I have cancer? I walked the dog twice a day around the Hutt River; I worked at my part-time job as a homebound librarian, choosing books for people who couldn't choose for themselves at the War Memorial Library in Lower Hutt; and I was working on a commission, a non-fiction book that became *Yin & Tonic*. I'd even cleaned out the garden shed. I didn't have time to have cancer. Cancer was for other people. I could not – would not – accept what the diagnosis meant.

But, like everyone else who gets news like this, I had to deal with it. So I did.

I was lucky. It was found early. I got lots of support from my partner, Bernadette, and my kids, grandkids and friends. Some people found the news difficult to deal with. After I told them I never saw them again. I found out later that this is normal.

I had a very good surgeon. I wrote in my diary:

> Excellent meeting. Very clear and concise explanation. Nothing can be no-risk but the risk of recurrence seems low. He spoke matter-of-factly, has the ability to convey meaning very clearly. A gift in his profession.

I would have a lumpectomy followed by radiation therapy. I had to remember I could never say I was cured. I could only ever say, 'I'm in remission.'

Before we got to that stage though, there was the mammogram, the biopsy, the going to and from appointments. Bernadette came with me to all of them because we decided that two lots of ears were better. What one of us didn't remember, the other one would.

One day I was driving to the Cancer Society car park on Riddiford Street, where I planned to park the car while I went across to the hospital for what was called an 'oncology orientation', and I went through a red arrow at the traffic lights. I wasn't paying attention. I was worrying about my roses. I'd been told that after the op I'd have to be careful of lymphedema and to avoid getting scratches or other little gashes on that right arm. Should I dig up all my roses, I wondered, and give them away? Could I?

As I parked at the Cancer Society, a police car came up behind me and two officers got out. I had to ask them what I'd done. One of them told me. I was in the wrong. I felt an idiot. I gave them the information they wanted, but the female officer still hectored me like I really *was* an idiot, while I stood wondering why she didn't save it for the real crims. There had been no danger, I hadn't been going fast, no other traffic had gone into that lane – sure I was in the wrong, but was there any need to make a three-act drama out of it? Eventually the lecture ended, and having got whatever was really annoying her off her chest, she calmed down. She said I could consider this a warning and they wouldn't charge me. This time. I said nothing. I couldn't be bothered. It was obvious I hadn't parked in the Cancer Society car park because I was going shopping.

While the cops sat in their car writing this part of their life stories, I locked my little red Honda, which was now on a list of other such criminal vehicles, and walked across the road to join the group at the oncology department. There the therapists were kind, patient and careful. They recognised this was a new and scary experience and it was okay to ask questions, nothing was too ordinary or too obvious. I drove home extra carefully.

Surgery went according to plan. I came home still attached to a HemoVac to drain the wound, but a nurse called daily, and after a few days the tubes came out and it was taken away. I finished *Yin & Tonic* and agreed to a request from Cancer Society co-ordinator Mary Collow to create some workshops on writing a life story. She wanted me to run them for cancer patients and survivors. This turned out to be a great thing to do both for me and for the participants.

On the Saturday Bernadette and I went with my niece Vonny to Te Papa, where they had these little mounds in their car park. I tripped over one and fell on the hard ground. My ankle swelled up like a balloon.

'We'd better go to A&E,' said Bernadette.

'It's only a sprain,' I said.

'It looks awful,' said Vonny.

After I'd had X-rays and was told that yes, it was broken, I said, 'But I can't have a broken ankle, I'm having radiotherapy and have to drive to Wellington every day and then Friday afternoon I fly to Dunedin for the Robert Burns fellows' anniversary.'

'The orthopaedic nurse will give you some crutches,' said the X-ray nurse.

I decided I was beyond comprehending things. It was all too much. Fate had me in her sights, so I determined to borrow the wisdom of Gertrude Stein – there isn't an answer, there never will be an answer, just put on a smile on your face and get on with it.

PATCH 20

I was twenty-nine, Laurie and I had left our jobs as general handyman and cook at Waipoapoa Station because the Maraetōtara School was a one-teacher school and I wanted more than it could offer our kids. We were living in Laurie's parents' house temporarily. His mother had died and his father was very ill. In a little while we'd move to a house in Greenmeadows, but meanwhile we were living close to the Napier Repertory Players theatre and Kay Mooney suggested she and I go to an audition being held there. Kay lived at Port Ahuriri with her husband and three kids. We met at a meeting of the Hawke's Bay branch of the New Zealand Women Writers' Society, where I was a new member. Kay was a great reader, highly intelligent, very funny and we'd become friends.

I didn't really want to go to the audition. I was tired. We'd had all the organisation and hard work of the shift, and on top of that the Maraetōtara/Waimārama Country Women's Institute fundraising concert was coming up, in which I was to star as Marilyn Monroe in a blonde wig, a pink negligee and pink high-heeled strappy shoes. Mercifully I can't remember which song I sang. I enjoyed CWI. I entered all the competitions: four scones on a plate, creamed sponge, a knitted jersey. They had poetry competitions and one year I entered and got third. The concert was a huge success, and we had to do it again the next night so those who'd stayed home babysitting could come along.

Kay was insistent we should go to the audition. 'The director's a play in herself,' she said. 'Everyone goes to her auditions just to see her performance.' Laurie didn't mind looking after the kids. He enjoyed plays but the thought of being in one was like asking him to climb Everest with no oxygen. Although later he did agree to take part in two plays I directed because I was desperate and said he had to. Each of my sons has been coerced in the same way. Tim got off best because all he had to do was lie in a hole, get out after half an hour, say one line and walk off. This was N F Simpson's play *The Hole*. As happens in theatre, a day or so before opening night, Tim got the flu and a girl stepped in, lay in the hole for half an hour, got out and then walked off without saying the one line.

'Stage fright,' I said to Tim.

'It was only *one line*,' he said.

Tim says he used the play to answer every drama question in every exam he sat after that. So all was not lost.

Laurie's first role in theatre was in a crime thriller staged at Wairoa Little Theatre, title now forgotten. I have cultivated this kind of forgetfulness. I only started keeping diaries in 1979 – before that I rely on my memory and the memories of my sons. I will always remember the last night of this particular play though. Near the end, the character Laurie was playing had to face up to the villain and was supposed to grab a pistol from the drawer in the desk and stop him doing whatever it was he was going to do. As it happened, on the last night the props person had forgotten the gun. So Laurie said his line, opened the drawer, found it empty, knew I'd kill him if he just walked off, so he launched himself at the surprised actor, tackled him and brought him to floor, from where they shouted the closing lines.

I was waiting in the kitchen ready to make the tea for supper and nearly had a heart attack when I heard the thumping and rolling around. It made a great story at many of the theatre parties. The only other time Laurie performed in a play was again in Wairoa when I directed *O Temperance!* by Mervyn Thompson. All he had to do this time was bang a big drum and smile, so that was okay.

The night Kay and I walked into the Napier Rep auditions and found two seats near the back, I had no intention of doing anything more than having a good laugh. The director, May Macdonald, was a huge personality. Tall, good-looking, with a commanding presence, she smoked incessantly using a cigarette holder, which she waved around to stress a point. And she had a beautiful deep voice, she knew how to use. May had worked as a professional in touring repertory, in England. In Napier I saw her play Regina in *The Little Foxes* by Lillian Hellman and she was magnificent. She was equally commanding as a director.

Tonight she was auditioning for a play that was called *Bonaventure* by Charlotte Hastings. A woman has been charged with murdering her brother and is on her way to the gallows, accompanied by two prison officers.

There is a huge storm and a flood and they have to take shelter at a convent where Sister Bonaventure realises the woman is innocent. Napier Rep chose it because they knew audiences would love it, and there were a lot of female parts and a couple of good dramatic scenes. Kay was right. It was fascinating watching May do the auditions. She went through every part, tried people out in various roles, mixed and matched, then she turned to the audience and said she needed people to audition for the nurse in her late twenties.

'No,' I said to Kay, 'I haven't got time.' But somehow, with May's eyes on me and Kay's voice urging me to have a go, I stumbled out to the front along with four other women who, like me, were wondering why the hell they'd hadn't stayed in the peace and quiet of their own sitting rooms.

May lined us all up and told us to scream. 'Think of someone you'd like to scream at,' she advised, 'someone who, every time they open their mouth, says something you disagree with but you have to smile and look pleasant while inside you're screaming.'

This was easy. I could think of a number of people I'd like to scream at. Just a matter of choosing who. Then one at a time we screamed. I screamed like a frustrated elephant calling to its mate. Some people laughed while others put their hands over their ears. May clapped. I got the part. In a dream I took a copy of the script, trying to work out how Laurie would feel about this. He would have to look after the kids while I was at rehearsals – three nights a week and Sundays.

When I asked him he didn't hesitate: 'Okay.' In fact Laurie never minded looking after the kids, which turned out to be my good luck because the part of the nurse in *Bonaventure* was the beginning of a serious interest in theatre. Getting to work with May, getting to know her, led me to reading plays, to acting in them, to directing them both for adults and kids, to being on theatre committees, choosing plays, emptying dunnies and digging holes to bury the contents, doing the hundred and one jobs that have to be done to get plays on, and eventually led me to the job I liked best in theatre: writing them.

PATCH 21

From *Setting the Table* (Playmarket 1982, published with *Secrets* in Theatrescript series, editor David Carnegie), first performed at Mercury Theatre, Auckland, on 27 September 1982, with the following cast:

> Rose Murphy ... Annie Whittle
> Sheila Jewell ... Frances Edmond
> Con Beath ... Elizabeth McRae
> Assy Carlsson ... Kate Hood
> Liz Keenan ... Heather Bolton
> Detective Inspector Maxwell ... George Henare
> Constable Roberts ... David Chilvers
> First man ... Roy Billing
> Second man ... Nathaniel Lees
> Director ... Aileen O'Sullivan
> Designer ... Amanda Lane
> Lighting ... John McKay

SCENE FOUR – after lunch

ROSE, CON, SHEILA, ASSY are having a meeting.

ROSE: Everyone got enough to eat? Good. Let's go.

CON: Sheila, you start.

SHEILA: Let's take what happened as read. I'm not

	sorry about this latest affair except as it affects Assy. But I think we need to talk about it.
ASSY:	You shouldn't do things in the height of passion.
SHEILA:	I didn't. I did it in the light of conviction.
ASSY:	You didn't take time to think.
SHEILA:	I didn't have time. And if I had I'd have felt the same.
ASSY:	You really believe that?
SHEILA:	We all despise the way the courts deal with rapists. Even when they're reported and charged, only a few, a very few, get jail.
ROSE:	Even now, with all the changes in the law, the victim still suffers – she gets the blame.
SHEILA:	She shouldn't have been out after ten.
ROSE:	She shouldn't have worn those kind of clothes.
SHEILA:	This particular woman was at home in her own bed, for Christ's sake. So I decided, because she told me who he was, that I should do something about it.
ASSY:	I know.
SHEILA:	Do you? Do you really understand why I decided that this time the rapist would know what it was like to be hurt and frightened?

ASSY: Yes. I do.

SHEILA: You and me and Rose and Con were all taught that nice little girls don't fight. So what happens when your friendly neighbourhood rapist comes along? We don't fight. Some idiot filled us up with the idea that you get hurt more if you fight back. Rubbish. You know it. I know it. If you don't fight back (a) the cops and everyone else think you were a willing participant and (b) you get raped anyway. You know what the father of that girl said? It was her fault for coming to Auckland.

CON: The eye for an eye mentality –

SHEILA: I didn't rape him did I? I hurt him and frightened him. Now he knows what that's like.

CON: And in doing so you attracted police attention. Well, that's your choice. But the one thing we don't need at The Haven is any extra hassles with the cops. Once we can't guarantee these women absolute protection the whole thing is useless. We give them a present if you like. We give them time. Time to think about what they're going to do.

ROSE: We know that.

CON: I'm frightened. That cop knows that the window was smashed by an angry

	husband. What say he gets frustrated, what say he says he'll do a deal? We tell him the name of the attacker or he'll tell that guy where to find his wife. He knows we know.
SHEILA:	He doesn't know who the guy is.
CON:	I bet he does by now. They'll be checking out Assy but they'll have their eyes and ears peeled. My name and number are on the roster board. It's not going to take an intellectual giant to figure it out.
ASSY:	All irrelevant. It's the use of the knife.
SHEILA:	How else was I to frighten him?
ASSY:	I don't know but I think if we all agreed that violence was not the answer we'd think of other answers because we'd have to. Violence is too easy. It's quick of course – and usually works. That's why it's used as a tool by the gangs, husband and the cops. But. Why should we use that kind of weapon?
ROSE:	It's always easy to sit around in a quiet room and theorise and *theoretically* you're right, Assy, but *practically*, sometimes we have to.
ASSY:	What about The Haven?
SHEILA:	So we're to sit back and do nothing. Like it's always been.

ASSY: Sheila. I think you liked using that knife. You liked it.

ROSE: *Assy*.

SHEILA: (*shrugs*) It's true. I know it is. Violence is power. I liked that.

ASSY: I don't give a bugger about that man. I do care about you.

Phone rings

SHEILA: It's got nothing to do with anyone else. It's part of the deal.

CON *answers phone*

CON: Oh bloody hell. Thanks (*hangs up*). Cops have been. Checked out Assy's alibi. Saw the roster of course. Saw my name. It was Maxwell. Asked about me. Now they're trying to pacify the three kids and calm the mothers. Part of the deal? A bloody poor hand wouldn't you say?

SHEILA: So we're to wave *and* drown?

ROSE: Yes.

PATCH 22

Saturday, 30 May 1981. The woman, fifty-one, dark, plumpish, glasses, packs a large suitcase. Every thirty minutes or less, she wipes her face. She has severe menopausal symptoms. She hasn't slept properly for three years. It has taken her fifty-one years to get to this moment.

The man, sixty, thin, balding, glasses, sits at the table, watching. He is not an articulate man or one given to emotional outbursts. He's basically kind, he does his best, he's faithful, he understands about good sex, he works hard, he loves her but he doesn't know how to say, Please don't go. I can't bear it if you go. Or perhaps he does but he knows she will go anyway.

She: There's food in the fridge.

He nods.

She: I have to go.

He nods.

She: It's not your fault.

He nods. He doesn't believe her. But she's right, it's definitely not his fault. It's not hers either.

She: I've stayed for thirty-one years, you can't say I haven't given it a good go.

He: We should never have come to Auckland. It's her.

She: It's not Auckland. It's not her. It's not you. It's me. I've had forty-eight years of being responsible for other people. Now I want to be responsible just for me. I haven't ever had any time to do things. I've had to ask for time. Had to ask if it was okay. I don't want to ask anymore. I want it to be my time. I don't want to have to arrange things to fit in. I want to just know that it's my time and I can do whatever I want with it. I don't want to have to fit in. Sorry, I'm repeating myself.

He: I thought you were free.

He looks to where a second, younger woman stands in the doorway, says: You've won.

The second woman says: It's not a contest.

The first woman thinks, Yes it is. It's a contest inside me and for the first time, I've won. She looks at the younger woman and thinks this won't last either, a year or so, she's too young.

She: I don't think I've changed, I think I'm just tired of having to fit in, of always having to remember you, the kids, others. Now they're grown-up, they don't need me. I don't want to just gradually grow old, be part of some background. I want my own ground. This is the only way I can have it.

He doesn't answer. He doesn't answer because he doesn't know what to say. He doesn't know what she means. All he knows is that something's broken in him but he doesn't know how to say that either.

She knows it. She knows it but she pushes the clothes down in the suitcase and forces the lid shut.

He: Can I come and see you?

She: Ring me. The number's by the phone.

She picks up the suitcase. It's really heavy. The other woman is leaving.

He: I'll carry it.

She: My own ground.
She carries the suitcase.
He begins to cry.
She walks out. It's not until she's shutting the gate that she realises she's crying too.

PATCH 23

When I applied for the 1989 Robert Burns Fellowship at Otago University, I made up my mind that if I got it, I would investigate my father Stan's family and also make an attempt to forgive him or at least stop hating him. I'd discovered a 1934 issue of *Truth* that reported the following:

> Stanley George Howard Jones was working as a farm manager on a farm at Pakowhai, situated between Hastings and Napier in Hawke's Bay.
>
> He left his home, ostensibly to go into Napier, he purchased a .22 rifle there, caught a service car to Palmerston North on the morning of April 29 and his body was found lying on the railway embankment in Wellington.
>
> How he covered the last stages of his journey – from Palmerston North to Wellington – is not known. Beside his body were two unopened small bottles of ale and in his pocket a broken glass.
>
> In a pocket also was a box of cartridges, 49 in number, the fatal fiftieth – and the only one missing – had been used in the rifle which was close to the body.
>
> Did Jones leave his home, his wife, and three young children, with the fixed intention to take his own life? From the subsequent events it appears as though he did, but neither his relatives, his wife, nor the police can find any possible motive for such an action.

These reported facts are duplicated in the depositions from the coroner's court. Rose's deposition bears these facts out – and there is a paragraph in her own handwriting at the end of her deposition. I imagine it was already typed out for her to sign, and she asked if she could add this last piece.

> He was not in the habit of drinking heavily – he was not in debt & did not gamble – he was not a sportsman and was not going duck shooting when he left his home on 29th April – he was very fond of his family & a good husband.
>
> Signed, Rose A Jones

The other depositions are from a man who knew Stan when he worked in the Post and Telegraph Department, the fireman who saw the body from the train, and the police constable who went to check out the fireman's report and located the body.

As a child, I'd heard various things about Stan, snippets, whispers, 'not in front of the children' type things. Suicide has nothing to do with voluntary euthanasia, which I regard as a human right. A separate argument. I don't have any religious beliefs so I have no problem with someone in agony wanting to put an end to it. We euthanise pets when they are very ill or in severe pain, surely we can treat human beings with the same kindness and love? Suicide is a totally different matter.

I got the Robert Burns Fellowship so now had to do what I'd promised I'd do about Stan. I was very tempted to break this deal with myself and for a while ignored it, but eventually I started searching. I thought maybe I'd find a clue to the mystery of why he did it.

I received a letter from Orm, Stan's youngest brother. Orm – Ormond Russell Jones – was a lovely man and I remember him with great affection. I wrote to ask him if he knew why Stan killed himself. He wrote back about his and my father's early life.

> Mum was Gertrude Knowles and I think she married Joseph Jones in Ōwaka. The first thing I can remember was living on a farm. I think it was at Mandeville. Joseph Jones' name was in a book with the Original Owners … we also found the old house in Wentworth Street, Gore … exactly as I remember it, along with six acres of land which would have been very valuable had we stayed.
>
> Joseph was away most of the time. I hardly remember him, thank goodness. Mum was a darling and he was a rotter. At that time he was managing a sheep station called Argyle – later on he had a butcher shop in Waihai. Les was working in Cheese and Butter Factories and Stan started work in the Gore Post Office. I went to school at East Gore …
>
> Joseph's father was Emmanuel Jones who lived with us for quite a while in a little bach we built for him and Mum gave him his meals.
>
> Joseph's trips home were always hell for Mum and as Les and Stan were working by this time, they, particularly Les, decided enough was enough and got Mum to get a separation and get rid of him. It was not all that easy as he still hung around, so that was what sent us to the North Island. Stan stayed on, later got a transfer to Napier.
>
> So there you are, Renée, I hope you can make head and tail of this … now I will close with a few lines more about your father.
>
> He was always very good to me and I liked him the

best of my brothers by a long way. He was always good to Mum and I know he was her favourite son. What he did has always been a mystery to me. However, he would be proud of you if he was around today. Anyhow that is life, I guess. My big regret in life is that when I grew up and could have done something for my mother she wasn't there.

Best wishes, Orm

Olive, Stan's sister, wrote to me six years later:

> Orm rang and asked me about Emmanuel. I went to the library and I think I told you I could only get as far as him arriving in Melbourne on the *Commodore Perry*. Many years ago when I applied for the superann, I had to get my birth certificate from East Gore and I didn't realise I had 3 names. What a ruddy handle, Olive Gertrude Lydia. I asked Les where the name Lydia came from and he said, 'She was your grandmother.' So there you are. You have your answer. Lydia was Emmanuel's wife's name. Did Orm tell you he would like to know where Emmanuel came from? It must be Portugal or Spain (olé), I couldn't get anywhere with that.

Emmanuel Jonis, my great grandfather, was from the Cape Verde Islands off the West Coast of Africa, which were colonised by Portugal. He could have been a Cape Verdean, or Portuguese, possibly Jewish. He'd been in New Zealand for thirty-three years before he applied for naturalisation. His surname was Jonis but when he went to see the JP and the papers were filled in, the JP changed the name from Jonis to Jones. Emmanuel may have been called Jones by the people of Ōwaka. He probably had an accent and the name might have sounded more like Jones than Jonis. However he signed his name as Jonis and the writing is clear and the 'i' is definitely an 'i' but the JP ignored that. Which meant his descendants were called Jones instead of Jonis.

According to a report in an Invercargill newspaper, Emmanuel died at ninety-three in Invercargill. Emmanuel and Lydia's son Joseph married Gertrude Knowles, whose parents were Thomas Knowles (from Edinburgh) and Jane Barrier (from Melbourne), and they had four sons and two daughters. I knew only the younger sons as adults – my uncles Cliff and Orm – and the two girls, my aunties Evelyn and Olive. Later I was to use the scraps I knew of Emmanuel, add a few bits and pieces of my own, and make him a character in my novel *The Skeleton Woman*.

I don't know much about Gertrude, my grandmother. She was badly treated by Joseph. She was hardworking, loved my father and (according to Olive) didn't like Rose because she was Māori. I was given her name as my second name. When I was a kid I hated it. But since I've read about Gertrude Jekyll, the highly regarded garden designer; Gertrude Bell, the intrepid explorer; and the wonderful Gertrude Stein; I like it. Gertrude, my grandmother, fifty-two, died in 1932 and is buried in Napier in the Park Island Cemetery, just up the row from Stan (twenty-seven in 1934) and Rose (forty-two in 1949).

Olive gave me some family recipes, including one for Gertrude's sister's fruit cake. Her name was Beatrice or Beat.

Great-Auntie Beat's Special (Light Fruit Cake)
4 eggs plus their weight in flour, sugar and butter
Half-pound of sultanas
Cream butter and sugar
Beat in eggs one at a time, beating each one for five minutes
Bake one and a quarter hours

Bishop Souter's Housekeeper's Christmas Pudding – 1854
2oz butter
6oz sticky raisins
2oz peel
2 eggs
3oz breadcrumbs
2oz currants
2oz brown sugar
Blanched almonds if wanted
Wine glass of brandy if wanted
Quarter teasp. ground nutmeg
Quarter teasp. mixed spice
Quarter teasp. cinnamon
Steam 4 hours (if any excess butter when cooked, tip off)

I made up a lot of material from these sketchy family bits and pieces, added some stories and wrote my novel *Kissing Shadows*. While I think readers thought it was all true, there was only a sliver that was true. The fact that he did what he did was true. The rest was fiction.

My attempts at forgiving Stan failed. I'd thought

and read about the act of suicide a lot from the point of view of someone affected by it. I felt (and still feel) a kind of impatient contempt for those who do what my father did. This is because we, particularly Rose, lived with its repercussions. I believe that this is what killed her at forty-two. I stopped hating him, though, which is, I suppose, a step in the right direction. I decided to remember he was only twenty-seven, very young really. But old enough, my inner voice always answers back, to know better.

I'd applied for the Robert Burns partly so I could have a look at the place where my father was born. So maybe I should thank him for that impetus. If I hadn't applied and hadn't got it, I wouldn't have come to know and love Dunedin, and I wouldn't have come to know and love the friends I made there. That place and those friendships have become part of the warp and weft of my life.

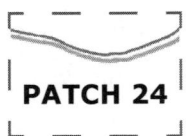

After you walk on water

After you walk on water
you remember Cygnus, the bird star
turned into a swan to trap Leda
you hear the sulky soft whine of the waves
lap lap – the strawberry sponge city's gone
the doll's houses – the silver foam eyes
the pretend jaguars floating high on iron
you remember you ran as Madame the Swan
how the pirouette slowed, preened at the shadow
where Hedda waits – I seen the little lamp, you say
just as the last brick takes the light
just as Antigone smiles and stands up
just as the sly knife slides out
you smile, and then you leave

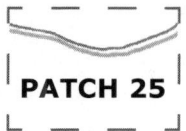

PATCH 25

Sunday, 1 January 1984. Got up early & gardened. Thought about a play. Different to the others but not really. I want the Playmarket week-long workshop this time. Not sure this idea will do it. Will write it anyway.

Saturday, 7 January. Worked on play. In my head and on the page. Guts of it in my head but looks a bit spare. Leonie to stay night so we can have early start on cleaning leaves from terrace. Sharon rang to say she and kids arriving Monday or Tuesday. Chris is in Wairoa and will give them a ride up. Pleased.

Sunday, 8 January. Leonie cleared leaves. Terrace looks much better. I did some more gardening, looks good. Bernadette to Trade Centre to do summary of submissions for newsletter. I planned new look for backyard. Leonie and Bernadette to paint shed roof and fence next Sunday. Worked on play. When I say worked, I mean I thought of a name for the main character. Tried out all sorts but when I thought of Iris, I knew. Rose. Iris. A flower. 4 letters.

Monday, 9 January. Name of firm whose bins weren't used on Springbok tour, Freeth & Brooks Bins Ltd. Rang Sharon. They'll be here tomorrow about 7pm. *Broadsheet*. Play.

Tuesday, 10 January. Rang Laurie re paint for shed. Rang Hirepool. Electric breaker, transformer, point and chisel for half day $22, 2 pr ear muffs $2, ext. lead $3 = $27. Could she make scones onstage? Why not? The night Rose died, around about eleven, Carol Hamilton came to tell us the hospital had rung with the news. Carol had a phone and we didn't. My brother had not long got home from the hospital. I made scones. Just the old simple recipe, flour, baking powder, salt, milk.

Wednesday, 11 January. Sharon, Naomi, Abbie, arrived at 10 to 1. Good trip. Sharon tired. Told her to sit on couch and read magazines, got her a cup of tea and gave her a packet of Matinée.

Thursday, 12 January. Collective meeting. Pledges. Dates of meetings. Workers' meeting. Play. Four generations. Wishful thinking.

Friday, 13 January. Feed Garbo. Play.

Sunday, 15 January. Painting shed, roof and fence. Remembered Bernadette's grandfather – he was called Granna. I loved the name instantly. And it can be male or female. He used to say, 'Monday today, Tuesday to come.' Why have I remembered that? Immediately I know. It's so wonderfully full of foreboding. You think today's bad? Wait till you see what tomorrow has in store. Wednesday to come? Even worse. Who knows what will happen two days away? Got it. Got it. Got it. *Wednesday To Come*.

Tuesday, 17 January. English conference forms 1 to 5. Panel discussion 7pm. Ring Hirepool, Freeth & Brooks Bins. Make cheque Freeth Disposals. Think about Molly.

Wednesday, 18 January. Stocktake *Broadsheet* bookshop. Ring Lynn re statement on finances for March issue. Car firm to ring back re contract ad today. Ring Bert, Elaine, Helen re booking ads. Pay TV and bills. Write to bookshop in Gisborne re stocking *Broadsheet*. Play. Sent to Playmarket for copy of *Setting the Table* to send to Oz.

Friday, 20 January. Send badges, stickers, posters for stall in Hamilton. Got electric breaker etc. Really hard work. Bernadette much smaller than the machine but she was determined it wouldn't beat her. It made a hell of a noise, which was good because the neighbours couldn't hear her swearing. Her face got redder and redder as she forced the damn thing to do what she wanted. Once the first bit of concrete was broken up she got the glory and didn't come in till quarter to 9. Bin doesn't look big enough.

Saturday, 21 January. All concrete broken up. Bin very full. Chrissie and Paula helped. Got trailer and they took some to dump. I'm worried the truck won't be able to lift the bin onto the tray. So is the truck driver. It's a real strain for the hoist. We all hold our breath. But it holds. A crash when it comes down on the tray but it settles. The driver takes off very carefully.

Have to get the way we talked in the 1930s. Not so many words. Lots of subtext though. We really had two languages, one spoken and one not. But we all understood both. We learned it when we were very young. The unspoken language of adults, the looks, glances, gestures, asides, understatement. Osmosis explains how we learned to read adults and understand their subtext but it doesn't do a thing for me when I want to put it on the page. One of the big differences between the middle and the working classes is how words are used. Working class are very careful how they're doled out. It's as if we think every word costs and we don't want to end up out of pocket and in debt. And maybe we think: 'Better store some away for a rainy day.'

Sunday, 22 January. Leonie's friends took some loads of dry fill. All big stuff gone. To beach for little while. Chris came at teatime, took Sharon and Naomi for swim at hot pools. Need a song for Iris. Mouth organ. That's the sound. Wondering about the reins. I mean for Christ's sake, Renée – a coffin and some reins?

Monday, 23 January. Worked on *Wednesday To Come*. Not there yet. The essence is there but something is not right yet. Sequence needs altering maybe? Chris brought veges and 2 apricot pies.

Wednesday, 25 January. Workers' meeting. Jenny – money for batteries, tapes and feather duster. End of stocktaking in sight. Work out headline for Muldoon's speech. Ring H&S for review copy of *Whina*. Send 100 badges and 25 T-shirts to Hazel for Sweetwaters. First draft not finished but it's not the story of my life so its free to fly any way I choose.

Friday, 27 January. Cough mixture. Dice onion, mix with honey in pan till warm and runny – strain and drink the juice. Rang Nonnita to ask for extension of time for playwrights' workshop. 'No,' she said. I'm not really surprised. They have to draw the line somewhere. I'm probably not the first or only one to ask.

Hungry Horse with Bernadette, Sharon and the kids – then a walk around Albert Park and university. Thought about Rose.

Saturday, 28 January. Worked on *WTC*. What will they think of a coffin onstage? Too late now. That's where it is. Or do they bring it on? Talk about suicide too. Silences about it too.

Sunday, 29 January. Went around garden centres, also to Deborah's & got plums. Bought honeysuckle, agapanthus, 2 lavender, blue creeper, others. Sharon gave us a Japanese maple and Leonie gave us a sacred bamboo and stake for maple. Nice day. I think Ted's good. I like Iris saying, 'What I need, Ted, is a hammer.' Bernadette likes it too. It becomes a catchphrase we use when we've got something hard to do.

Monday, 30 January. Worked on *WTC* until 4. Got Naomi and Abb to weed the garden by throwing some small coins around. So cute. I wasted some time laughing. Only needed one to find a coin and it was all on. Tomorrow is the closing date of applications for playwrights' workshop. Bernadette Xeroxed *WTC*. Bit late to start worrying now.

Wednesday, 1 February. Sharon and kids to airport. Up at 5. Early night.

Sunday, 5 February. Worked on the backyard. Leonie, Bernadette and I shifted bath in backyard. Every spadeful of earth has rocks and rubbish.

Monday, 6 February. Massive house clean. Felt good.

Tuesday, 14 February. *Amazon Mothers* launched. Made short speech. Seemed to go well. Feel a bit withdrawn from most people at the moment. Nancy and Bev to dinner. Gazpacho, cauli & cheese pie, avocado, lettuce and nut salad, fruit and cheese.

Saturday, 18 February. Worked on backyard.

Sunday, 19 February. Got a long way towards end of backyard slog. Planted maple, sacred bamboo, kōwhai, replanted tree tomato, feijoa, oleander, citrus trees, jasmine, blue creeper. Peppers, broccoli, lettuce, parsley, silver beet. Hard slog.

Monday, 20 February. Cleaned side corner. Went to Palmers. Rang lawn place for details. Agreed to do talk in March.

Tuesday, 21 February. Planted viscaria, alyssum, night-scented stock, radishes, cranberry bush, dahlia, passion fruit, antirrhinums, pansies, ageratum, primulas, sweet william, black-eyed Susan.

Things to do. See Jenny about New Plymouth. Wire netting and nails. Book a trailer. Measure for lawn and arrange delivery. They'll come Friday. 26 rolls $78. Chris came round with silver beet, fish, tomatoes, courgettes, spring onions.

Wednesday, 22 February. Rehearsal for *Bludgers on the Dole*.

Thursday, 23 February. Ready lawn arrived late afternoon, a day early. We had to lay the bloody stuff because otherwise it would dry out. It also has to be watered in.

Both of us were sick of it by the time we finished. But it looked good.

Saturday, 25 February. Unemployment conference and *Bludgers on the Dole* went down very well. Rose's birthday. How old would she be? She was born in 1907 – so 77.

Sunday, 26 February. Finished hard labour on backyard today. Buggered.

Monday, 27 February. Talk about bookshop organising with Caroline. Rang WEA re weekend courses, what has been arranged, times etc. Incinerator, wire netting. Laid paving stones.

Tuesday, 20 March. Tried to mow back lawn but think we've left it too long. Came home to find Heather had mowed lawn. While I was at *Broadsheet*, Nonnita rang. Playmarket has accepted *Wednesday To Come* for the New Zealand Playwrights' Workshop 11–19 May.

I am so chuffed. So chuffed.

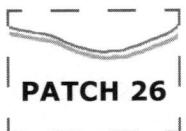

PATCH 26

My political views were formed very early and have remained strongly left, although I've never joined any party. It's clear to me when I look back at the girl I was, that for years her ideas were unformulated, and unsupported by much reading or discussions of political strategies or policies. I knew we were the have-nots and others were the haves. Naturally the haves didn't want to give us any of their wealth, open up any of their schools to us, share their comfortable lives. We were the Great Unwashed, the kids with snotty noses, dirty clothes, sores, nits, bare feet, rotten teeth, hungry bellies, staring eyes. We weren't attractive. Most of us left school at twelve and did the jobs the haves didn't want to do. We were cheap too. And we needed the work.

The only ones who offered us a way up were the unions. Their message was basically that collective power works better for have-nots than individual efforts. I marched with joy when the forty-hour week was passed. We gathered up Dickens and Emerson Streets in Napier and celebrated the fact that we didn't have to work on Saturdays anymore, and that if we did it would be counted as overtime so we'd get more pay. There was a belief that weekends were for families, friends, sport, gardening, social activity and, for most people then, church and/or Sunday school.

There were great divides between Catholics and the rest. These started in primer one (or before) and continued forever. I base this assertion on the fact that when Laurie told his family I had agreed to marry him they were aghast. There were three strikes against me: 'Her mother is Māori or "half-caste" and a Catholic, and Renée goes to dances.' I don't know which one they thought was the worst. They were nice people really – they just had fixed ideas. Exactly like a large strata of society does now when they think of beneficiaries or immigrants.

In any case, whatever their initial response had been, when Rose got sick about a month before the wedding and we were told she was not expected to live, Laurie's family rallied around. We cancelled the planned reception in Napier and Laurie's mother and sisters organised an afternoon tea at Laurie's parents' house in Nelson Crescent. We were married at the Baptist Church in Napier. My friend Joy, a choir mistress and singing teacher, played the organ, and my uncle Cliff had elected to 'give me away'. I had to pull him back because he walked too fast. I didn't know anything about theatre then, but I knew I had to make an entrance, not rip down the aisle like we were in a race.

The doctor said we should feel all right about going away, my mother wouldn't know. But I would, I told Laurie. We'd go to Taupō for four days because, if we had to, it was easy to get home from there. That was a good decision because we'd only been back a day or so when Rose died. Val had fainted at the hospital and she fainted again at the funeral home, so it was decided that she shouldn't go to the funeral and that I should stay with her. I couldn't be bothered arguing so I stayed, but

I've always regretted this. It's like something has been left unfinished.

I began reading about political matters well before Rose died, probably when I went to work at Venables Willis, the printers. They were on Dickens Street, which was very convenient for visits to the Napier Central Library in the lunch hour. I read without thought, plan or strategy. I started at one end of a shelf and hoovered my way round to the end of that shelf. In this way I read about opera, ballet, dance, jazz, theatre, you name it, and in the same vein I read Locke and Smith and various others whose names I've forgotten. If it was next on the shelf it got its turn. I had a mad desire to be educated and I thought this would do it. I didn't realise that to be educated, people need discussion, argument and opposition, so they can be made to think for themselves. You have to learn to defend your patch, to reason. It took me years to understand that I would never catch up with my contemporaries' experiences and a lot longer to accept the difference that class makes even in a country that prides itself on being classless. Class is always going to matter because people born into one or the other have totally different world views formed by being either a have or a have-not.

When I read Vera Brittain's *Testament of Youth* and re-read Dorothy L Sayers' *Gaudy Night*, I began thinking about feminism as a political stance, not only a personal one. I already knew the basics from other reading, and this was a name to give my jangled thoughts on the role of women in society. At one stage I didn't even know it had a name and I wouldn't have used those words. What was obvious was that all the men I came into contact with – except for Jimmy and Orm (and who knew what they were like when I wasn't there?) and, later, Laurie – thought it was fair to make rude jokes and put-downs, compare breasts and bums, shout out lewd suggestions. If you turned round and swore at them, you were called 'lippy'. It was not considered a good thing to be lippy, either by men or women. Naturally I never thought I was lippy – I saw it as having my say. I thought I had a right to have a say.

I see now that my main advantage was that I was brought up by a woman. She was in charge. If there was trouble, she solved it. She was the one we asked permission to do things, the one we had to answer to, the one who ruled the house. She was why I had great difficulty allowing Laurie any say at all when we first married. It was only when my sense of fairness (a damn nuisance but I must have been born with it) kicked in that I realised he had a right to his opinion. That his opinion could be different from mine and the world as I knew it wouldn't end. A new thought.

Laurie was different in other ways too. I didn't know any other man who would have read Marie Stopes' book *Married Love* before he got married because I said he needed to. I got it out from the library again and he read it. It talked about contraception and about the need for both parties to find pleasure in sex. The language is a bit stiff and old-fashioned to read now, but the advice is still good. While I read almost anything, Laurie read mainly Louis L'Amour westerns, *Best Bets* and *Friday Flash*, and he liked to read the *Daily Telegraph* each day if he could. Then Dick Francis came along with novels centred around horse-racing, crime and a good story, and Laurie read them all. So did I. He enjoyed and was good at sport – rugby, cricket, basketball – and he got good reviews of his performances from the newspaper's sports reviewer. Laurie also enjoyed sweets, while I had strict ideas about how many the kids should have. Often on a Friday he'd come home with a bag of toffees, some licorice straps and a bag of peanuts and share them out, and I'd shut my mouth.

Laurie read Marie Stopes because I pushed it at him and said he should. I don't know for certain, but I'd be willing to bet I'd read somewhere that reading this book before one got married was a good thing. As Rose never talked about menstruation or sex, it was unlikely she told me to read it. It would have been someone in a book mentioning it or I might even have thought of it myself. Wherever I got the idea from, it was very good advice.

Rose liked Laurie. She didn't get enough time to know him very well, but she said to me after we got engaged that I had done the right thing. I was so surprised to hear this that I just stared at her. 'He loves you more than you love him,' she said, 'that's the way it should be.' Then she added, 'And he doesn't drink.'

A woman I know said to me recently that she'd been thinking about her mother and me in relation to other women she knows of our generation and about why her mum and I are so stroppy. She decided it was because we'd been brought up by women who were in charge of the household, so it seemed an ordinary thing for us to take charge. We didn't seem to have the same patience for putting up with bullshit as the rest, she said. I pointed out that sometimes this worked the other way. I'd noticed that sometimes daughters who'd lived with a mother who took charge could revert very quickly to the biddable, ready-to-please, peace-at-any-price, always-smiling woman, hoping for a knight on a white horse who would swoop in and take charge of her life so she'd never have to worry her head about a thing ever again. It's a nice dream. I love it in Georgette Heyer novels, but in real life?

It wasn't until I began reading the British women writing between 1920 and 1940 – Dorothy L Sayers, Vera Brittain, Winifred Holtby among others – that I realised these unformed and scattered ideas had a name. *Feminism*. I didn't read about New Zealand feminists because there weren't any books about them on the library shelf. I didn't know names like Kate Sheppard or Ettie Rout until the 1970s.

In 1972 I saw the first copies of *Broadsheet*, the New Zealand feminist magazine – foolscap, cyclostyled – and bought two. Then in 1975 I saw an advertisement about something called the United Women's Convention, which was to take place in Wellington. I checked with Laurie and yes, he'd look after the kids, so I booked to go, in spite of the fact that I was directing a play for Wairoa Little Theatre at the time. I can't remember which, but I do remember that one of my neighbours was a little shocked that I was going to something called the United Women's Convention and supposed there would be feminists who shouted a lot there. She added, 'Is your husband really letting you go?'

Bernadette was in the play and asked if she could come too. At the time, apart from working on the play with her, I didn't know Bernadette very well, so all I said was she'd better get cracking because the cheaper hotels were well booked. Bernadette's surname is Doolan and when we got to Wellington, she ordered a cab. It arrived, and the driver stood at the doorway and shouted, '*Doolan.*' Bernadette was furious. As we walked over to him he said, 'I'm a Presbyterian myself.' Not the best start for her, but it turned out to be a wonderfully exhilarating weekend for us both, and I loved every minute of it.

It was absolutely and positively the worst weather Wellington had ever turned on – freezing, heavy rain, wind – but inside the Winter Show Buildings the weather didn't matter. I don't remember which workshops I attended. I didn't know anyone at either of them, and the other participants all seemed to have gone to uni or teachers' college or both, and many seemed to know each other. They were inclusive, though, and while a bit overawed I remember my enjoyment of the workshops. It seemed that although there was a difference between me and them we could discuss issues without the differences mattering. I was very naïve. I didn't see that while it might not matter to them it would always matter to me.

At the end of the convention, Margaret Mead told us that if we believed that women were equal to men and deserved equal rights, we should go home and do something about it. I met up with Bernadette on the plane and after we discussed the workshops, we talked non-stop about what we would do in Wairoa with everything we'd learned.

PATCH 27

Tall woman in a frame

Your eyes narrow to keep out the intrusive sun
your mouth a line firm against God, life, a stone
caught in your sensible black shoe.

You marry a widower twice your age, two children
to head the twelve you have, the two who lie
in beds of quiet inside the houses of the dead.

Behind the line of your mouth red slippers
dance under purple satin shawls, embroidered skirts
tease violins, a silver flute signals your entrance.

Sunflowers turn their heads as you climb
triumphant in the high celebratory air,
platters of pomegranates, pears, pale juices

lush on another's lips – bluebirds play with bees,
leopards offer sweetmeats, pour wine in glasses.
Back here in the frame, enclosed, caught, held,

you stand – behind you a trellis fence, beyond that the tree
under which you were born and where that line began
to carve itself into the newborn pink of your mouth.

PATCH 28

On Friday, 13 November 2015, I had a bilateral mastectomy. Yep. After seventeen years the cancer came back. This time in both breasts.

I'd felt a lump in my right breast two months earlier, the day I'd put in four tomato plants: two Moneymakers and two cherry. I put the Moneymakers in the corner of the trellis, where the sweet peas were already growing green and lush. It's a nice, sunny corner and I expected the sweet peas would shelter them from the winds of October. Gertrude Jekyll had buds with pink showing and Ingrid Bergman was just about to burst into the extravagant dark red, which I love seeing when I'm working at the bench in the kitchen. The broad beans, planted on Anzac Day, were on track, covered with flowers and some already showing baby pods. *Oh shit*, I thought, when I felt the lump.

That the local GP found one in my left breast as well was a surprise. I was given an appointment with a surgeon very quickly. We met in Horowhenua Hospital where he has a clinic once a month. He arranged an ultrasound appointment but we both agreed it was almost certainly cancer. He said medical processes had moved heaps in seventeen years. How long would I be in hospital? He shrugged. 'Couple of days? Maybe three.'

The right breast where I'd had cancer before would

have to be removed, and he wasn't sure about the left one before he saw the tests, but probably. I asked if I could have both done at once and he said it would depend on tests. 'It's a three-and-a-half hour major op,' he said, 'and you are eighty-six, so tests will have to prove you're up to it.' A mammogram, ultrasound, biopsies, all showed it was cancer. The tests showed I could handle the op. I was fit and healthy (not counting the cancer) and I didn't have a lot of choice anyway, so it was all on.

I had told one person. Miriam came round one day and we had a cup of tea, and she said, 'You've lost weight.' As it turned out I hadn't, but the opening led me to say what I knew so far, and she said immediately, 'I'll drive you wherever you have to go.' I asked her to tell no one else, but after a week or two, when I knew for sure what was wrong, I told my family and a couple of friends. The reason I didn't tell everyone was because I'd done that last time and had not liked some of the reactions to the news. I didn't want to subject myself to that again. I decided I'd tell everyone after the operation.

Aquilegia, columbine, granny's bonnet, take your pick. They seed themselves and each year I leave them in a different place. The lavenders and borage attract bees galore – busy, busy, busy – and irises swell ready to bloom. Irises are for me the signal of spring. I grow daffodils, freesias and lachanalia in pots, so they can be placed around the garden to bloom, then removed to the back once the flowers die down and the leaves start looking like dried grass. They all come out early because they're fed well and they like where they are. The end of winter is the signal for the first ones.

I love those first signs of spring. People walking past

comment on the garden, which is lovely to hear, but the truth is I grow this small garden for me. If other people get pleasure too then that's a bonus.

Christopher and Zuzu live in Wellington now, so he's the son nearest to Ōtaki. He told me his current contract finished soon and another one started five days later, so he was free between those dates to help me out, but he could also make time for me around that as well. David and Tim, and Naomi, Andrew, Abbie, Saskia, Sharon – everyone I told was shocked but staunch.

I got the op date. Monday, 16 November. So I emailed Mary-Jane at Whitireia Polytechnic and said I wouldn't be able to do the launch of the online journal *4th Floor* – for which I was editor – on the fifteenth, and then I emailed the same thing to Michaela McGuire, who had invited me to be part of the TED Talk event *Women and Letters* on the same date. Both replied immediately and said reassuring, supportive things. I emailed Kirsten, who'd asked me to do a weekend teaching at the Kahini Kāpiti Writers Retreat in late January, and explained I had a health issue that needed to be sorted, but as far as I knew I would still be able to do the weekend. I figured I'd be well over the op by then. She was understanding. Heather Joy contacted me about the *Your Life, Your Story* weekend I was due to do for a Whanganui group she was organising in the third weekend of November, and I told her and her daughter, actor and playwright Fiona Samuel, what had happened.

I was teaching a ten-week *Your Life, Your Story* workshop in Ōtaki that finished on the last Wednesday of October. We'd arranged to meet up in early November for a 'skite session', where the participants bring the hard copies of the ninety or so pages they've written over the time of the workshop and show them off. I was determined not to miss it and I was right to go. It was a happy, laughter-filled hour.

Uncle Walter had one deep red rose out, and a Tequila Sunset too, and I steamed a little kale and liked it. I'd tried it some years before and hadn't enjoyed it at all, but this one seemed different. I went to a jazz concert where Andrew was playing bass guitar in the second half of the programme and enjoyed that very much. So did everyone there. People sang, got up and danced their delight in the music, all women so far as I could see. All of the generation that loved dancing and moving to music and knew these songs.

All the time Miriam had been taking me backwards and forwards to Palmerston North for appointments, and Chris said he'd come up and take me to the hospital for the operation, so all was arranged. I'd had an ultrasound, mammograms, biopsies and more consultations.

On Wednesday, 11 November, the phone call came: 'Hi, Renée, Emma here, just to say your operation date has been brought forward to Friday the thirteenth. It'll be an early start from Ōtaki I'm afraid. Also you have an appointment tomorrow at 3pm for a procedure at the Nuclear Medicine department. Okay? Hospital at 7am Friday and tomorrow Thursday at 3pm?'

'Okay,' I said. I looked out the window at Ingrid. She and her girlfriend had luscious, deep red flowers, and around them the Canterbury bells were showing blue and pink. Not a great combination with Ingrid's red, you'd have thought, but in a garden the most unusual colour mixes seem to work. I'd read up about various things – post-op fatigue, for example. I'd read the Cancer Society booklet from cover to cover. I wondered what the outcome of the op would be. Had the cancer gone to my lymph nodes? Or anywhere else?

I set the alarm for 4.30am on the Friday and Chris got up after I'd showered. We left Ōtaki around 5.40am. Kim would come later and do any deadheading the garden needed. This was the time of the year when deadheading was the job. If you didn't do it, you wouldn't have any new growth or many new flowers coming on. I dislike the way people let their flowers almost rot on the stem because they can't bring themselves to lop off the deadheads.

It was a pleasant morning and there were few cars on the road. We didn't talk much. Chris said when we got there he'd organise a motel and then wait.

Palmerston North was just getting into gear for the day when we arrived. We parked in the car park – surely the cheapest hospital car park anywhere. (Paying less for a car park is a huge boon for friends and relatives of those who are sick – Lower Hutt and Wellington charge much more.) Anyway, Chris lugged my gear into the hospital general area, and we were directed to the day-treatment reception. There were a lot of people already waiting – all ages, sizes, ethnicities. We waited too. Names were called out and people got up and left, some with whānau or friends, some on their own.

My name was called. Chris picked up my gear and in we went. I got changed into a green cotton smock and put my gear in a patient property bag, and then Chris and I followed the nurse to a bed in a cubicle. It was a long, tall room with lots of cubicles and someone in nearly every bed. Chris sat while I answered the same questions everyone was asking me: Name? Date of birth? Address? What are you in here for? All of the questioners carried papers and all of them smiled and said it wouldn't be long.

I met two or three members of the medical team, which was good, and the anaesthetist, who said he would do his best not to injure my vocal cords any further. One had been injured during a previous anaesthetic, which is why I sounded even huskier than before and why I lost my singing voice. I can still sing but nowhere near as well (the members of my ukulele group have been very kind about my drone). The anaesthetist assured me that although he would have to use a tube down my throat he would take great care. As it turned out he was successful and it's no worse. The nurse told Chris she'd ring him as soon as the op was over and I was in the recovery room. He thanked her, smiled at me and left.

I lay there for a while longer then a nurse came and got me. I was wheeled into a room where the anaesthetist and a couple of others in green gear greeted me. Then on into the theatre, 'just a small prick' and I went out.

When I woke I was in recovery and someone was smiling at me and asking me my name, birth date, address. 'Good,' she said, 'good. Well done.'

I was trundled along to a ward. Ward twenty-nine, room ten, bed three of four beds. They pulled the curtains around me, and Chris and my friend Sarah Delahunty came in. Chris had been waiting in his motel for the call and as time went on and on, well over the estimated time, he said it was not a pleasant wait. Sarah, driving from Wellington, had received Chris's text that I was out of theatre and all was well. It was good to see them. There's something about a familiar face that is so reassuring. The world hasn't entirely shifted on its axis.

I didn't feel groggy, but I was very thirsty and Chris got me a glass of water. I drained it instantly and asked for more. And more. I had a tube with a little pad on the end that I could press if the pain got bad. I pressed it once while they were there. I didn't like the effect, and Sarah says I said, 'Well, I won't be doing that too often.' After a while I said, 'I'm going to sleep now,' and Chris and Sarah left.

Chris could walk across the road to the motel and read or watch TV, or he could walk uptown and see a film, look about, choose a place for dinner, watch the world go by, think about waiting. Sarah had to drive back to Wellington that day. Yes, I know. Both of them. Stars.

I kept waiting for the pain to get worse but only had to press the little pad twice more, and the next day they took it away. Surplus to requirements. I blessed the medical team. Outside the windows was a panoramic view of this part of Palmerston North. Trees, bushes, buildings, a road snaking and looping around the green. I must have been five or six storeys up.

I had two tubes each side of my body with bottles attached, so every time I turned I had to do it very carefully. The tubes allowed liquid to drain away – if they weren't there the area would swell up and be very uncomfortable. I was afraid that I would dislodge them somehow and pull the tubes out. Ha. I discovered it took more than an unwary turn to do that.

Bedpans and bed washes and decisions about food. An engaging young woman came round and took orders. You ordered blind of course and just hoped the description matched the actual dish. No salads on offer, though, and I thought of the lettuce, spring onions and spinach at home, wondered about the broad beans. The first year I was in Ōtaki and the garden was just a black patch, I planted my first broad beans there. When the little tips appeared I got very excited. I grabbed the phone and rang Sunny and said, 'Sunny, Sunny, they're up. Three.'

Poor Sunny, it was probably 7.30am, but she gallantly took up the challenge. 'What's up?'

'The broad beans, the broad beans. Three.'

'Great,' said Sunny, 'what are you going to call them?'

I was visited by the medical team. They all seemed pleased. The surgeon said, 'You'll probably think the wound looks terrible but we think it's beautiful.' Now that I was compos mentis, I decided it was time to start texting and telling people what had happened. What could I say? *Hi darlings, I had a double mastectomy yesterday. How was your Friday?*

I also wanted to answer family messages. Chris had let everyone on the list know that the op had gone well, but I wanted to send a message from me. I blessed my cellphone, which makes all this possible. Before I owned one, anyone enquiring about me would have had to ring the nurses' desk and ask them about my progress or ask to speak to me, and the nurse (if she had time) would have to trundle the phone to my bed. A great user of precious time and now completely unnecessary. A perfect example of why I love technology.

I traversed the visit to the bathroom lugging four drainage bottles without any drama. The Cancer Society supporters make little cotton shoulder bags that hold two bottles, and I had two of those. The surgeon's breast cancer nurse, Cheryl, visited me so I'd know who she was, she said. She brought some pink satin, crescent-shaped cushions for putting under my arms. They were made by members of Zonta, a professional women's organisation, who also beavered away making little shoulder bags. It's amazing how much random kindness there is in the world. Cheryl had all the info on prostheses should I want them, and told me there was a government grant towards the cost. I'd already decided not to do this, but it was still good to know that if I did there was help.

I was in hospital four days. It would have been three but I needed a blood transfusion and an iron one too. I've always tended towards anaemia, so no real surprises there.

There are three reasons why people don't spend so long in hospital after an operation now. Firstly, medical procedures have advanced so the progress towards being able to walk and use the bathroom is much quicker. Secondly, hospital staff and medical teams are aware that there's always a risk of infection in a large place like a hospital, so they think it best to remove that possibility. And the third reason? We recuperate faster at home in our own surroundings and in our own beds.

On the last day of my stay, I was visited by a trio of helpful women: a physiotherapist, a welfare person with details of home help should I need it, and a third to talk about what I needed when I got home. 'A stool for the shower and a bedside table,' I said. And lo, they were brought in later that morning, and Chris packed them into the car.

The plan was that Chris would stay with me the first night and then we'd see how I was. The district nurse would call and the breast cancer nurse. The ukulele group was in recess at the time but I knew the members would call. I knew other friends would call.

A nurse took out two of the tubes at the hospital and it hurt. It shouldn't have hurt. I discovered that a couple of weeks later when the other two were removed without incident. I was given a little talk at the hospital before I left. 'Take it easy, no work for a few days.' That last was a triumph. I can't be the first person my age who gets irritated when the medical person ticks 'retired' without asking first, but it feels like it. One of the helpful hints in the Cancer Society booklet about after-operation processes was the warning that I might get irritable and impatient. Not to worry, that was perfectly normal. Yes. Always.

I got the discharge papers and a prescription, and the nurse packed my gear. 'Be sure to put Freddie's card in,' I said. I didn't want to leave it behind.

An orderly brought a wheelchair and we rolled down to the main entrance where Chris waited with the car. I was going home. I wanted to shout out to everyone but decided perhaps not. The orderly might just turn the wheelchair around and take me back in. So I smiled instead. Is there any feeling to beat going home after a hospital stay?

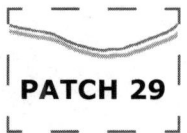

PATCH 29

And as we gather

Let us thank the stranger on the train
Let us agree to smile at everyone
Let us buy one hundred books of poems
Let us pick roses and common thyme
Let us create seven chocolate desserts
Let us pour red wine into glasses
Let us dance our way to the room
Let us sing those old forgotten songs
Let us celebrate this shining moment
Let us sit down at the table

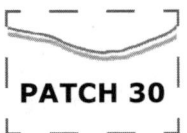

PATCH 30

The garden looks amazing. The sweet peas are tall and abundant, all colours, even some purple. They are trampling over everything in their path but their blooming is for only a few weeks so I let them. Roses, roses everywhere. Anyone who passes smiles. People stream by on their way to a concert at Ngā Purapura and some stop and take photographs. Broad beans ready to pick.

'Sensational,' says Sunny, who pops in on her way to the concert.

I came home from the operation with a drainage tube each side, and even with the little bags to hold them they've been a trial. But I can sit on the white stool and shower myself and that feels good. Being home is like I've been given the signal to get well. I follow instructions to the letter. I get lots of texts telling me to rest. Not one from my friend Pam though. She saw me through the first op when I broke my ankle as well, making sure I followed the instructions on resting and exercise. I'm impatient and quick-moving but not stupid – I did what I had to do. I dug all my roses out that time because I needed to be careful not to get scratched. Danger of lymphedema, they said. Won't do it this time.

Within the human body there are two different types of circulatory systems: the cardiovascular system, which pumps blood around the body, and the lymphatic system, which carries waste and fluid from the tissues in a fluid called 'lymph'. Cancer cells spread through these channels. For this reason, the part of the lymphatic system in the areas affected, like nodes under the arm, are removed during surgery. A side effect of this is that the fluid that would normally drain from the area can become trapped in the limb. Symptoms are a full and heavy sensation in the arm, skin tightness, decreased flexibility in the hand, wrist or elbow. Clothes can feel tight and so can bracelets or rings, and scratches from rose bushes can easily get infected.

You can see why I'm fussy about not getting scratches and cuts, but of course they happen and the world doesn't end. The physiotherapist tells me that tapping the keyboard is good exercise to help avoid lymphedema. I liked her before, but I like her even more now.

I text a couple of friends to see if they have any large T-shirts I can borrow. I want loose garments and I only have one that fits that description. Jill and Joy come to the rescue and bring me six lovely T-shirts. Have them as long as you like, they say. They have political slogans on them, which I love. Lounging in bed telling everyone else to save the earth seems a good way to go. Yes, I know, no work for a few days. I keep to that but the veto is up now.

I've been to three clinic visits since the operation, and each time the surgeon studies the wounds and looks inscrutable. When I said once that I got these little prickles of pain from time to time, then they went, he said, 'I'd be surprised if you didn't.' Which was reassuring. Run-of-the-mill stuff. Obviously. 'One more clinic visit then you'll be out of the acute stage,' he said. I didn't know I was in it. If he can be inscrutable so can I.

So, three and a half weeks from the op, one more clinic visit and a bone density test. I don't have to have chemo and can't have radiation on the right side anyway, so hormones have been prescribed. There are two kinds apparently, one of which works better with estrogen-driven cancers, which mine was, but can cause bone troubles, hence the bone density test.

I can read and work. I have good friends and an extra-special whānau. There's a famous comment attributed to Russian feminist and anarchist Emma Goldman (but is in fact only a paraphrase), 'If there's no dancing at the revolution, I'm not coming,' and then something she did say in one of her essays, 'Love is free; it can dwell in no other atmosphere.' Homai te pakipaki to that.

PATCH 31

What led me to try and become more comfortable around te reo was the legacy my mother left me through her whakapapa. Rose, like a lot of her generation, both female and male, thought their kids would do better to live solely in the Pākehā world. She discouraged any friendships with Māori kids, and I didn't dare tell her that the old Māori women who sat on the footpath in the sun outside Martin's butcher's shop in Taradale had yelled at me, 'You Rose Brown's daughter?'

I heard Bub Bridger talk about this once and she was right. It's no good blaming our parents for doing what they thought was best for their kids. But when Laurie and I and the three kids went to live in Wairoa in 1964, I thought it was time to start looking up my whakapapa. Laurie's employer and friend, Ron, had invited him to set up a pre-stressed concrete yard in Wairoa, so we left Avenue Road, Greenmeadows, and went to live there. A house to rent on Hunter-Brown Street was found for us by a guy from Wairoa Little Theatre, who was very pleased to welcome us to the town. We'd look for a more permanent residence once we'd settled in.

Wairoa is divided in two – North Clyde and the other side, which gets called the 'town side' among other things. The college is on the town side. On my first walk up Marine Parade, the main street of Wairoa, on one side shops, the other side river, I was hailed by a stout man standing outside his shop. Mick Barrett, then Mayor of Wairoa, said, 'You must be Rose Brown's daughter. Heard you were coming to town. You look just like her.'

Turned out Mick had attended St Joseph's along with Rose, her sister Mary, and her brothers. Turned out he donated the dux medals every year. Turns out Sharon, who would marry David one day, has one of those medals. Granddaughters Naomi and Abbie went there, too, for their primary schooling. On their first afternoon the girls were brought home in a police car. 'Fighting in the street,' said the policeman. Apparently he managed to say it without grinning at Sharon. Turns out one wanted to go one way and one the other, and next minute a police car came along and here they were.

It felt strange looking at the school building where Rose had been so unhappy, and where she'd learned to despise the people who taught there. She remembered being strapped with a piece of leather that had smaller strings of leather on the end of it. Attitudes of those in charge – the nuns, the priests, parents – were much the same. Children were strapped and caned to teach them not to lie, not to answer back, and to love God and the teachings of the church.

No wonder it only worked superficially. No wonder the legacy of the beatings made these kids use the same methods on their kids. If your father had a position in town and donated generously to the church you might be lucky and not get treated so hard, but kids had to be seen and not heard and that was that.

Chris had had only one year at Napier Boys' and I had a few misgivings about moving him to another college, but he's never reproached me for it. The younger ones, David and Timothy, seemed to enjoy Hillneath Primary School. We rented a house nearer the school, then I saw a house for sale in Kabul Street. We managed to scrape up the money for a deposit and moved in. It had a big backyard and it was there, when Tim was around fourteen, that I made my first garden. There was the lemon tree, of course – everyone had a lemon tree – and the tamarillo.

About a week after we arrived in Wairoa, I started reading old copies of the *Wairoa Star* and began visiting the courthouse seeking information from birth, death and marriage certificates. Nothing online in those days but the woman in charge was very helpful. She'd lived in Wairoa all her life and knew lots without having to look it up. I had to pay for every certificate copy I wanted, but sometimes she took pity on me and gave me two for the price of one. I also borrowed *The Story of Old Wairoa and the East Coast* by Thomas Lambert from the library. The kids gave me my own copy some years ago, which was just as well because now it's out of print, and if you can find one secondhand it costs a fair bit.

The woman at the courthouse told me about the name Harmer, and later I discovered it in the Lambert book, where I also found the name Lewis. Charles Harmer owned the Wairoa Hotel, and when he sold it he bought premises along the road, around where the cinema is now, and called it Harmer's Emporium.

So there was the newspaper, the book, the records at the courthouse and the memories of people in Wairoa. I was also getting to know the town and some of the people in it, and especially those who worked for Wairoa Little

Theatre. I already knew Grace, Rose's youngest sister, and I had met Bill, one of her brothers, who lived with his family in Hastings. Our relationships with uncles was much stronger with my father's brothers, Ormond and Cliff.

We settled into the house on Kabul Street. Laurie dug a garden and I baked every Friday. Two lots of biscuits (peanut brownies and Anzac biscuits were favourites), a fruit loaf and a cake of some kind. For a few years, on Sundays, I also made a sponge that I filled with jam and whipped cream, dusted the top with icing sugar and served it for afternoon tea or as a treat after our evening meal.

I joined Wairoa Little Theatre and was asked to direct a play. The editor of the *Wairoa Star* asked me to write a humorous column, copy deadline every Tuesday at lunchtime. I'd sent him something in the hopes he would publish it and he must have liked it. I used a pen-name but after a while it seemed everyone knew it was me. Searching through courthouse records and old newspapers for my ancestors had to take its chances among all the balls I was juggling in the air. The family had to be fed, food had to be bought, clothes had to be washed and ironed, shoes purchased, lunches packed, beds made and the house cleaned.

So I became a part-time detective, though progress was slow because I was learning about Wairoa as well. What I did discover was that Puti Mary Lewis married Charles Harmer when she was nineteen and he was in his early forties. He was a widower with two children. I also discovered that she was one of the three children – Puti, Maata and David – of David Lewis, once a whaler, and a Māori woman with a high-ranking father, whose name I didn't yet know. I knew that Puti's brother, David, had ridden horses in the New Year races, and at some stage he and his horse went over the cliffs at Marumaru, when he was coming home from the pub. Most of this I learned from the book, although Charles Harmer had regular advertisements in the *Wairoa Star*, extolling the virtues of the 'Wairoa Hotel, Prop: Charles Harmer', and later The Emporium, which sold everything anyone could want.

Slow progress, but I knew more than before we'd come to Wairoa. And this was the sixties. Bob Dylan, Joan Baez, The Band, The Beatles. Guitars began to be the musical instrument of choice, surfing the activity of choice and hitch-hiking the way to get around. Jeans and bare feet came in, boys began to grow their hair longer than the short back and sides their fathers thought was the only way to wear it. It took more time for attitudes to change, and boys growing their hair long had a few ups and downs with teachers at Wairoa College.

But the times were a-changin' all right, a huge unstoppable wave. The revolution was here. 'Get with the programme,' said the kids. The papers told us about sit-ins at American universities, protests about the Vietnam War and draft dodgers, and then the second wave of feminism arrived. Given the tumultuous events of the next twenty years or so, it's a wonder I kept up the search for my whānau at all, but I did, although in the end it was a stranger who finally gave me the answers I was looking for.

PATCH 32

Someone asked me a question recently. The question was, 'Were you frightened?' It referred of course to my most recent cancer diagnosis, operation and recovery. My answer was no, I didn't feel fear. But I'm not sure this answer was satisfying.

When you're doing the medical dance, people only look at the figures. Many medical professionals have conventional ideas about what being seventy-five, or eighty-one, or eighty-eight means. They're right to see me as old, but they're wrong when they expect me to be the same as everyone else my age. They mirror the conventional ideas of the rest of society of course. What comes as a surprise is when the occasional doctor treats me like a functioning, intelligent human being who happens to be eighty-eight.

Maybe I was lucky, but this time round I struck more of the latter than the former. Perhaps it's merely reflecting changes in attitude over the seventeen years that have elapsed between one bout of cancer and another? The people who see female and old and call me 'Mrs' are, in the main, receptionists. I say, 'I am not Mrs, call me Ms if you must, but I prefer Renée.' Do I get sick of saying this? Yes, I do.

I always expected to die at forty-two. Rose died at forty-two, but both my grandmothers died in their early fifties, so why I plumped for forty-two I don't know. An early death seemed inevitable somehow. So now that I've lived twice the number of years Rose did plus a few more, is it any wonder I didn't panic when I felt the lump? I felt more irritated than fearful and I know exactly why.

There is a framed photograph of the Hawke's Bay branch of the New Zealand Women Writers' Society hanging on my wall. I'm not exactly sure when it was taken, but in the photo there is a semi-circle of seated writers looking towards the centre of the group, where one of our number is reading a book. Outside this circle looking on, I stand at the back, my glasses in my hand, instead of in front of my eyes, and there is a considered expression on my face as I look at the others posing. It's a very good group photo and I am glad I have saved it.

Why did I choose to stand at the back looking on rather than being one of those sitting grouped around the woman holding the book? Why did I place myself outside the circle? Did I not want to be in the photo? Maybe I didn't like the posed nature of it? Then I remember – of course – I was the one who staged it, and just before the photographer clicked I rushed to the back and smiled benignly on my work. So what irritates me most about the medical dance? Obvious. I'm not in charge of it.

PATCH 33

Wairoa Hotel, Marine Parade, which Occupies a Valuable Position in the Heart of this Town and stands Unrivalled for the Extent and Quality of its Accommodation, has Private Suites for Families in this House of Call for Travellers as well as good stabling and sectioned paddocks.

From the *Wairoa Free Press*, Saturday, 2 June 1877.

The proprietor of the Wairoa Hotel at this time was Charles Albert Harmer, my great-grandfather. His death certificate tells me he died 29 July 1894, aged sixty. So when this advertisement was put in the paper seventeen years before that, he would have been forty-three. The certificate states his occupation as storekeeper, which would be right because he sold the pub and set up what he called an emporium just a little bit further back along Marine Parade. He was born in London, the surname of his mother before her marriage is 'not known', and his father, it states, was a merchant. Charles (forty) married Puti Mary (age unknown, says the certificate, but I was told she was nineteen).

Charles was a widower so Puti was his second wife. If she was nineteen, that makes her around thirty-six when he died. Can this be right? It seems young to me now but it probably wasn't then. If she'd had nine kids in the seventeen years, that's one nearly every two years, I should think that's pretty ageing. She probably felt like she was a hundred, but there would be kids to feed, clothe, send to school, so no time to think about herself. I wonder if he was good to her.

Charles Albert Harmer lived in New Zealand for forty years, but as far as the certificate is concerned there's no knowledge of his mother's name, nor his usual place of residence (huh?), and they don't know the age of his widow. The certificate states that his issue was three males (ages not known) and six females (ages not known). Nine children. *And no one knew his 'usual place of residence'?* How come? Did he die in hospital? Was he living apart from Puti Mary and the family?

Charles is buried in Wairoa Cemetery. I never found his grave but that's not surprising. I'm surmising he was a Catholic because the other members of Rose's family were, so I searched in that part of the cemetery a few times when I lived in Wairoa but I never found him. If he had a gravestone it could have fallen over. The 1931 Napier earthquake would have made a lot of the old stones tumble down, but there were smaller quakes before then as well as floods and great storms. Or maybe he didn't have a gravestone? I should have asked at the council offices, but I would have had to pay and I didn't want to. The woman at the courthouse was very generous but asking her to search for his burial site number would have taken her hours – this was the days before computers – and I just didn't have the gall to ask.

Death certificates are notoriously unreliable because the information is supplied by family members who just go on what they've been told, and often this doesn't include details like ages. Even more often, the information's a bit garbled because they were told it some time before as a passing remark and weren't interested enough to ask for more details. It continues to puzzle me that Charles's usual place of residence is stated as unknown, and that his widow's age is not known either. How could this be? Wasn't she living right there in Wairoa? Well at some stage she'd moved to Hastings. I know this because Rose and her brother Jim stayed with Puti Mary on separate occasions for brief periods. Even if she was living in Hastings when Charles died, the funeral director or the coroner could have sent someone to ask her how old she was, surely. Charles, according to the certificate, died of granular contracted kidneys and chronic gout, and his attending physician was Dr Ross. It goes on to say Charles was buried on 30 July – the day after he died.

Like all detective work, the search raises more questions than it answers. I know some of the names of these children. There was a Charles (Charley Brown) and an Edward among the boys, and a Grace and a Rosabelle among the girls. I surmise Grace, my grandmother, named Rose after her sister Rosabelle. I feel pleased she didn't go with her sister's full name.

Had I the inclination, I'm sure I could have found out more about Puti Mary and her nine kids. Perhaps they were adults when she left? I had two uncles (my mother's brothers) who lived in Hastings when we were living in Greenmeadows. I met one of their sons briefly once and then Mary, Bill's daughter, a few years ago and we exchange Christmas/New Year greetings – more thanks to Mary than to me. Maybe the funeral director couldn't be bothered, perhaps he was in a hurry. If Charles Albert Harmer died one day and was buried the next, it doesn't sound like there was much of a funeral. If not, why not? He'd owned two businesses, one a pub, so he must have been known to a lot of regulars as well as visiting travellers. His kids had gone to school, almost certainly St Joseph's. So – again – why was his usual place of residence not known, and why was the funeral so quick? Do I care? Not sure that I do. Not enough to continue the search anyway.

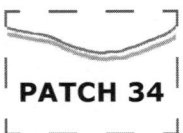

PATCH 34

Porohiwi was the grandfather of Puti Mary Harmer née Lewis, who was my great-grandmother. Puti's mother was Kokotui, daughter of Porohiwi and his third wife, Wheoro. The following story is based on unpublished research compiled by Jan Hughes in 2001, which included newspaper reports from the 1860s.

On Monday, 19 September 1864, Porohiwi was sitting outside his whare when Hotene and Paraikete walked over to him. While one entered into a conversation, the other – standing about five or six yards away – shot him. The ball entered Porohiwi's right temple and came out just below his left. Before dying, Porohiwi put his hand to his head, spoke to children who were nearby then slumped to the ground.

A coroner's inquest was held the following day before a jury with Mr Carroll (has to be Sir James) as foreman and presided over by CH Brown. The coroner's report has not survived. Following an examination of the witnesses, a verdict of wilful murder was returned against both Hotene and Paraikete. During the inquest, the murderers and their people were under arms half a mile away.

Large numbers of Māori gathered, and in the two days after the inquest shots were fired in the air all over the river as people came and went. By Tuesday, 4 October,

Hotene and Paraikete had not been sighted. It was believed they had gone into the bush armed, ready to put up resistance if pursued. No moves were made to arrest the pair. This lack of action was attributed to the fact that the authorities were reluctant to invite a disturbance. Another reason might have been a desire for more land.

On 26 October 1864, just five weeks after the murder, the superintendent of Hawke's Bay – Donald McLean – was in Wairoa to buy Māori land. He'd already bought half the Māhia Peninsula and had put in an offer from the government for the rest of the peninsula as well as the land from Māhia to Nūhaka.

A meeting was held at Waihīrere on Thursday, 27 October, to discuss buying a block that included a small part of the river frontage from the mouth of the river inland. The deep-water frontage on the eastern side over from Spooners Point was excluded from the sale as a group of Māori referred to in newspapers of the time as the 'King' or 'Kahu' (clearly Ngāti Kahungunu) had claims to all of the lower part of the river.

The reports said Ngāti Kahungunu knew they had broken European law and were willing to negotiate some form of settlement. Mr McLean agreed to meet them. On Friday, 28 October, the government sighted the flag of 'His Majesty the King' waving from a flagpole on top of a hill. Through field glasses it was revealed that Ngāti Kahungunu were armed. They advanced down the hill to the settlement of Ngāti Kurupakiaka, who were strongly in favour of selling the land, and spent the rest of the day with them establishing individual claims.

The story goes that the next morning a messenger arrived at Mr Lockwood's house from Ngāti Kahungunu saying they were ready to meet. Meanwhile another small group of six to eight people, who had a claim and were referred to in news reports as the Ngāti Moewhare hapū, arrived to oppose the sale. They lived just behind Mr Lockwood's house and owned the land he occupied. Putoko was the elderly head of this hapū, and it's reported he told Mr McLean that he intended putting his spear through a young chief called Taiepa, who had been active in arranging the sale.

At 'Kai Rakau' (presumably Kairākau) two hundred people gathered, including Ngāti Kahungunu and others. A number of speakers asked the government what they intended doing about the Porohiwi case. They contended that he was a 'magician' who deserved his fate and made it clear that if action was taken against the murderers or their iwi then the land would not be for sale. They pointed out that as it was a very special piece of land, the price was high. A figure of thirty thousand pounds was floated.

Mr McLean's response was that although he did not know what the governor would decide to do in the Porohiwi case, a life taken because of a charge of sorcery was ridiculous and it was clear that the law must be upheld. Mr McLean said the asking price for the land was too high given that it was only eight hundred to a thousand acres. He offered eight hundred pounds. The offer was rejected. After negotiation McLean's offer of twelve hundred pounds was accepted.

There is another side to the story of my ancestor Porohiwi. Porohiwi had mana on the block and it seems that in 1839

– twenty-five years before his murder – he may have been one of the sellers of a large tract of land to the Crown. The deed of sale is in Turton's Deeds of the North Island.

Daniel Cooper, a merchant of London; James Holt, a merchant of Sydney; and William Barnard Rhodes, a master mariner of Sydney; claimed to have bought land that went from the north bank of the Wairoa River to north of Table Cape (Kahutara Point) – around a hundred and sixty kilometres of coastline, totalling over a hundred and thirty thousand hectares. It was alleged the land was purchased from those named Wanoga, Tebatu, Eappe, Maraicowa, Erapa and Poroiwi (sic).

The big question is whether or not Porohiwi had the right to sell the land in the first place. It's clear land was gifted to him at some stage – but was it gifted to him only for his lifetime or was it an outright gift to do with what he liked? I haven't seen any proof that he did in fact sell this land to Cooper, Holt and Rhodes, but it is known that he dug his heels in about selling a smaller piece of land, and that could have been the reason behind his murder later on at the hands of Hotene and Paraikete.

It is possible the murderers wanted to sell some land themselves and were unable to because Porohiwi would not agree. Perhaps they believed the land wasn't his to make decisions about. Claiming he was a sorcerer gave their action some semblance of righteousness. The murderers, while charged, were never brought to trial and the land was sold in the end anyway. I have no way of knowing and neither do I have a consuming interest in the motives of my ancestor's murderers or those who wanted the land. There are many such stories in this country. Land has always mattered – whether you regard it as a saleable commodity or you believe it's in trust to be handed on to the next generation – and violence over land has occurred throughout history. It's one of the reasons why there are wars.

Mā te wahine, mā te whenua, ka ngaro te tangata. By women and land do men perish. So the old whakataukī goes. That proverb was probably created by a man. It's a nicely balanced sentence but it's fairly obvious when one looks at history that it's not land or women that men fight over. With the occasional exception (Helen of Troy perhaps), the reason men fight and kill each other is over land and religion. Look around.

PATCH 35

From *Does This Make Sense To You?* (Penguin 1995).

She plants the bay tree, carefully freeing the roots from the mound of earth they'd grown in.

'I'll get a couple of thymes,' she tells Annie. She has a bright image of a clump of common thyme next to one with striking variegated leaves. She tells Annie about it.

'Oh yes,' says Annie, 'cool.'

Flora sets the sprinkler softly on top of the barrel and lets it dribble down.

She feels pleased with all this effort. She thinks of that long-ago time and her mum and dad walking away from her at the bus terminus. They weren't bad people, her mum and dad, just typical of their time like the rest of us. Her mother had invested a lot of hope in Flora's future and all the plans she'd had in her head had been wrecked. A white wedding, a couple of grandchildren, the excitement of buying three-ply white wool and number thirteen needles, knitting intricately patterned matinée jackets, comparing progress with other grandmothers. Although she got her dream in the end.

I don't know why Dad went along with Mum's plans, Flora thinks. I don't know why he hardly ever spoke to her. I don't know anything about his years in the POW camp. I thought I knew Mike but I don't. I know he can be a bully and a bit mean with money but I would have sworn on the Bible he was faithful. But all last year he was lying to me. We slept together, made love even. Why did he do that? So I wouldn't suspect? Out of kindness? Pity? Because Verna was busy with Charlie?

'When you think about it,' says Flora to Annie and the bay tree, 'even a detached observer, looking at me, would advance as their objective opinion that there goes a woman who's definitely a sandwich short of a picnic.'

Annie shakes her head. 'Tell me about it. I went for an audition for a parlour job. He said he had to try out what was offering. Bastard. Didn't give me the job either. So you're not the only one who's thick.'

'Is that true?' Flora is sceptical.

Annie touches the leaves on the bay tree. 'Bit of a waste of time if you're going to be leaving isn't it?'

'Shut up,' says Flora, 'just shut up.'

Annie stretches and rubs her back. She scratches her head then inspects her nails thoughtfully.

'You were at the Home with Ka,' she says.

Flora looks at her.

'Ka said,' says Annie. 'Why did you run away?'

Flora shrugs. She goes inside and puts the jug on. Annie follows.

'It's just,' says Annie, 'it seems so funny, I mean someone your age, running away.'

'What's age got to do with it?'

It's Annie's turn to shrug. Any fool would know that, says her shrug. You don't run away when you're old. Running away is for the young.

Flora fumbles with the tea tin lid and the tea leaves

spurt out all over the bench. '*Bugger,*' she says and throws the tin on the floor.

Annie giggles, a spontaneous child's giggle of enjoyment as though an adult having a tantrum and throwing a tin of tea leaves on the floor is genuinely funny.

Flora can see the lovely child Annie has been, still is probably. She can't help smiling. Annie's giggles are infectious. Flora's irritability, a moment ago so intense, now seems petty, unreal.

'Let's take this outside,' she says, 'and admire our handiwork. Did I tell you I was asked to go to a play-reading?'

'Oh yeah,' says Annie, sounding knowledgeable but not having a clue what Flora's on about. 'You know anything about shitting?' she says.

'Are you constipated?'

'Haven't been for two days.'

'Did you tell the doctor?'

'Course not. Why would I tell her? What I want to know is, did you run away because of your baby?'

PATCH 36

Rain

Below me, cars do their morning run,
ambulances practise scales, buses
meditate on tourists and tour guides
and the way luggage takes off
without even leaving a note.

On the balcony, parched pots –
sage, thyme, chives, parsley,
geraniums, begonias, succulents
all plead for water. Wellington's
winds show no mercy and neither

do I. I have a play to finish, a poem,
a monthly progress report, a book
review, journal entries, guests
to dinner, no food. I'm on a marathon,
out of steam and losing it.

I fill the watering can, race smooth-footed
through the space between the windows,
out to the space in space, and tip. It's okay
on mint, sage, thyme, chives, parsley, but
at the geraniums it turns nasty.

From below I hear, 'Fucking hell –
was that rain?'

I creep backwards through the space
over space and, tea towel over my giggly,
snorty, five-year-old response, reflect
on guilt and how rain falls on the just
and the unjust and, it seems, the just passing.

PATCH 37

From *The Snowball Waltz* (Penguin Books 1997).

Sullivans in Christchurch seated sixty. A huge barn, plenty of space between tables, appealing to nuclear families and larger groups, according to its advertisements. One day, on one of those hot Christchurch days, a northerly, all of the staff running with sweat, faces red, feeling like they'd die if they moved one more dish or shot one more bright, happy smile, something terrible happened. It was well past lunchtime but one table of patrons had stayed on and on. Just one more glass of wine, one more piece of that divine chocolate cake.

At quarter to four, all patrons had drunk their coffee, visited the toilet, redone their lipstick, straightened their ties, prepared to go back to work or crash in flats or houses with or without the someone they'd had their eye on for the last three hours.

The silence was like slipping into soft comfortable garments. While the rest of the staff went off to have a swim, Clive, Heather and Souvie enjoyed a cold beer. Souvie had just rinsed her glass and put it in the dishwasher when the door to the restaurant opened. Heather leapt up, was back in two seconds, eyes staring, mouth opened.

'Thirty five Japanese and their tour leader.'

'*Fucking hell.*' Then Clive rallied. 'Tell them the kitchen's closed.'

'I did but their leader says they've been everywhere. No one's interested in such a large number. Some of them haven't had breakfast because they won't eat porridge. They'll pay double.'

Clive looked at Heather and Souvie, dollar signs lit up his eyes. They both turned to Souvie.

'They pay double, I get double.'

'Done.'

Souvie washed her face and hands, pulled a comb through her hair, replaced the smile on her face and together, she, Heather and Clive provided service and food for thirty-six tired, hungry, irritable people who behaved like tired, hungry, irritable people the world over. They took it out on the waitress.

Souvie and Heather carried jugs, tall glasses, plates of bread. Where's the orange? The tea? The coffee? Any butter? Will the entrée be long? More bread – are you deaf? I asked for more bread.

With muttered curses interspersed with passionate appeals to Jesus, Clive defrosted trays of sushi, and flung lettuce, sliced tomato and slivered spring onions onto entrée plates. He chopped the defrosted boned chicken, put rice on to steam, snarled impatient commands at the two women.

'This is what you call getting it both ways,' Souvie whispered to Heather, who gave a shout of laughter, quickly subdued.

When she got home just after eleven that night, Resa borrowed a bucket from their landlady, took Souvie's shoes off and gently eased her swollen feet into hot water. Souvie didn't know whether to laugh or scream. Resa kept refilling the water until Souvie was almost unconscious with relief, then she undressed her, held her under the shower, dried her, then led her to bed where she slept for twelve hours.

PATCH 38

The first time we worked on Waipoapoa Station, Maraetōtara, out the back of Havelock North in Hawke's Bay, Chris was a baby. So it must have been 1950. Laurie and I had applied for a job that asked for a general handyman and station cook. I can't remember why but it wasn't because he needed a job. He had one and I'd given up mine in Monarch Motors Office when I married (as you did), and we managed well on his wages. Maybe I just wanted to get away from our Moeller Street house, I don't blame my young self for that at all. Maybe I thought it would be good for Chris.

I say 'I' because I think most of the changes and moves we made were at my instigation. There is a restless streak to my nature and a liking for change. I am notorious among my friends and family for moving the furniture around, and Laurie used to joke that when he came home after working night shift he never knew whether he would hop into the bed or into the wardrobe.

The station was at the end of Maraetōtara Road. From the gate with the sign on it, which I had to get out and hold open while Laurie drove through, there was a winding road, not much more than a track really, on which our old Chrysler bumped, lurched and struggled its way to the house. The first time we drove over Maraetōtara Road it was a marathon of metal road, dust, crying baby.

We stopped for me to change Chris, and I thought, Does this road never end? He was an easy-going baby and only cried if he was hungry or wet. I breastfed him for nearly nine months, and at the end of that he was quite happy, or at least appeared philosophical, about going straight on to a cup.

We used only fabric nappies then, so every time I changed a baby it meant more washing. Washing nappies was like running a marathon for which you had not trained – every day. If the nappy was only wet, you soaked it in a bucket. If it was pooey, you folded the nappy and edged the poos into the toilet (a dunny) and then soaked the nappy in a different bucket. By the end of twenty-four hours you had a swag of dirty nappies and were hoping the night man would not miss picking up the can from the dunny as he had last week.

Around 8am after my two slices of toast, and two cups of strong tea, each one laced with four drops of milk, the baby safely asleep, I began filling the copper. I filled buckets of water from the tap on the laundry tub and lugged them to it. Wash houses were designed so that the tubs were the longest possible distance away from the copper the builder could devise. I learned to put paper and kindling in the fireplace under the copper before I started, and once I'd half-filled the pan with water, I lit the fire and kept it fed with wood as long as I needed to.

If Laurie had time, and he usually did, he cut a pile of wood at the weekend. If he forgot (rare) or didn't have time (very rare), I cut it. I took the hand-wrung nappies out of the soaking water and washed them with Velvet soap by hand in the tub. Then I lifted them, heavy and wet, over to the copper. It was a bit like a dance, only my partner was a copper stick holding a sodden lump of wet, heavy nappies. Once you got into the rhythm, it worked okay. Sometimes I got careless and sloshed water on the floor, which made me really wild. I hated having to interrupt the swing of things to get the mop and dry it up straight away, and it was a rising temper, ten-star drama having to slow down and make sure I didn't slip on the wet floor. I was always in a hurry. I think I spent most of the years between birth and forty running.

Into the water in the copper went grated soap. It was thought the flakes were better than powder for the baby's bum, and that even with two rinses the powder clung to the fabric while soap flakes didn't. Then you got the copper stick and gave it a stir every now and then. One of the problems was that I was short: five foot three inches as I knew it then (around one and a half metres in today's measurements) and five foot one inch now. My granddaughter Abbie Marie has told me why this happens but it hasn't helped.

Anyway, the top of the copper was at the level of my chest, so using the copper stick was awkward and transferring the nappies from the tub was pure slog, although it was marginally better than lugging them back when they were 'done'. Lifting the boiling nappies out from the hot, furiously spitting water (think raspberry jam on the boil) and then transferring them back to the tub was an exercise certain to result in nasty little spits adhering to any part of the arms or face where they landed.

I would have already filled the tubs with cold water. If you had two tubs you filled them both. One for the first rinse and one for the last. If you had a wringer, you put the nappies through; if you didn't, you wrung them out by hand. Then you put the clean wrung nappies into a basket or bucket, took them out and pegged them on a long line, with wooden props every few yards to hold the weight. Washing was hard labour, but I was young and fit and that's what you did. It was no good slumping after the washing dance either, there was still the house to clean, preparation and cooking to be done, baking once a week, and a baby to sing to. And reading. There had to be time for reading. One of my friends, eyeing the pile of library books, told me that before she got married her husband asked her to promise that she would never read in the daytime. I found it incomprehensible that she'd still gone ahead and married him. That she kept to it was astounding.

Once the line of stark white nappies was flapping and fluttering, I felt a huge wave of pleasure. If it was a blue-skied sunny morning, even more so, but even if it was a grey day it still gave me the same feeling of happiness. And how lovely to take them inside in the afternoon smelling of warm air and fluffy with cleanliness. What a delight to fold them up in piles and know that you were right for another couple of days.

The house on Waipoapoa was painted woolshed-red, and it sat hunched on a flat piece of land at the top of a small rise. It had three bedrooms, a bathroom and toilet, a kitchen with a large wood and coal range, and a wooden table and chairs where we ate. Off the kitchen was a long room with a long wooden dining table and chairs where the men ate, and which had its own outside entrance.

On the other side of the back door was the wash house with the copper at one end and two wooden tubs at the other. There was a wringer too. Through a wall at the end of the wash house was the dairy, with its own outside entrance. A lovely long verandah along the bedrooms' side of the house looked a great sunny place for a baby to crawl and play. There was no electricity. Kerosene lamps lit the rooms when it got dark. There was a phone at the manager's house and if you wanted to ring anyone you had to tramp over there, quite a way, to their much nicer house and ask if you could use the phone.

The job offered a house, a small wage and 'all found'. This meant you got wood, meat (mainly mutton, the occasional chook or turkey, and a side of bacon that hung in the dairy), milk, cream, eggs and basic groceries, which were delivered each month. This sounds very generous but I was to cook for the shepherds and anyone else who turned up, and Laurie would do any jobs they wanted him to do and work as many hours as needed to finish them. We took the job and I felt a real excitement, although I'd never cooked for anyone apart from family members before. Given the mush I'd made the first time I cooked potatoes three years earlier, I must have either learned fast or had incredible optimism. Hastings was forty miles away so you couldn't run out to the grocer if you'd forgotten to order something.

I had the *Edmonds Cookery Book* though. I still have it. Stained and battered, its recipes fatty and sugary, but it was my Bible till Alison Holst came along. She became my star and still is. There are other writers of recipe books I am very fond of and use a lot, but Alison, for me, is the queen. She came along just when I needed her.

I started work at 6am and breakfast was served at 7am. I made the shepherds porridge, toast, and bacon and eggs for breakfast. Lunch was soup (winter or summer), bread and butter, and either cold meat, beetroot and salads, or I'd make a shepherd's pie, which they served themselves with great sloshes of my home-made tomato sauce. Sometimes I made rissoles, which were also very popular. For dinner, it was either a roast or a stew, accompanied by big dishes of potatoes, pumpkin, silver beet, cabbage, carrots if you were lucky and, once a week, tinned green peas. This was followed by a pudding either with cream or custard, usually both. Laurie milked the cows, separated out the cream and made butter, but there was usually enough cream for the table as well. Steamed pudding, rice pudding, stewed or preserved fruit, apple pie or apple shortcake (rhubarb ditto). All swallowed hastily as though the house was on fire and they had to get it down before they escaped.

There were morning and afternoon teas to provide. Morning tea was scones: cheese, plain, date or raisin. Afternoon tea was more scones or maybe buttered slices of a fruit or ginger loaf, sometimes a plate of pikelets, always a cake of some kind, something heavy that 'stuck to the ribs' like fruit cake.

How the shepherds managed to eat as much as they did and then five minutes after they left the dining room get stuck into hard physical work, I don't know, but they did. They were very appreciative of my cooking and always yelled out, 'Thanks, Renée,' as they left. Sometimes a young guy might have to be nudged by an older one into remembering or perhaps learning his manners, but it was a ritual that soon became automatic, just as cooking and baking every day became mine. I had, and still have, an excessive anxiety about people being hungry or cold, so I always over-cater for family and friends, but those men and boys were a match for me. They never won though. There was always more if they wanted it because I thought they deserved good food and plenty of it.

The shepherds' cottage was cold and badly furnished, their bedrooms small and icy. Beds were wire stretchers with knobbly kapok mattresses. There were sheets and some thin grey blankets and sometimes a pillow. Some of the older ones knew to bring an extra blanket but the young ones had to endure whatever conditions were offered. There was a living room, a fireplace, a bathroom with a bath and basin, and unlined walls. The shepherds worked long hard hours, and on Sundays had to do their washing and cleaning (if they liked being clean) and chop wood for their fire. If it rained on a Sunday, tough. Laurie worked hard, too, but he had a clean house, clean clothes, good food and a warm bed to come home to.

I liked the life and the work and even the cold wet winters weren't too bad. There had been a garden once, now fenced off by an old wooden fence and gate, and in the spring it was covered with violets. Violets are colonisers, so never grow them if you're not prepared to be ruthless about cutting them back. I used to look at the violets and wonder about the woman who'd planted them. Laurie's vege garden was on the other side of the fence, near the house, but this area got very cold in the winter and it was hard to grow anything.

It might have been the unceasing work that made us leave that first time, or it might have been the stink of kerosene lamps. When we went back a few years later, we had three kids and the house had electricity, which meant only that there was electric lighting and maybe a power point. This time Chris was old enough to go to the one-teacher school halfway down the road, and I had a typewriter which seemed to be a surprise to the manager's wife. 'What on earth do you want a typewriter for?' she asked.

'I write,' I said. 'Book reviews, articles.'

'Really?' she said, as if this was a bizarre kind of joke.

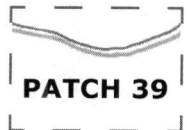

PATCH 39

Whatever gave me the idea I could write anything anyway? Especially something someone else would want to read. What hidden well of arrogance made me start? I know what made me have a go at plays. A dangerous mix of love for theatre coupled with the mad belief that the world – specifically the New Zealand part of it – needed plays that had women centre stage. And I'd turned fifty. What did I have to lose?

Maybe it was those lethal flagons of cheap sherry I used to buy from a shop on K Road? You had to queue because there was a limited supply. Those of us in the know were there at 4pm for the 5pm opening, when the truck arrived from West Auckland. You had to hand over the money and the empty flagons to replace the ones they charged you for. You were actually losing while you thought you were winning. We drank the sherry in beer glasses, and watered it down with lemonade. Occasionally we'd splash out and buy a bottle of wine or a cask of some unidentifiable pinky-red liquid. You don't want to know the labels. Times were hard. I smoked then too.

Perhaps the idea I could write plays stemmed from the same sort of logic that made me jump in the river each spring and investigate where the river had changed. This was on the basis that if I was struck on the head by a hidden rock, got pulled by a giant force into some rapids or sucked under by a whirlpool, all the other kids would know not to swim there. The beginning of this jump into the unknown of writing began, as most things in my life have, with reading. I read articles. Jillian Squires wrote very funny stories that were loosely based around domestic happenings. Maybe I could do this kind of writing? I had a go and it turned out I could.

Writing is basically solving problems. Problems of story, structure and style. Which one of the characters I've been thinking about will be the main one? Where do I want to start and where do I want to go? Huia Publishers contacted me recently to ask if I'd write a story for an anthology; I said yes because I've got a lot of time for Huia. I'd had a character in my mind for a while. She would do perfectly for the idea I had.

So I started writing 'This Day Was Different'. All I knew for sure was I would write something from the point of view of an old woman who was the opposite of all the stereotypical words and images used to describe old women. Yes, she would be old, and have some physical difficulties to contend with, but she would have a sense of humour, be a bit cynical, a hard worker. She would not be stupid or doddery or – bloody hell – *feisty*. A radical thought if you listen to the panels of experts trotted out to talk about what it means to be old. Anyway, Huia accepted it and the *Stories on the Four Winds* collection arrived in my letterbox. I remember thinking, So now I'll see how my old woman does on the page and how much better everyone else's stories are. (That's another thing about writing. Everyone else is always better.)

I like what James Lee Burke says about a story growing out of incremental discoveries, but I can't rely on those to start me off because incremental discoveries only appear after I've started the work. I heard Kim Hill interviewing Ian Rankin recently and was interested to hear him say that when he starts writing a new Rebus novel he doesn't know what is going to happen two pages away.

When I first began writing articles for newspapers and magazines, I knew I liked reading and I had a fair idea what I liked to read, but I had no idea how to make one turn into the other. No sherry involved at that stage. Only strong tea with four drops of milk in it. And maybe a couple of my peanut brownies. A lot of dreams. My aim was to make a bit of extra money, which just shows how naïve I was. Writing has the exciting, mind-changing, hallucinatory effect of a drug with all the highs and lows that come with this risky enterprise. It's not the beginning, it's not the end, it's the bit in between. Once caught in its thrall, there has been no going back. I need a daily fix. There are no courses where I can be taught how to ween myself off it. There is no room where I can stand up, face a group of people, and say, 'Hello, my name's Renée and I'm a reformed writer.' Even if there was such a course I wouldn't join it. Writing is a habit I can't break. It's a habit I don't want to break.

Of course I fail more than I win. Of course I set out with an idea that I can't make work, although it takes me ages to find that out. And sometimes it works and it's published, and years later when I re-read it for some reason – like I need to save my life – I think, I could do that better now. Or once or twice I think, mmm, yes, that wasn't too bad.

Every year I pick a horse in the Melbourne Cup. This once-a-year splurge (five dollars – two dollars for a win, three for a place) has never done more than recoup the outlay plus a dollar or two, and that rarely. My horses lose more than they win. Writing's a bit like that.

PATCH 40

Leafy greens: a fairy tale

Once upon a time there was an old woman with a garden the size of a shoebox. Everyone knew her as Nanny, and while she was generally happy with her life, she had so much pain at night that she didn't know what to do with herself.

Nanny had read about a woman called Helen who used leafy greens to deal with her own terrible chronic pain. Helen said the greens worked so well that everyone in pain should consider giving them a go.

Nanny started asking her friends and family and the people at the local shops where she could find some leafy greens just like Helen's, but nobody seemed to know. They didn't want to know. Growing leafy greens was something people frowned upon.

Then one day when Nanny was outside digging her garden, she saw some spiky leaves sticking out of her letterbox. There were three small plants in there. It looked like somebody had left them for her.

That same day a man knocked on the door, and when Nanny opened it, he said he was a community volunteer, and if there was anything she wanted help with to just let him know. He gave her a card with a cellphone number on it. 'Stick it on the fridge,' he said.

Nanny was a good keen gardener, but she didn't know anything about growing leafy greens of the sort left in her letterbox. It can't be that hard, she said to herself. Her soil was good, and if the plants needed watering she would do it. They were a bit like tomatoes weren't they? Without the tomatoes of course.

Nanny put one of the small leafy greens in a pot near her door and two in the garden. She worked on the assumption that no one looked that closely at the plants in someone else's garden – they saw the scene but not the particulars.

A friend came round to visit and Nanny made them both a cup of tea. When the friend was leaving she said, 'Where are they?'

'You just walked past them,' Nanny said. Meanwhile she was still having trouble sleeping, her joints were so sore. She longed to try the leafy greens, but she'd have to wait.

It wasn't a particularly good summer but there was enough sun for the three leafy plants to grow luxuriantly. Then under the heat of the occasional summer day, they began to smell. A neighbour over the fence said, 'Must be that boy next door.'

Another neighbour at the back said, 'Must be those people on the other side of us, or maybe it's old Nanny with the shoebox garden?' She said this to her teenage son and they both laughed heartily.

Nanny read the card on the fridge again. She texted the volunteer. He came round and had a look. 'Needs picking,' he said.

Nanny frowned.

'You want me to do it?' he said.

'What happens then?'

'You stick it in the hot-water cupboard to dry out.'

Sounded reasonable. Nanny got a plastic bag and picked the spiky leaves. It was half full when she put it in the hot-water cupboard.

When she opened the cupboard the next morning the blast of the smell just about knocked her over. Shit, she thought. She opened the back door and all the windows, and then reversed around and shut them again.

Nanny didn't want to be caught growing leafy greens when she had class notes to write and students to teach the next day. She opened the back door and all the windows again and waved a towel around.

She texted the volunteer.

Gotta be really dry so you can crumble it, was the message back. What the fuck did that mean? Nanny scratched her head.

If she had to crumble it, where would she do it? Couldn't do it in the kitchen. Too near the back door. She texted him again.

He replied immediately: *How do you intend to use it?*

Biscuits.

You know about making the butter?

Huh?

The volunteer brought round a recipe for making the butter. They crumbled the dry leafy greens. The smell was very strong. Nanny became a little anxious about heating it in the butter – she imagined the smell wafting all round town. But when she spooned the crumbled stuff into the melted butter there was no smell at all.

Phew. She was faint with relief.

'Look,' said the volunteer, 'I think if it works and you want to bake some more biscuits it might be an idea to buy the stuff ready-made.'

'Where?'

He sighed. It wasn't easy being a volunteer helper of old people.

'You want some biscuits?' She wanted to cheer him up.

'Christ, no.' Then he said, 'What do they look like?'

'Peanut brownies without the peanuts,' she said.

So he took four. His mother used to make peanut brownies and he wanted to see if Nanny's brownies were as good.

He texted the next day: *You tried these?*

Tonight.

You might want to think about just taking half a biscuit.

Why?

Just do it.

So she did. Half a biscuit. And after a while Nanny fell fast asleep.

When she woke in the morning, Nanny swung her legs out of bed and stood up. Yes they still hurt. But she'd slept all night. 'I can handle the day if I get a good night's sleep,' she told her mirror. 'What a gift,' she said to herself as she walked outside to her garden. 'Blessings on you, Helen, and on your leafy greens.'

That day she heard that the volunteer had moved away from community volunteering for old people and joined a support group for new parents. Looking after old people was too stressful, he'd told the organisers.

And Nanny lived happily ever after.

PATCH 41

From *The Skeleton Woman* (Huia 2002).

'You'd better go to the lav,' said Rose. They crept through the wash house to the lav. Well, Rose crept. Maisy lumbered. Their piddle sounded very loud. Don't think about it, she told herself. She was spending half her life telling herself not to think about things.

'What's going on?' Ada's voice sounded loud and fierce. The suddenness of it coming out of the dark made Rose jump and Maisy gave a terrified yelp. 'Come on Rose, what's going on? Who's this?' Ada peered at Maisy, then shone the torch. 'Jesus, God,' said Ada.

Maisy put her hands over her eyes and tried to shrink behind Rose.

'She hit someone with the shovel.' It sounded so bald when said out loud, but it was the truth and that was the only thing left now. You told your mother the truth only when anything else was plain useless.

'Why?' Ada's voice was sharp, disbelieving. She addressed Maisy. 'Well, girl, why?'

Maisy shook her head and said nothing.

'She says he was following her and saying things like, "Come on, girl, I won't hurt you."'

'He wanted to take my pants down,' Maisy volunteered.

'She says she hit him, then she heard someone being sick.'

'Boom boom,' said Maisy.

'*Shut up*,' Rose was angry with Maisy, angry with Ada, angry about everything. 'Just *shut up*, Maisy Beacon.'

Maisy cowered back and Rose felt mean, but she was sick of everything.

'Oh Jesus,' said Ada, 'where is the bugger then?' She limped around the backyard, the torch swinging in a wide arc in front of her. The two girls followed. Rose heard Maisy's hoarse breathing, loud in the night air. Ada peered into the shed, nothing stirred. 'He must have gone,' she said finally.

'What's up?' yelled an indignant voice from the fence. 'Who are you, what are you doing?'

'It's me, Mrs Miller,' said Rose, 'and Mum.'

'What are you doing at this hour of the night, for God's sake? Nearly had a heart attack when I saw that torch. Oh Jesus, sorry, shouldn't have said that.'

'What is it, Mum?' Jo joined her mother at the fence.

Ada never said more than hello to Thelma Miller anyway, but she hadn't even done that since Sim died in Thelma's bed. Rose saw Ada open her mouth to say mind your own business, when Jo gasped, 'Mum, *Mum*, there's a man lying on the grass. By the tree.'

Thelma scrambled over the fence but Ada was at the tree before her. A man was lying there all right. Ada shone the torch on him. He lay very still as though he was playing dead. Rose couldn't see his face, just his red-purply hands. She knew those hands.

'Christ almighty,' said Ada.

'Holy hell,' said Thelma.

'I didn't mean to,' Maisy burst out crying, 'I didn't mean to – he shouldn't have, he shouldn't have. All I did was give him a belt with the shovel.'

Looking as though she wouldn't mind giving Maisy a belt with the shovel, Ada knelt down by the man. Maisy snivelled and huge trails of snot ran down from her nose. Just as they got near her mouth Maisy gave a huge sniff and dragged them part of the way back. Rose's stomach heaved violently.

'Here, Rose, give her this.' Ada held out her handkerchief.

Ada and Thelma looked at each other across the man lying on the ground. 'Oh for God's sake, can't you even wipe your nose properly?'

She grabbed the hanky and wiped Maisy's face. 'Now blow,' she said, holding the hanky to Maisy's nose. Maisy blew. 'Get rid of this,' Ada said to Rose. But that was too much. Rose turned away and was sick onto the lawn.

'Oh for God's sake,' said Ada. She looked at the hanky with impatient disgust. 'Stop it at once, Rose. If this is the worst you ever see you'll have a very good life, believe me.' She threw the hanky on the ground.

'I'd just like to know what I've done,' Thelma said, looking up at the sky. 'I'd just like to know what I've bloody done.'

Ada looked at her contemptuously.

Thelma bent over and listened to the man's chest. Then she stood up, looked at Ada, didn't say a word.

'Oh for Christ's sake,' said Ada.

The two women looked at each other for what seemed like a long time. Thelma's eyes were shadowed and she looked tired, as though she didn't sleep well. Ada's eyes were brighter, fiercer, the way they'd been since Rose told her about Sim. As she and Thelma looked at each other, something of that sharp intensity spread to Thelma. She nodded.

'What are you standing there for?' Ada said finally, as if just remembering Jo, Maisy and Rose were still there. 'Get her a clean hanky, Rose.'

'Pooh,' said Maisy, 'smells like he pooed his pants.'

'Mum,' said Rose, 'is that Ha–'

Thelma overrode her words. 'Jo, you get Maisy a hanky from our place. Take Maisy and Rose and go home and make some tea. Stoke up the fire then stick the griddle iron on and make some scones. The girls can help. And watch the noise, eh? Any more people round here and we might as well sell tickets.'

'What are you going to do?' asked Jo.

'I'm going to wake up this rooster and give him a piece of my mind. And then I'm going to see him off the property. And Mrs Anthony's going to help me. Right, Ada?'

There was a tense pause, then Ada nodded.

'Then I want to talk to Mrs Anthony.'

PATCH 42

Being old. What's it like? How does it feel? How do you do it? There are no maps, no guidelines, you have to make your own way. A lot depends on your idea of what being old means. I had no examples in my family because they nearly all died early, and Puti Mary, who lived to seventy-three, and Emmanuel, ninety-three, were before my time. Although they could only have told me how they managed, not how I should.

I have never been good at reading maps and even if I was, there are no charted pathways for this one. Ours is the first for each of us and no other map will be exactly like it. I didn't have any plans for being old – I just got here because I lived long enough. What this odyssey is like is largely up to me.

I've arrived at this place called old age. It's not uncomfortable. It's like it's always been waiting in the wings. When I hear politicians and others refer to me as 'the elderly' like we're all the same height, the same size and genderless – the *other* – then I feel like having a tantrum. Saying 'I'm old' has vigour. There's a faint tinge of 'so what?' about it.

The truth is we old people are a motley bunch. We differ in health, income, education, working lives, our taste in clothes, our physical ailments, our physical activities (or not), our desires, the way we deliberately challenge our brains (or not), whether we love technology (or not), whether we like reading or watching TV, whether we are social or antisocial or somewhere in between. We differ in our sexuality and how we meet sexual desire – I'm under the 'girls can do anything' umbrella.

My physical decline is slow but noticeable. When I was seventy-nine I came to live in Ōtaki and made a garden. I couldn't do that now without a lot more help than I needed then. I'm a better and more adventurous cook than I was at seventy-nine (I say this every year), and now that I've got a food mixer with a dough hook, I enjoy making and eating my own bread. My skin is more lined and my hair greyer. My eyes always got tired when I read too long. Too long meant all day and half the night. Now it means half a day and a little bit of the evening. I have age-related macular degeneration and although I'm told I'll always be able to find my way around, reading and working will become more of a trial for my eyes.

Work is still a pleasure and I still have the willpower to delete large chunks of my writing and start again if it's not the way I want it. I am mortified to discover I left typos in a printed book when I thought I'd done a good job of proofreading it, but that's a different matter. A lesson too. Won't allow that to happen again. 'Pay a proofreader and look happy about it' will be my motto. So obviously I still make mistakes.

I still teach, and I can make a joke against myself and say I like being the boss, but really it's more the adventure, the excitement, the thrill of seeing something I say click in someone else's mind. I can walk briskly on the flat but I'm unsteady going downhill or up and down steps. If there's a rail or an arm I'm much happier. A friend,

Marilyn, gave me a walking stick this Christmas. She said I needed one with a bit of style and she did all her homework, and lo, that's what I've got.

I am often appalled at my own ignorance. For example, I knew nothing about the gut. No teacher or medical professional mentioned it until I got something wrong 'in the gut', and I realised I hadn't learnt anything about this eight or so metres of intestine until it started giving me problems. I now think everyone, at any age, should learn about the gut because it's a hundred to one you'll have a problem with its workings at some stage. Next to the brain, the gut is possibly our most important organ. When we say 'I've got a sore stomach', we often mean the gut area. Old age is a whole lot easier if you understand the workings of that part of the body, why it goes on strike sometimes, why it overworks other times.

My brain has got better. I said this at fifty and now again in my late eighties. The reason for this, I am convinced, is that I feed it. I work it. I ask a lot of it. It forgets the occasional word. Like, what is the word when you use the first letters as shorthand for the name of an organisation, such as UNESCO. Antonym? No. At least I know that's not right. Think. Go on, *think*. Acronym. Whoo – I can feel the relief right down to my toes.

My joints, hips, knees, ankles are sore most of the time. I still walk every day and I'm on my feet a lot at home. I take pills for blood pressure, Panadol for pain in my neck if it's during the day, and codeine at night if it's severe. Naturally every damn pill makes you constipated. My brain took a while to accept this as a 'here to stay' problem that had to be dealt with, but good little machine that it is, it eventually got the message. I have stronger drugs for the neck pain I get (very common, half the world has neck pain) but very rarely take them because I don't like how they make me feel. I am taking Tamoxifen as a barrier to cancer coming back. It won't necessarily stop it because it depends where it appears in my body, but it's a safeguard. Sort of. Tamoxifen tablets have brought back some menopausal symptoms. Heigh-ho. Swings and roundabouts.

It's been interesting over the last couple of months to dress for a different shape and to realise that there are now a few fabrics the scarred skin on my chest will not accept. Two garments – one I bought new before I had the operation and one I've had for a while and always liked – have, both times I've worn them, became so unbearable against my skin I've had to rip them off and find something else. However, this new shape is not a result of being old, it's the result of cancer and that can happen at any age.

A while ago I realised it was senseless to beat myself up when I left something in the bedroom instead of bringing it through with me to my workroom or the laundry. I should be telling myself all movement is good because it is. I should be saying to myself 'well done', when I forget to take the clothes through to the laundry and have to go back for them, or when I walk away without the cup that held my morning tea instead of carrying it through to the sink to be washed. *All movement is good.*

Walking out with a banana skin to throw under a rose is good, walking to the letterbox is good, and no need to try and do everything in one trip. Walking to the library is good, although I had to learn that lugging a heavy load of books home in my arms is now just plain silly. Use your brain, I tell myself. Make two trips or use the trolley. Yes, I, who once dismissed Chris's suggestion with a contemptuous shake of the head, now have a shopping trolley, and am glad of it to lug home my heavy groceries or books.

These two hands that have done so much for me are still active – tapping the keys has probably seen to that. They still prune and weed, and they still cook and bake, although the kitchen bench seems higher and my arms get sore if I stand there too long. I have help in the house two hours a week and help in the garden two hours a week when the weather's right. I figure I'd have to pay one way or the other and this is a way of making sure I stay here as long as I need to.

So that's how I am. How do I feel about it? I feel lucky.

PATCH 43

From *Willy Nilly* (Penguin 1990).

'We'll be married here,' Polly announced, 'on the back lawn.'

'Holy shit –' Sonja stared at Polly.

'On the back lawn?' asked Evvie.

They surveyed the dreary lavenders, the dusty red geraniums, the huge spreading flax and the lusty mounds of oxalis and comfrey, which surrounded a lawn composed mainly of kikuyu grass and couch. A narrow concrete path, pitted and scarred with age, took the eye straight to the rickety circular clothes line, which, at the moment, supported a few towels and a number of brightly coloured pegs.

'I told Gran when I rang. She thought it sounded all right.'

Sonja snorted. 'If you said you wanted to get married on Queen Street during rush hour, she'd think it was all right.' Sonja got up from the table, carried her cup to the sink and turned the tap on so the water gushed loudly. She flicked a tea towel viciously at a wasp, 'Damn things.'

Polly smiled at Evvie. 'I must change. Luke's parents will be here soon.'

'The only good thing I've ever done, as far as my

mother's concerned,' said Sonja, 'was to have Polly, and if she could have taken her away from me, she would have.'

I wonder what Luke's parents are like, Evvie thought. I've never met a dentist before – socially I mean – not that I've ever wanted to, but if everyone feels like that they must lead a very limited social life.

Polly, back in a blue checked shirt and cotton pants, eyed her mother warily. 'We should talk about invitations.'

'I wish you'd stop going on as though everything's settled.'

'Are you going to invite your ex?'

'Am I what?'

'My father. Are you going to invite him?'

Round the corner of the house and up onto the porch came Luke, and a man and woman in their late fifties. The man was short and pink with remnants of red hair on the sides of his head. He looked confident and already had a smile, implying great pleasure, securely in place.

The plump dark-haired woman wore a loose navy and white dress and matching jacket. A chain attached to bifocals hung round her neck. She wasn't smiling.

Luke, except for his frizzy hair and glasses, didn't resemble either of his parents. He was tall and tanned. He kissed Polly and kept his arm round her as he made the introductions.

'Sonja,' he smiled cheerfully, 'meet my parents, Daphne and St Clair. Mum and Dad this is Sonja and her friend, Evvie.'

Not a bad effort, thought Evvie, well-rehearsed.

Daphne managed a smile and St Clair stepped forward and shook hands firmly. Sonja opted for cool civility.

Polly had eyes only for Luke. Evvie smiled encouragingly.

'What about a drink?' asked Polly.

'Just fruit juice.' St Clair laughed heartily. 'Just a couple of old wowsers, that's us. Alcohol's so bad for the teeth.'

There was an uneasy pause.

Evvie saw St Clair's eyes on the bookshelf opposite. The copies of *Pure Lust*, *Lesbian Women* and *Desert of the Heart* seemed to leap out at her so God knows what they were doing to St Clair.

'Luke tells me you work at the Post Office?'

Sonja admitted she did. 'I'm a supervisor in the sorting room.'

'And what about you – um – Evvie?'

He's game, thought Evvie. Aloud she said she'd been a teacher until recently.

'I'm sorry.' It was St Clair's turn to go pink.

'No,' said Evvie, 'I didn't get the sack. I decided I needed some time off so I applied for leave without pay.'

'Good idea,' agreed St Clair fervently.

Sonja took the initiative. 'What about you, Daphne?'

'Just a housewife and mother,' Daphne said. 'Not very trendy I'm afraid.'

Evvie looked away from Sonja.

'That's not true,' St Clair looked around proudly, 'Daphne's a stalwart of the local gardening club, the secretary actually.'

'I've always hated gardening,' said Sonja.

Daphne and St Clair gazed in a kind of resigned horror at the dreary backyard. Evvie made herself useful, as her mother would have said, and set out glasses.

'We thought, Daphne and I, well only if you feel it's appropriate, that we could talk about the actual ceremony?' St Clair nodded enthusiastically. 'We've always gone to the Presbyterian church so of course Luke went right through Sunday school there, but we don't want to be dogmatic about it.'

'So they haven't told you about the back lawn,' said Sonja.

There was a flurry of explanations from Luke and Polly, the gist of which appeared to be that neither of them wanted a big ceremony.

'I don't want any ceremony,' Sonja pointed out sharply. 'Why can't you just live together?'

'We thought we'd make up the service ourselves,' said Polly.

Daphne's eyes were, despairingly, on the backyard. 'They can't just live together. Luke has his career to think about.'

'They've been living together for weeks,' Sonja looked aggressively at the bubbles in her glass.

'Why don't you want Polly to marry Luke, um, Sonja? Do you have anything against Luke personally?'

'He's a man.' Sonja drained her glass and Luke hastily refilled it.

'Yeees?' St Clair waited courteously for further revelations but there were none. Sonja considered her answer to be self-explanatory, self-sufficient, needing no more explication than any of the other great maxims which seek to sum up complex issues in a few words. God is Love. All Men are Created Equal. Spare the Rod and Spoil the Child.

Luke said, 'If it's all right with you Sonja, we thought we'd ask Mum and Dad to pay for the drinks and the musicians.'

'*Musicians?*'

'Won't be too loud, Mum,' said Polly, 'definitely no amplifiers.'

'I won't be bulldozed,' said Sonja.

St Clair clicked his lips and leaned forward. 'No hurry is there?'

There was a small pause. Then Polly spoke. 'Luke's had the offer of an assistant's job in Dunedin. I want to go with him. It starts in four weeks' time.'

'*Luke.*' Daphne was appalled.

'You knew this job was only temporary, Mum.'

'Oh Luke, oh Luke.'

'Dunedin?' Sonja was pale with rage. '*Dunedin?*'

'It's not outer Mongolia, Mum. They do have electricity and postal deliveries.'

Sonja got up and stared with loathing out at the backyard. 'Kids,' she said.

St Clair had no difficulty understanding her this time. 'Exactly,' he said and put an arm round his wife's shoulders.

'I want my father invited to the wedding,' said Polly.

'You've never worried about him.'

'I'm getting married. I want children. There are things I need to know. Surely you can put up with your ex for a couple of hours.'

'He's not your father,' Sonja said.

'What?'

'We can talk about it later.'

'You do know who he is, I presume?'

'Oh dear, oh dear.' St Clair was reduced to repeating this phrase over and over like a mantra.

'Yes, of course I know who he is,' said Sonja. 'I asked

him to be the donor, didn't I?'

Evvie gave a bellow of laughter, which she tried to muffle in her drink. She needn't have bothered. No one was taking any notice of her.

'Are you telling me, Mother, are you telling me that my children's grandfather was a bloody teaspoon?'

'Only one of them,' said St Clair.

Sonja sat down. 'If you want to put it that way,' she said. 'In any case it was a meat-baster.'

'Oh dear, oh dear,' said Daphne.

'Polly,' Luke put out a hand.

Polly's face contorted and with a gasping sob she ran out of the room. They heard her bedroom door slam and the key turn in the lock with a loud screech.

'Needs some three-in-one,' said Evvie.

Sonja shot Luke a venomous glance. 'I hope you're satisfied.'

'Me?' A flush of astonished anger spread over Luke's face. 'Me?'

Evvie opened the cupboard over the sink and pulled out a bottle of Napoleon given to her by friends in the English department to help her through the rigours of temporary retirement. She poured generous amounts into four glasses and carried two over to St Clair and Daphne. St Clair waved the drink away.

'Medicinal,' whispered Evvie with a meaningful jerk of her head in Daphne's direction. St Clair nodded and took a large gulp. He took another.

Sonja sipped some brandy and pulled a face. 'I was going to tell her. I wanted to tell her. But the agreement was not until she was twenty-one.'

'At her twenty-first birthday party, I suppose?' The

brandy only fanned Luke's hostility.

'She never showed any interest. Never.'

Beside St Clair, Daphne sipped her drink and sought for something to say. She looked across at her son and her face softened. 'Never mind, son,' she said, as though he was a small child again.

Luke walked outside. He appeared to be lost in a study of a particularly fine heap of oxalis.

Inside conversation died. The first drink finished, they started on another. Evvie had a brainwave.

'What say,' she said into the busy silence, 'what say I rustle up some food?'

PATCH 44

In the early 1980s the British feminist magazine *Spare Rib* ran an article on the menopause and quoted from *Everything You Always Wanted To Know About Sex – But Were Afraid To Ask* by Dr David Reuben. It's an example of the arrogance that abounded amongst those who specialised in women's 'problems'. I wrote about it at the time in New Zealand's feminist magazine, *Broadsheet*. I've compressed that article here. First here's some of David Reuben on menopause.

> As the oestrogen is shut off, a woman comes close as she can to being a man. Increased facial hair, deepened voice, obesity, and the decline of the breasts and female genitalia all contribute to a masculine appearance. Coarsened features, enlargement of the clitoris and gradual baldness complete the picture. Not really a man, but no longer a functional woman, these individuals live in a world of intersex ... sex no longer interests them.
>
> To many women, menopause marks the end of their useful life. They see it as the onset of old age, the beginning of the end. Having outlived their ovaries, they have outlived their usefulness as human beings. The remaining years may just be marking time until they follow their glands into oblivion.

As far as I was concerned, back in those days the only problem women had was men like David Reuben. With gems like this, though, it's no wonder I approached my own menopause with some trepidation.

One day I was busy teaching when I suddenly became aware that I was sweating profusely and was extremely hot. Shit, I thought, as I continued to discuss the finer points of *Romeo and Juliet*. I've got the flu. At lunchtime I described this 'turn' to my colleagues. Not one of the four over-fifty women there said, 'That, my dear simpleton, is a hot flush!' Various explanations were offered, but not that. I know now that they were terrified to acknowledge their own menopausal state because they would be seen through Dr Reuben's eyes – washed out, on the scrapheap, half-people.

Although I didn't realise it at the time, I had actually started menopausal symptoms a few years earlier when I began to experience severe flooding for the first three days of each period. I looked forward to the cessation of these periods as a condemned prisoner looks forward to release. I'd heard a few stories about 'the change of life', usually to the effect that a woman has gone crazy or, worse, was exhibiting 'nerves' and driving her family crazy.

This wasn't going to happen to me of course. I was busy, I had many interests and, in between periods, I was very fit. And I was ecstatic when the last of my kids left home. That's not quite true. I missed Tim when he left but I also loved the feeling of freedom. Anyway, imagine my anger and resentment when none of these things meant a damn. It became clear I was at the mercy of my hormones and there was little I could do about it.

After the classroom incident, I started having severe hot sweats. I use this term because 'flush' seems to me to be too pallid a word for that drenching, debilitating experience. Nights became a true nightmare. Every thirty-five minutes I had a hot sweat. I know this is accurate because on the night the Air New Zealand plane crashed on Erebus, I stayed up all night and listened to the radio and at the same time recorded my hot sweats in a little red notebook, which I still have. I also recorded that each night I had to change both the sheets and my clothes, which made me so wide awake that there was little chance of getting back to a restful sleep again.

Teaching is a demanding job and it didn't make it any easier when drops of water fell from my face to the desk in the middle of a lesson, or when my glasses fogged up as I was taking roll call.

Debilitated, irritable, tired and resentful, I turned to books for knowledge and comfort. There was some knowledge but little comfort. I tried ginseng, vitamin E, vitamin B, vitamin C, bought a fan. Nothing worked. I did discover that hardly any research had been done on this stage of a woman's life, probably because men don't experience it. I travelled all round the country putting on shows and doing talks with a roll of paper towel beside me, so I could wipe my face when I needed to. I was menopausal and everyone knew it. I probably wrecked the psyches of a lot of younger women as they looked at me and realised what they were in for.

My physical symptoms were severe but so were my mental and emotional reactions – I experienced times of deep depression – but on the good side I had improved mental efficiency and creativity. I wanted to be alone a lot of the time. I turned fifty and began thinking about what I wanted to do with the rest of my life. Did I want to lie on my death bed and think of all the things I hadn't done?

I started writing what I wanted to write and didn't worry about what people thought. I began to realise that many of the things I'd thought and said were true, and that I wasn't 'being silly' or 'twisting the facts'. Although I was still left with irritation and miserable physical symptoms, I began to alter my situation so that I could cope with menopause a lot better. I opted for celibacy and that was great. I also had a D&C and finished my periods completely.

It's a wonderfully liberating thing to do. To think about what is best for the person that is you. I spent a lot of time caring for plants, seeing they had the right situation for maximum growth and blooming, but how often did I put even a quarter of that time and concentration into my own growth and blooming?

I recognised my love for women and for one particular woman, and I looked back to all the times my sanity had been saved by the love and friendship of other women. I changed my job to one that was less stressful because of the fewer hours involved, but it was also, of course, less well paid. So I frequented the op shops and grew my own vegetables.

The menopause did not mark the end of my useful life as Dr Reuben asserted it would, and as a matter of fact I am grateful for that stage of my life where physical symptoms forced me to face up to other changes I needed and wanted to make and did make. These changes didn't come without pain, self-questioning and doubt, but I knew one thing for sure – I wouldn't go back.

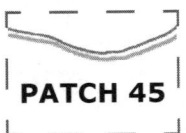

PATCH 45

On 29 May 1988, in what was turning out to be a memorable year, my sister, Val, rang me to tell me that our uncle Cliff had died and, as a kind of afterthought, that she'd been diagnosed with secondary emphysema. 'Don't know what I've done,' she said.

This had to be wrong. She was younger than me. When we were little and whenever we were anywhere strange or different, I always said to her and Jimmy, 'I'll go first.' I was always the one who tried out the new currents in the river in early spring until Jimmy was older. That was my job. To look after them. I didn't always like it but I did it. Now here was Val telling me she might go first.

Cliff, who had advanced to drinking a flagon of sherry a day, had always had a foul mouth and repelled most visitors. It wasn't only his swearing. He said nasty things about people, and got angry at the slightest hint of disagreement. He had a terrible stutter so maybe the explosive Fs and Bs helped him get the words out. He and I never really got on. I didn't hesitate to answer him back and he didn't hesitate to call me names for having the gall to do so.

We had a standup, all-stops-out, shouting match when I turned up a few minutes late for cleaning the hall after Val's wedding party. He called me names. I was furious. I had cleaned the entire kitchen before I'd left the night before and was tired and in no mood to hear him describe me as a lazy, lying bitch. I marched off steaming.

Jimmy kept up visiting Cliff out of duty, but Jimmy's wife, Lillian, didn't – she had never been keen on his being around the kids because of the swearing. My family is composed of those who swear a lot and those who don't swear at all. I'm in the swear-a-lot group.

There was another side to Cliff. He had been such a help to Rose when he was young. He'd made sure we had wood and that it was chopped. When Jimmy was old enough Cliff taught him to chop kindling with a little tomahawk and – when it was time – how to use the big axe. The only thing I remember about my father shooting himself was seeing Orm cry and hearing Cliff shout at him, 'That woman in there's got enough to put up with without listening to your bloody shit.'

At the wake after his wife's funeral, Cliff, barely stuttering, said to me, 'I only ever loved two women, my mother and yours.' I sat there hoping like hell no one else had heard him. Good line, though – nicely balanced. I used it in *Kissing Shadows*. You can't waste a good line.

And now Cliff was dead. And Val had emphysema.

The year had started out well. My revue *Born to Clean* had a four-week season at Belvoir Street Theatre in Sydney after a great run in New Zealand. I'd already written three revues for the theatre before I started on this one: *What Did You Do in the War, Mummy?*, *Asking For It* and *The MCP Show* – all of which had sketches and skits, and old songs to which I'd written new words (and for which I got rapped over the knuckles by APRA). But when I had the idea for *Born to Clean*, I decided to ask Jess Hawk Oakenstar and Hilary King to come up with songs. And they did. I remember ringing Jess and saying, 'I need a song called "Dear Gertrude Stein".'

'Okay,' she said. And wrote one.

Dear Gertrude Stein
I just want to thank you
For going so far out, going so far out …

Limbs studio theatre, Ponsonby, 1986, and the first night of *Born to Clean* was packed. I was so nervous I couldn't stay in the theatre. Revues were one thing but a show with original songs was quite another. Once the lights over the audience went down, I walked up and down in the dark, listening and smoking. This was of course before the day in 1986 when I gave up smoking forever. I had reason to be nervous. I had written a scene about using a tampon for the first time, and apart from a little dialogue to get the scene going, the three main characters just repeated the instructions on the piece of paper that came with the packet. I might have gone too far this time, I thought.

When loud noise erupted from the other side of the closed door, I knew I was right. I had gone too far. Rape, murder, assault, yes, but not menstruation. Shit, were they storming the stage? Then I realised it was laughter. Laughter that went on and on while the actors couldn't get a line in because the audience wouldn't let them. They were so busy laughing at something that recalled their own difficulties when faced for the first time with a tampon, they couldn't stop.

Hilz told me later that she tried and tried to make herself heard because she couldn't stand there all night with one leg up on the toilet seat, holding a tampon and a piece of paper. Finally, in a tiny pause the audience needed to take a breath, and using all her power, she yelled, 'And insert the *tampon*.' The place went wild. No one onstage could say anything for at least five minutes, after which the cast managed to get through to interval. Greg McGee came out then and saw me. 'Relax, Renée,' he said. 'You've got them.'

The next day the queue to the box office stretched from there, down the stairs and out onto the street below. It was well before the days of Twitter and Facebook.

The script is about three young women who meet at school, become friends, drift apart and come back together again. There were great performances and great singing. Throughout the piece there are advertisements about cleaning products and how women of the time were taken in by the claims. Now it would be run-of-the-mill, then it was new and smart.

Born to Clean did well around the country and had a great run in Sydney, although the review in the *Sydney Morning Herald* was terrible. Basically, we were a bunch of New Zealand feminists who couldn't sing or act our way out of a paper bag, and as for the script – well, *he* didn't think much of that either.

We had the last laugh. Full houses most nights and close to full on others. Some of the full houses were 'very full', the box office admitted. We got good reviews everywhere else. I did loads of interviews. I concluded that to get a bad review in the *Sydney Morning Herald* had been very good for business. Best of all we attracted lots of people who didn't usually go to the theatre and we made enough money to pay everyone properly. We were invited to lengthen the season but decided against that. We were all pretty tired. Besides we'd stayed with friends who were wonderfully hospitable but were probably very pleased to see us go.

That was January 1988. Two months later, on 8 March, Wairoa's bridge was down because of severe flooding. Sharon, Naomi and Abbie rang to say they were okay. After that came the New Zealand Festival of the Arts. In my diary I wrote:

> Enjoyed Greg [McGee] and Roger [Hall]. Spoke briefly to Dorothy Hewitt from Australia [*The Man from Mukinupin*] and John McGrath from Britain [*The Cheviot, The Stag and the Black Black Oil*], two playwrights whose work I admire very much.

On 21 May, Hoot (David's second wife, so-called because when she was little she had a pet owl) rang to say David was in intensive care. He'd had an accident in the car, broken a shoulder and was suffering from exposure. Eight days later I heard the news about Cliff and Val.

I was working on a novel that year and Bernadette still had her secondhand bookshop, The Book Stops Here. I helped out in the shop on Thursdays and by going to garage sales on Saturdays looking for stock. I had a good eye for books.

I received an invitation to be one of the three keynote speakers at the First International Women Playwrights

Conference. Should I go? What did I have to say to a large conference of strangers?

I was also asked if I'd be interested in adapting Keri Hulme's *The Bone People* for a TV series. I used exclamation marks in those days, and the line in my diary where I recorded this invitation has four. When I look back over my unpublished and published works from that time, I see I used exclamation marks like a drunken sailor uses booze: 'Just one more and I'll be all right.' This TV series to-ing and fro-ing with Ray Waru and Larry Parr and others on Te Mānuka Trust was a dead loss, and ended with me getting more and more frustrated and eventually losing interest altogether. Probably that was their trajectory too. 'God, I hate this shilly-shallying,' I raged in my diary.

By the time I sent the draft of *Willy Nilly* to the publishers, Heinemann, David was much better. I went down to Wellington for George Webby's farewell and wrote in my diary that I felt very distanced from a lot of the theatre people. Later on I made up my mind to write something from my point of view about an attack on playwright and lecturer Mervyn Thompson, which had imitated events in a play of mine.

I see with at first disbelief, then amusement, an entry in my diary in April that year: 'I received a snotty letter from Jill Abigail in answer to the snotty letter I sent her.' But there's no clue as to what the correspondence was about. 'At least I had the grace to admit I started it,' I told Jill when I rang her the other week to ask if she knew.

'I will find out,' she said. She probably will.

I decided to accept the invitation by Anna Kay France to speak at the women playwrights conference in

Buffalo, New York. Bernadette sold the shop so she had the money to come too. We both got temporary jobs to have more money to take with us: Bernadette at Social Welfare and me at Inland Revenue. I applied to the New Zealand Literary Fund for travel assistance to the conference. The Ministry of Foreign Affairs contacted me and asked if I would lengthen my travel to include speaking at universities in Europe and England, and at the Commonwealth Institute meeting in London in October. Chris, who was working in Sydney at the time, gave me a thousand dollars to spend.

I sent off an application to Otago University for the Robert Burns Fellowship, and around the same time Heinemann turned down the novel I'd been writing, so I rang Geoff Walker at Penguin. I'd met him once when he came to one of our garage sales and bought curtains. I said I wasn't submitting the novel to him, but would he read it and tell me what was wrong with it. And he said yes, he would.

In June I'd started the job at Inland Revenue as a temporary assistant. I had to organise IRD numbers. There was a backlog of stuff to do, and another woman and I began on the pile. At the end of each day whatever rubbish there was had to be ripped up into small pieces. Repetitive, monotonous, but we didn't mind. Now it's become a habit of mine to rip up anything I put it in the paper rubbish. I used to catch the bus and my colleague travelled on the same bus. She talked about making cakes and icing flowers, buying a new dress and shoes for a son's wedding in the Catholic church, all very normal and sometimes dull. Then one day she told me about her other son who'd hanged himself because he had AIDS antibodies, and how she'd never talked about it because of what people would think. Her husband had forbidden anyone to mention the son's name. She was telling me, she said, because she knew who I was. I felt ashamed of my quick judgement of her as dull, and resolved not to be so hasty in future – a resolution I've broken many times.

This wasn't the first or the last time a woman has confided in me when she knows who I am. Their lives are often completely different from mine and they know it, but they have no one who won't judge them on the basis of a suicide or an old pregnancy out of wedlock or a mistake they made they haven't told anyone about ever, till now. It's mainly suicide or adoption, and that's come out of *Wednesday To Come* (suicide) and *Does This Make Sense To You?* (forced adoption in New Zealand). People feel they can talk to me in perfect safety, and they're right.

On 9 August Val went into Waikato Hospital and the next day she had an operation to see if something could be done. She had always been an asthmatic and emphysema made breathing even harder. But she was going to be all right. She had to be.

In October, near the end of a tumultuous year, Bernadette and I left for New York City for a few days stopover before going on to Buffalo.

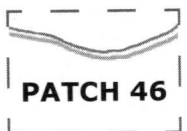

PATCH 46

I fell in love with Dunedin when I was sitting, tired to the bone, in a spa pool at the top of City Road, sipping champagne and looking out at the night sky. It was snowing, which added to the magic.

We arrived there on Wednesday, 14 July 1982, to give a performance of *What Did You Do in the War, Mummy?* I'd begun writing it in Auckland when, on Thursday 11 March at 11.30pm, I'd got a ring from someone at *Broadsheet*. Phone calls late at night usually mean bad news. Although no one I knew in Auckland back then considered 11.30pm late.

The first party I went to in Auckland was a real shock. There was only one light on, a lamp in the corner. You had to grope your way to a space and if you didn't sit down immediately, someone else took it. Lots of people were sitting on the floor, talking and arguing about feminism, Gloria's latest book, Jill Johnston's wrestling match with Norman Mailer, domestic abuse and what we were going to do about it. This was a party? Where I came from a party meant lights, laughing, joking, singing songs like 'I'm Just a Poor Cinderella', while someone (me if they were desperate) played the guitar and people who had to work the next day started making going-home noises around 11.30. Which meant they left about 1am, but their intentions were good. There was always food:

plates of sandwiches and lots of cheese, and nearly always someone would go up the road and get fish and chips. In Auckland they all drank wine and you were lucky to get a cracker. They had minds above food. I was intrigued, amused and a little wary.

Now this caller at 11.30 at night was asking if I could do something to open a *Broadsheet* seminar in Auckland, because the woman who was going to do something had just rung to say she couldn't.

'Do something?'
'You know – theatrical?'
'When's the seminar?'
'Twentieth.'
'Of March?'
'Yes.'
'You mean this March – *1982* March?'
'Yes.'
'Nine days away 20 March?'
'Yep.'
Fuck, I thought.

Laurie didn't swear and I had managed to refrain until we got an agitator washing machine, the kind where a hose from the tap filled the bowl of the machine with water. I was always forgetting I had the tap on because I'd go away and start doing something either with Tim, such a cute little baby, or David, such a bright little boy, both very keen on things that made them laugh. Like stories, songs, or Mum being silly and pretending to be a dazzler from a fireworks display. But the funniest thing was the time I remembered I'd left the washing machine filling and when we got to the laundry, there was water all over the floor. I yelled, 'Fuck,' ordered the boys to stand still, rushed to the hot-water cupboard, grabbed towels, chucked them on the floor and jumped up and down on them.

My friend down the road had solved this problem by drilling a hole in her laundry floor, but although I admired her creative problem-solving, I didn't have the nerve or the tools. So I shouted 'fuck' and 'fuck you' at the machine. Very satisfying. But I still had to get the mop out and clean up the mess. 'Fuck,' said David, trying out the word, and Tim laughed. He laughed at anything so probably wasn't marked for life, I hoped. They definitely thought the whole performance was my best ever.

'Make the most of it,' I muttered, 'it's a one-off.' I had hoped they hadn't heard me but there's an immutable law – kids always hear the things you don't want them to hear.

'How long a piece were you thinking?' I asked the woman from *Broadsheet*. This was a question she was not prepared for. But she gave it a stab. 'Half an hour, twenty minutes?'

I made up my mind. 'Okay, twenty minutes, twentieth of March, see you at Auckland Girls' Grammar hall, 9am,' and hung up.

My first impulse after I've made this sort of decision is to panic. This is a good thing. I get it all over before I've even started so I'm free to concentrate on the work. Panic means unanswerable questions. Why had I said yes? I loved and admired *Broadsheet*, but hello? I had to write the play, find a cast who could sing and play an instrument, find rehearsal space, rehearse … Twenty minutes? Does she understand how long, in theatrical terms, twenty minutes is? If she didn't, I did. Twenty minutes is a long time when the show is only eleven days away and at that moment I had nothing, not one word, not even an idea, to fill those hungry minutes.

Okay, I thought, as I always do. Okay, eleven days. Divide it up, make it manageable. Four days to write it and seven to rehearse it.

Write what? A play? A monologue? No, a revue. Skits, sketches, songs and maybe, if I'm lucky, some dancing. About what? I'll think of something. Okay. Settled. A twenty-minute revue called – ?

I tossed and turned all night, then noted in my trusty diary:

Saturday, 13 March, 1982. Wrote most of the theatre piece *What Did You Do in the War, Mummy?*

Monday 15 March, 1982. After false start [no idea what this means], I conned Lois Haynes, Christina Milligan, Marylin Eccles and Bernadette into coming in on this mad enterprise.

The public performance was on Saturday, so we had a week. I forget the details – one of the cast had a baby or a toddler I think and wasn't as free as the rest to come to rehearsals – but through that week we met every spare minute, hour, half-day, evening … and finally it was Saturday. Performance Day.

These women were stars. Hardworking. Talented. So quick on the uptake. How or when they found time to learn their lines, I have no idea. Every breathing minute was focused on rehearsals. It never entered their heads, or mine, that we couldn't do it. We knew the idiocy of the whole enterprise but ignored it. Who cared if our legs, bodies, arms were sore and our voices tired and hoarse? Who cared if we were so tired we could barely think? As long as the cast could get the lines, come in on cue, sing the songs and do the dances, as long as we were still all upright, all would be well. Sleep? We'd sleep next week. The show must go on.

'*What Did You Do in the War, Mummy?* opened the *Broadsheet* seminar on Saturday, 20 March, as promised, and was a great success,' I wrote in my diary, with commendable restraint. Actually the audience went mad. Claps, smiles, yells of approval. Then they implored us to do it again at lunchtime, but it wasn't possible because the one with the toddler had other calls on her time. And fair enough. Her partner, mother, sister had all held the fort, but by lunchtime Saturday they were haddit and the little toddler was wondering where the hell this woman called Mum was.

Lots of things happened in 1982. Bernadette was cast in *Give Us a Kiss and I'll Tell You* by William Dart, which was to tour. The title comes from an old joke. Two men meet at a party and one of them asks the other, 'Are you gay?' And the other says, 'Give us a kiss and I'll tell you.' I got a job at *Broadsheet*, but before that they asked me to tour *What Did You Do in the War, Mummy?* to celebrate their tenth anniversary. I got a cast together. Hilz King and Jess Hawk Oakenstar were the singers and musos, and Jude Wishart and Bernadette the singers and actors.

We rehearsed, fractionally less frantically than we had in March. We were to take it to the big centres and generous readers offered billets. Miriam Saphira organised the van, the billets, the publicity, everything. One of the Nelson billets was Mary O'Regan, Pauline O'Regan's niece who was to become the head of the Ministry of Women's Affairs. Sister Pauline O'Regan was one of my heroes because of her stand on social justice issues, and she was also a favourite writer, who'd taught Bernadette history at Villa Maria College in Christchurch.

By the time we got to Dunedin we had passed the exhausted stage. There is a whole other story about 'Five in a Van' plus musical instruments and luggage for a week or ten days or whatever it was. My memory is mercifully blank on this point. I'm pleased about that. We were at Marama Hall – or was it the education department? – exhausted out of our minds. We sat on chairs and stared dully into space while we waited for a representative of the Dunedin Feminist Collective to arrive. We had a performance to do that night but none of us had the energy to even check where we were to actually stage the show, and as for checking the lights, who cared?

Then in came Jocelyn Harris. Great smile. 'Give me all your dirty clothes,' she commanded. She had a huge plastic bag. 'Come along,' she said. So we did. We didn't have the strength to argue. If she was a thief and was preparing to run off with our clothes, we were past caring. Jocelyn washed and dried a week's worth of clothes and brought them all back neatly folded. Jocelyn, we discovered, was a feminist, taught as a professor in the English department, wrote about Jane Austen, and was the most hospitable and helpful woman in a city that seems to specialise in this sort of woman.

The format we used was to present the show in the first half, then in the second half, we'd sit on the stage while the audience asked us questions. We finished with that great song by Robyn Archer of 'Dicks Don't Grow on Trees' fame – 'That Good Old Double Standard', about the differences in what we expect of men and women. Everyone joined in and after that we had a delicious supper organised by Anna Marsich at her home.

Bernadette and I were billeted with Shirley Child on City Road. It was snowing. Cold as only Dunedin can get. I'm not sure whether Hilz or Bernadette drove, but eventually we arrived at the top of City Road. We got our bags, said goodbye and the van took off. Bernadette and I slipped and slid on the snow as we found our way to the house. I grabbed frantically at the fence so I didn't fall over. I was very cold, very tired, very much in the mood of 'why the hell did I do this? I'm never doing this again'. Shirley said, 'Put your bags in there, get undressed, grab a towel, the spa pool's up the stairs – it's warm and waiting.'

So we sat in scrumptious hot water and gazed out the windows at the skies of Dunedin. Shirley came through with two glasses of champagne. 'There,' she said, 'everything okay?' She handed us the bottle, nodded and left us to it. The pleasure of sitting in the little spa pool thinking over the successful performance, the generous feedback and the delicious supper was like a happy ending to all the rush and rustle of the last weeks. We lingered and toasted Shirley, the other members of the cast and ourselves, and I thought – I could grow to like this place.

PATCH 47

In London, in 1903, with two shillings and sixpence from the housekeeping money, Frances and Albert Mansbridge set up an association to educate working men who'd missed out on educational opportunities because of lack of money or opportunity. Two years later, when it became obvious that not only men wanted to be educated, the name was changed to the Workers' Educational Association (WEA), and in 1915 the WEA was set up in New Zealand.

It used to be funded by government grants, which helped towards paying tutors, materials, equipment and room hire, but in the 1970s the government made cuts, and further cuts were made in the 1990s and in 2009. So now, instead of paying a small sum to study *Antony and Cleopatra* by Shakespeare or 'The Beginning of Astrology' – courses that have been offered by my local WEA in Kāpiti – participants have to pay a much larger sum. And for many of us, larger fees put the courses out of contention.

Do I want to know about *Antony and Cleopatra*? It's not a play I'm attracted to but maybe if I know more about it, I might like it? Or at least appreciate it. For someone who attended and taught many WEA workshops and is a strong advocate and participant in life-long learning, I was cheesed off when the cuts happened, and even more so when one of the arguments for cutting the funding was that the courses really just catered to a bunch of old people who wanted to fill in time.

This is patently untrue. Many courses offer classes in subjects that help people improve their work prospects and reading skills, but even if it were true – so what? Far better for old people to do something constructive like studying painting or geology, history or philosophy, broadening their knowledge of the birds of New Zealand or learning how to make a chair, than sitting at home lonely and bored.

Whatever age we are, there is a drive in us to learn. Sometimes (too often) this desire is snuffed out by lack of opportunity, our own laziness or fear that we'll be embarrassed because people will know we can't read well, or simply because we are frightened that everyone else will be cleverer, smarter and more knowledgeable than we are. Or for other reasons. I received an application form to join the University of the Third Age, but as I filled it in I saw that I had to be retired to qualify. I have no intention of ever retiring, so I didn't go any further with the form.

We want to learn what's happening to people in other countries, we want to learn what's happening in our own, we want to learn how to make bread, we want to know what quantum physics and chaos theory mean. So we go online or we go to listen to a live person explain these mysteries.

'What's that?' A woman pauses by my front fence and points to the crabapple tree, which is loaded with fruit this year. I tell her what it is and that you can't eat the fruit unless it's cooked, and the juice (with some sugar added) is made into crabapple jelly. I used to get one jar from that little tree and now it's five. 'Use it with cheese or meats,' I say. She nods and I can see her deciding to look it up when she gets home.

'Mum, what's that?' asks the little boy, seeing someone on a mobility scooter for the first time.

'Did you hear about that new thing by Apple?' someone says to someone else on Main Street, and all of us passing by decide to go online when we get home. But sometimes we don't need the spur of a strange-looking fruit, a funny-looking machine or a new piece of technology, sometimes we simply read about a course or a topic we've never ever considered before and think to ourselves, this is the time.

We breathe, therefore we learn. 'But surely,' someone says to me, 'you can't possibly remember everything you learn? I mean what's the point of learning a whole lot of stuff if you're going to forget most of it?'

I shrug. Make up my mind. I'll do the *Antony and Cleopatra* course. Learning is a many-pointed star – some of the points are lost and some drop off, but the light remains.

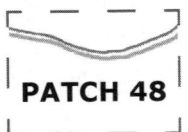

PATCH 48

Late October 1988 we left for New York, where we were to spend twelve days before going on to the First International Women Playwrights Conference in Buffalo. It was the first time I'd been to the United States, and I was looking forward to seeing this fabled city, but I was apprehensive about making a speech at the conference. It wasn't that I hadn't spoken in public before – I'd been teaching for years, given talks at the end of plays, held workshops, made other speeches – but this was different. Most of the women there, I felt, had much more illustrious careers than I had and a much larger claim to speak to their peers. However, I'd agreed to do it, so no good grizzling.

Bernadette had rung Urban Ventures in New York City to secure an apartment for us for the time we had there before the conference started – she says she wouldn't dream of doing that now. Her brother and his wife had given her five hundred dollars towards the trip, and with the thousand dollars Chris gave me and the money we'd saved, we thought we should be more than okay. Foreign Affairs had offered airfares and billets in Europe so I could do lectures at various universities and talks at conferences. It was a working trip, but I thought I should also be able to see some of the countries I was to travel through. Patricia Grace and her husband, Dick, were to accompany us through Europe, where she would be giving talks and lectures too.

We had a brief stopover in Los Angeles and boarded another plane to New York. I remember feeling overwhelmed in La Guardia airport – so big and so many people. Bernadette had booked our seats in a taxi-van to take us into the city. The van was driven by a large West Indian man, who suggested I have the front passenger seat and laughed when I tried to get into the left-hand side of the cab – the driver's seat in this country, where obviously they do things the wrong way round. He asked where we were from and when I said New Zealand, he smiled. 'Good cricketers,' he said. He was really kind and pointed out various points of interest, none of which I remember, before he dropped us right outside the apartment building.

I'd noticed banks of rubbish on the side of the streets, some in bags, some just chucked on the footpath. 'Rubbish men on strike,' said the driver, 'been a week.' The apartment was on the eighteenth floor of the building and we had to use a code to open the locked front doors. We were goggle-eyed to see an armed guard sitting in the foyer in front of a bank of TV screens. Welcome to New York, I thought.

The apartment was fine, if a bit dark. And it was small, basically one room plus a tiny kitchen and bathroom. There was a couch in the living room that you made into a bed at night. On the kitchen bench was a plate with a bag on it. In the bag were some cakes or what looked like cakes. Muffins? It was breakfast time. They ate sweet cakes for breakfast? With icing on them? And they were big. This was my introduction to the large servings that are taken for granted there. Still, it was a kind thought.

'We need to stay up as normal, then we'll sleep as normal,' said Bernadette.

She was right, but by four in the afternoon we were both practically on our knees. I could barely keep my eyes open. She wasn't much better. We'd have an early dinner, then come back and fall into bed, we decided. We found a café, which I think was called Teachers. It served the most wonderful little loaves of wholemeal bread they made on the premises and a little bread saw to cut slices as you wanted. The butter wasn't butter of course. I never eat any of the margarines, soft spreads or any other of the horrible chemical imitations of butter, but, when in Rome ... It was nasty, which confirmed my prejudices. If I can't have butter, I won't have anything, I decided.

'Where you from?' asked the waitress, the latest in a long line of people to ask the question that day, although one or two had said, 'You from England?' And I'd thought, I bet that would please the English. Not.

'New Zealand. We're from New Zealand.'

'Where's that?' was the second question of the day.

In Auckland when we'd mentioned we were going to New York, we were told that it was crowded and that no one cared about anyone. You could fall down dead on the footpath and they'd just walk over you. As it happened, we did see a woman fall over on the footpath and immediately a small crowd gathered. A man said he'd find a phone. A young woman took off her coat, knelt down, lifted the woman's head and slipped her rolled-up coat under it. It was established she'd tripped and hurt an ankle, and it was swelling rapidly. A young man got water, another woman said she'd ring the son, and the one who'd used her coat as a pillow talked to the woman on the ground when she came round. She had a bruise on her face from the fall, but she would be okay.

We got back to the apartment and in a daze of tiredness, managed to pull the couch into a bed and make it, shower and collapse. A moment later the buzzer on the door was pressed firmly. Huh? Visitors?

The sister of the woman who'd let the apartment through Urban Ventures had popped in, she said, because she just wanted to check all was okay. Then the true story poured out. Her sister rented the apartment from their brother who owned it. He was overseas. The sisters thought up a plan because the one who rented the apartment needed money. *Credit card* – she rolled her eyes. They discussed what her sister could do and came up with this bright idea: she would rent the apartment out to overseas travellers and go and stay with her mother, who, conveniently, had been sick.

She didn't tell her mother or her brother she was renting the apartment out through Urban Ventures, because they wouldn't understand. Now the brother had rung their mother, learned she hadn't been well and said he'd see if he could cut his business short and come home early. His sisters were frantic. If he came back and discovered the double-dealing, he'd chuck the sister out. They were also worried, the woman confided, that we would trash the place and she'd have to pay to have it fixed and all the money she was to make from renting it out would go on repairs. And she'd have no home. Her eyes were darting around the room to make sure we hadn't tagged the walls or ripped up the carpet. Who knew what people from a place called New Zealand did?

We got a bit worried too. We had visions of an angry man arriving and throwing us out onto Amsterdam Avenue in the middle of the night. But commonsense came to the rescue. We'd paid. We had the receipts. And we didn't point out that the bathroom was already cleaner than it was when we arrived. She left and we went back to bed, which seemed to be the signal every police and fire siren in New York was waiting for. From then on, they screamed non-stop all night. I didn't fall into the uneasy sleep of exhaustion until the early hours, but of course woke at the same time I always did.

The apartment block was in a great location on the corner of 89th Street and (I think) 7th Avenue and had buses just a short walk away going both ways up and down Manhattan. On our first foray out into NYC, we were puzzled that no buses were going in the downtown direction we wanted to go in – until we realised we were waiting on the wrong side of the road. We loved the kneeling buses, which made it easier for people with disabilities to get on and off. NYC also had a really great system of transfer tickets, so we paid for our daily fares once and were able to get on and off buses at will without paying again that day. We mainly used buses and walked our feet off because we didn't trust the subway system, which we used only once from memory when we were going to the reception for the international women playwrights.

I wanted to see Christopher Street because of the Stonewall riots in 1969. The Stonewall was an inn on Christopher Street frequented by gays, lesbians and transgender people, and here – on 28 June 1969 – they refused to run from the batons and fists of the police and, for the first time, fought back. It had been a decade of social unrest with the Civil Rights movement, anti-war protests, the contraceptive pill and women's right to choose all upsetting the status quo. There had been student sit-ins at universities and harangues disguised as letters to the editor about 'long-haired louts' and 'communes'. And then Woodstock, An Aquarian Exposition: Three Days of Peace and Music happened in August the same year. It didn't turn out quite as the advertisements suggested it would.

Two months earlier some of the people who met at the Stonewall Inn realised that lesbians, gays and transgender people had to organise themselves. It was decided they needed a place where they could meet in safety, where they could have fun socially, be themselves and not always live in fear of being raided and beaten up by the cops. They couldn't go on leading lives where they were never safe. So on 28 June 1969, when the police raided the Stonewall Inn, the people there fought back, using whatever they could grab to defend themselves, and if they had nothing else, fists. The cops, after their first shock, fought the crowd, but the message had been given and received. Some people were arrested, some beaten up, all had bruises and that included the police officers.

The police tried again on two subsequent nights and the fight back was the same. So gradually there came to be an understanding that the inn and the area around it was the territory of the lesbian, gay and transgender people who hung out there. Nothing in print, nothing legal, that all came later, but an understanding nevertheless. Organising themselves as Gay Pride became not just a matter of urgency but of survival.

Nearly twenty years later when I walked down Christopher Street it looked like an ordinary suburban street where nothing ever happened – quiet, living its life in a humdrum sort of way, but I could imagine that night, that decision, the degree of determination and willpower it took to see it through. I thought of all the times in New Zealand when those in charge had pushed just a little bit too hard and far and people had stood firm. I had joined protests about Bastion Point, marched against the Springbok Tour in 1981 and for the Homosexual Law Reform Bill in 1986, and been as scared as I'll ever be by the faces and batons of those who were determined to stop us. It was inspiring and affirming to walk down Christopher Street and reflect on the courage of those people who said: *We have a right to meet, we have a right to socialise, we have a right to be ourselves – just like anybody else.*

Bernadette and I became intrepid sightseers – in Times Square, we queued for cut-price tickets to see *A Chorus Line* and goggled at the passers-by like the country cousins we were. New Yorkers were very kind and patient. Most had difficulty with our accent, but unlike the French waiters we were to meet in Europe, they weren't rude or impatient and they never ignored us.

We saw *The 10% Revue* in a theatre in Greenwich, presented by a gay and lesbian theatre group, funny and very political, and a play written and played by a black cast, the title of which, to my shame, I've forgotten. Noel Coward said that in writing a play, the construction of the situation matters more than clever dialogue, although you need both. I think he was told this by the great impresario Charles Cochran after Coward's first efforts at scripts were just pages of clever-clever dialogue and no structure. This play had both solid structure and great dialogue with lots of subtext. Someone knew how these people spoke and had caught it exactly. The response of the audience said so.

I've always been fascinated by the things we say and the things we don't say. New Zealanders are very good at subtext, so a lot of our communication is not by what we say but what we convey, the message that lies underneath the words or the expression or the stance. I suppose this is why learning another language is often very difficult. You can learn the words, but it's the mysterious subtext and its signs that often defeat us. And the slang.

Bernadette and I loved the garment district around 14th Avenue, and it was sales time, so we bought jackets and coats, and when the guy in one shop asked us where we came from and we said New Zealand, he took it upon himself to educate us on the history of the district by marching us out onto the pavement and showing us that the 'pavement' was actually huge concrete blocks that had been there since the year dot. Or since the settlers came. This area of Manhattan had always been the place where garments were made, but he said that once the German and Central European immigrants came in the nineteenth century with their business skills and experience in the trade, it really took off. 'Great history here,' he said, 'someone will write about it one day.'

He asked us where we were going for lunch and did us an enormous favour by recommending The Dairy Company, a Jewish café, which served the most amazingly gorgeous potato soup. We sat and sipped and watched wealthy Jewish women in their diamonds and furs (it was late October, after all, and getting a bit cold). They had come down from the Upper East Side to eat kosher food, drink glasses of warm cream and leave lavish tips. I love cream but I never thought of drinking it warm. And we couldn't afford large tips, so we kept to the ten per cent, which we were told was the correct amount. Not lavish, but it would let you get out the door in one piece. I don't blame the waiting staff, they get such poor wages that without tips they'd never be able to pay the rent.

The waiters at The Dairy Company were older Jewish men who made their entrance by banging through the swing doors from the kitchen with three to four plates covering each arm, yelling out the dishes at the top of their voices and getting really cheesed off when people like me didn't answer immediately. Even when I did catch on to the routine, it was still difficult to understand what they were saying, because they spoke so quickly. So theatrical. I loved it. We went back a few times simply because of the drama of the place. The waiters played their parts to perfection. The café itself wasn't exactly inviting – it was in what looked like an industrial area – and we had to queue to get in.

'Queue? For lunch?' I was incredulous.

Inside the walls were grubby, streaked with grime and

condensation – who knew what the kitchen was like? – but the food was absolutely amazing. And I never got sick from eating it.

We walked around the Lower Manhattan financial district and Wall Street, looked at the buildings and walked around the park, where noisy, creepy squirrels ran all over like black woolly rats. They weren't afraid of human beings at all. We ate amazing sandwiches with everything in them – a whole meal in a sandwich. But one day I ordered scrambled eggs and when the dish arrived it looked like someone had dumped a thick round of yellow leather on the plate and then poured hot not-butter over it. The first bite tasted like that too, so I didn't eat any more.

New York offered so much to see and discover but you'd need a lifetime, and even then you'd probably only know a part. It's a great place to be on holiday and we didn't want to leave. Then one day I was contacted by the organisers of the conference, who asked if I could possibly stay another two or three days. They'd decided to have the reception for all the playwrights in New York. We could be billeted, no trouble. Both Bernadette and I had experienced billeting, but that was in New Zealand where we spoke the same language and had the same customs as the people having us to stay. It's quite a big thing to be invited into a stranger's home and be part of that household for a short time. We were going to be billeted in Buffalo for the four days of the conference, but New York? Of course we said yes …

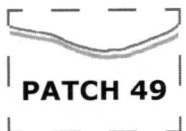

PATCH 49

It's 2015, and I've been asked to write a play to celebrate the hundredth anniversary of the formation of the Labour Party in 1916. The request is from the Ōtaki Women's Branch of the party, and they want the play to be about the ten Labour prime ministers. I'm not a member of any political party but I'm an old leftie. And I'm a playwright. Rose would have cheered me on because, like a lot of working-class people of her era, she thought Michael Joseph Savage was a saint. I had also been told at Methodist Sunday school that every good deed I did was another star in my crown when I got to heaven. So I said yes.

I decide my play about Labour prime ministers will start in 1934, the year when there should have been an election but the Reform Party cancelled it. A mistake. In 1935 the Labour Party romped in. Then, as always, instead of sitting down and starting to write, I do something else. 'I go,' as I said once to Huia's Brian Bargh and John Huria, 'all round the pig's arse.' Which means having a little panic then deciding to read around the subject, something I first heard when I was an extramural student and that I discovered was exactly what I did anyway – a training run around little side alleys before I do the big race.

The writing of the period between and during the two wars has always fascinated me. The plays, the novels, the non-fiction, the politics, the writers. I've already read just about everything on the subject on the shelves of the Napier Library, so I re-read *The Autobiography of Alice B Toklas*, which informs and amuses me all over again. I love Stein's sublime indifference to commas and what I was taught to call 'inverted commas' but which are now referred to as 'speech marks'. I love the way the famous names pour out in sentence after sentence. Fernande (Picasso's lover) is as always very large, very beautiful and very gracious. She offered to read La Fontaine's stories aloud to Gertrude Stein to amuse her while she posed for the great artist. Picasso meanwhile sat very tightly on his chair and very close to his canvas. On a small palette of uniform brown and grey, he mixed some more brown and grey, and the painting began. This was the first of some eighty or ninety sittings. Picasso said once, 'Inspiration exists but it has to find you working.' Good to have this affirmed.

I've always hankered to write a play about Gertrude, so I think to myself that maybe after this one, I'll do it. I will call it *The Ghost Writer*. She is probably the most eminent ghostwriter we have – though perhaps not a proper one because she put her name to Alice's autobiography.

The time I first read him, I thought Ernest Hemingway was the best, because up till then he was the only one I'd read who talked about writing in words I understood. I thought then and I think now that the language used by a writer when they're explaining their ideas about writing or when they review another writer's book is a pointer to the readers they're writing for. It is always a pleasure to read writers whose aim is clarity. Here's Hemingway from *A Moveable Feast* on getting yourself out of the pit called 'I can't do it': 'All you have to do is write one true sentence. Write the truest sentence you know ... then go on from there.'

Continuing my reading around the pig's arse, I start on *Murder in Montparnasse* by Kerry Greenwood. Her diligent research of the times and her understanding of and skill with the genre she's chosen is admirable. *Razorhurst* by Justine Larbalestier, another Australian writer, is also great at context and never loses focus on her indomitable heroine, Kelpie, and her two cohorts, Snowy and Dymphna. Grim at times but it has an engaging, interesting structure, and a sustained and well-judged control of events. Both books are set in 1928.

I read *Present Indicative*, Noel Coward's first autobiography, and slide effortlessly back into the world of English theatre he describes. He talks about writing plays and acting, and reading him this time around I am struck all over again by how hard he worked. I admire some of Coward's plays immensely but I am in awe of his truly formidable ability to work. I've never seen his *Cavalcade* or *Bitter Sweet*, but I played in *Blithe Spirit* and also directed it later at Wairoa Little Theatre. I like the structure of *Cavalcade* and the way he melds history, music and song around the lives of two families. Thornton Wilder's *The Long Christmas Dinner* does the same without the music, and so does Kiwi playwright Robert Lord in his *Joyful and Triumphant*. I think about these plays particularly because of the play I'm going to write, and up until Saturday night, I think I'll use the same idea. I'm not happy about it though.

At Circa's fortieth birthday brunch, I see a writer I know slightly and force her to listen to my muddle of ideas. She is very kind. She doesn't say, 'Piss off, Renée, I'm trying to enjoy myself.'

That night I decide no, definitely not happy, change it. Think of something else. *Think of one true sentence.* Think how you tell students that if the car's parked on the road, it's not going anywhere, so get in and drive. Inspiration will be waiting to hitch a ride. What else can I use for continuity? I wish I knew. Okay. *One true sentence*. I muddle through various ideas. Nah. And the next morning I wake up and – *ping* – there it is. An idea. Good old subconscious at it again.

When I get up I don't start work on the play straight away. Best to let my mind mull over it, be pleased about it, take some lull time. I'll have to research more, but the good thing is I already know people to talk to and I already have some knowledge. I lived through those years, for God's sake.

I'm just about to start reading a book about Simone de Beauvoir, Jean-Paul Sartre et al: *At The Existentialist Café: Freedom, Being and Apricot Cocktails* by Sarah Bakewell, whose *How to Live: A Life of Montaigne in One Question and Twenty Attempts at an Answer* I like a lot. Once I've read this I reckon I'll be ready to begin my play.

PATCH 50

The year 1992 didn't start off that well. New Zealand playwright Robert Lord died, and his funeral was on 9 January. He was young, only in his forties, and a talented writer. His play *Joyful and Triumphant* had another season at Circa just last year. He left his cottage on Titan Street to be used as a writers' residence and it's still being occupied by them on short or medium term residencies. I've been there twice since I left Dunedin and loved it both times. Robert's ashes are in a little wooden box on a table in the sitting room, so he's a beneficial presence in the cottage.

The year got better. I was working part-time at SPAN, a creative community group funded by Presbyterian Support Services aimed at encouraging contact between different generations, and I was artistic director at the Globe Theatre, organising its programme and newsletters with the help of a very good committee and people like Reg Graham, the renowned photographer. I was also involved in IRIS, a small theatre group consisting of Hilary Norris, Bernadette and me. We'd had a very successful run of *Touch of the Sun* the previous year, a play about two sisters returning to the house they grew up in to clear out their dead mother's clothes. During the play, Bernadette wore a red wig, courtesy of Terry McTavish, and at some stage a red petticoat. Her character Mugro quotes poetry all the time. Hilary, who played Lillibet (they were named after the two princesses Elizabeth and Margaret Rose), wore a dull dress and a pissed-off expression as she wrestled with wire coat hangers taken from their dead mother's clothes and tied them up into bundles of ten. It was a test of not only Hilary's acting ability, but also her good nature. That she could smile and say she loved being in it was a bonus.

I read the script again today. I think it would still play well but it would need to be brought up to date in parts. Bernadette and Hilary were younger than the two sisters when they did it; it's really a play for two older actresses. It's always a salutary experience reading stuff you wrote a long time ago, but this wasn't too bad. Pages 36 and 37 are missing so I've emailed Playmarket to see if they're also missing in the copy they hold. I think I'll type it into my laptop and play around with it, update the mentions of the Queen.

Richard Norris, Hilary's husband who lectured on geology at the University of Otago, did front of house for us and said, when asked, that he was happy to do it. What was better, he sounded like he really meant it. I started to relax after the first few nights when it became obvious we were going to have good houses. We used a lot of clothes from wardrobe, and the hangers came from everywhere.

I was writing *Te Pouaka Karāhe (The Glass Box)* for a production at Taki Rua in Wellington, and the first part of 1992 was full of trips there. I stayed with Rona Bailey and re-acquainted myself with Wellington, a city I didn't know all that well then. I'd been getting to know Dunedin, though, and I was loving it. I liked living in

Sawyer's Bay and I liked working for SPAN in North Dunedin. Both Brett Shand and I had been appointed as co-ordinators by Merania Katene. In my 1991 diary there's a red piece of paper taped to the page. I'm not sure who wrote the words on it, maybe Merania or one of the women from the community.

The newest member of our team – a whizz is she
The SPANners are still puffing from their outing spree
She led them all around the town
And up and down the stairs
The SPANners think she's great
She is Renée – who cares and dares.

I'm not surprised I feel a bit weepy when I read this. An accolade indeed from these North Dunedin women who, I'm sure, wondered what they'd struck when I first turned up. But they recovered, and occasionally SPAN would hire a bus, and they'd come out to our place at Sawyer's Bay and have a look around the garden I was making, and we'd shout them tea, sandwiches and cakes. Bernadette and I, and our next-door neighbour Jean, spent all morning baking or making sandwiches. The staunch women who joined SPAN grew very fond of us, and they loved Brett and his cooking.

They were terrified of touching the computer, though, and I remember telling one of them: 'You can't hurt the damn thing unless you take an axe to it. Anything you do will be fixable.' Some of them had never written a cheque, never learned to drive, never hired a handyman and didn't know about accounts. It was our job to answer any questions they had and to teach them anything they wanted to know. In fact they taught me a hell of a lot more than I taught them.

In the old villa rented by Presbyterian Support Services, we offered free lunches on Thursdays – Brett did the food, he had a cookbook called something like *Poverty Cookbook* – and I organised a series of speakers, one of whom arrived with rocks, compost and a large piece of tarpaulin that he spread on the floor. He then demonstrated rock by rock and shovel of dirt by shovel of dirt how to make a rock garden. They loved him. So did I because he cleaned up everything before he left. We had someone from the Orchid Society and I got really interested in growing orchids. People came to play the piano and sing the old songs. I'm not sure they all signed up for afternoon tea with two lesbian feminists, but they grew to love us and took a great interest both in the progress of the main garden and in the no-dig garden I made down the back end of the section. It grew great carrots and parsnips.

I planned to direct *Wednesday To Come* for the Globe, so I held auditions and cast it with Hilary as Mary, but her father died and she had to fly to England so another Mary – Mary Sutherland – took over the role. My sister, Val, rang to say she'd be coming to stay in late May. This was good news not only because she was coming to stay but also because she'd never seen *Wednesday*, and now she could.

She arrived on Tuesday, 26 May, and came to all the rehearsals. She helped with publicity by delivering lots of little posters and joined in the bigger poster pastes. She said she was okay and slept well in our spare bed. She didn't look sick and her use of the inhaler and asthmatic breathing was very familiar. At least the air at our place wasn't polluted by cigarette smoke.

One night one of the actors said, 'Have you always directed, Renée?' I opened my mouth to say no, when Val said, 'Oh yes, she's always loved it. When we were kids she used to organise concerts down at the river and God help anyone who didn't come in on time or sang in the wrong places. And if we got too giggly from nerves when we were waiting to sing or recite, she hit us with a toetoe.'

Everyone laughed and so did I – eventually. Hell, I thought, I hope I used the fluffy end. And I hope I've lost a little of that bossiness. No guarantees there.

Val came to the Access Radio Air Awards. Brett and I had been running a radio programme called *SPANner in the Works*, which was a mix of news about SPAN, music and interviews with locals. It had been a learn-as-you-go kind of exercise. Brett was very good on air and could keep talking through every crisis we had. He chose good music and he liked my choice of music too. I did a lot of the interviews, mainly with local people who were a bit shy at first but warmed up as we went on.

Val, Bernadette and I drove into town for the awards, parked and climbed into the big limousine sent to collect us, so we could be part of the group walking on the red carpet. I was so thrilled to be giving Val a ride in a limousine and a walk on the red carpet into the Glenroy Auditorium, where Brett and I received the Access Radio Award for best new programme. Now that was a surprise, and an exhilarating one too. It seemed amazing to be given a prize for talking to people and playing your favourite music.

Wednesday To Come went very well, the scone-making onstage especially, and there were gasps when they saw the harness. As always, Iris's words to Ben as he lies in the coffin had that true, listening-to-every-word silence. I have big capital letters all through these particular 1992 diary pages saying: MAKE SCONES. We got good audiences and Val went home. I didn't want her to go but was so pleased she'd come.

The day after my birthday, I got a call from Jimmy to say my sister-in-law, Lillian, was very ill from a cancerous tumour on her brain, and on Friday, 24 July, she died. She was fifty-nine. I'd known Lillian for a long, long time, and I thought of the many occasions where she and Val and I had loved singing together. I play the guitar a bit, four basic chords if you can call that playing, so I would play and we'd all sing. People loved us, our auntie Glad especially. She loved the song 'Whispering Hope', and even though none of us liked it, we sang it because we didn't want to hurt her feelings and because we had no choice. Our lives wouldn't have been worth living if we'd said no. When I think of Lillian I remember her smile and her welcome whenever we arrived at their place; she was a very pretty woman, a good cook and a fabulous baker. She, Val and I giggled over things whenever we got together and Jimmy, George and Laurie weren't always quite so comfortable about that. Perhaps they felt left out.

Now at her funeral, I thought of Lillian's laugh and that smile. I could see my brother was grieving. Their kids, now grown-up, were staunchly beside him. Lynda made a great speech. I felt so proud of her when she stood up, very pale but composed. I remembered her and Vonny, Val and George's daughter, perhaps around age ten, dressing up in stuff I gave them, makeup and all, and how they hobbled into our small grocery dairy on high heels to show me their glorious transformation. Now I watched the grown-up Lynda get through what she wanted to say without faltering and end by saying, 'I've not only lost a mother, I've lost a friend.'

I spent a lot of time thinking about Lillian and Jimmy. He'd had such plans. He retired from his job at sixty – big mistake – but he didn't realise that then. It was what everyone did. He got a good present and a good bonus from his employer and looked forward to his retirement, for which he'd saved all his life (unlike his sister), and within six months his plans were crushed because Lillian was dead.

Then 1992 got even worse. On Monday, 28 September, Vonny rang just as we were sitting down to dinner. 'Sorry, Auntie Renée, sorry …' and she burst into tears, then said baldly, 'Mum's dead.'

Val had been out to bowls all day and had been offered a ride home so she said yes. In the meantime, George and their granddaughter had gone to collect her. The vehicles must have passed each other on the way. So when Val got home, there was no one there. And there was no one there when she died on the floor by the bed, her hand reaching up for her inhaler. Vonny was hardly able to speak, and neither was I when I got back to the kitchen.

First Lillian, and now Val. Why had these younger ones gone first? Val was only sixty-one. I went to Tokoroa and I walked around the outside of their house, talking to George, who was in shock. He said, 'When Val and I met, that was it. We took one look and we knew.' I said something comforting as we turned a corner, and one of his sons jumped up looking very pale. He saw me and said, 'Christ, I thought it was Mum.' Our voices were very similar.

I was distraught, unhappy and very, very angry. It wasn't fair. But like everything that connected me and Val there was a fine line between heartfelt and farcical. Vonny, Bernadette and I followed the hearse to the crematorium. We were driven by Vonny's boyfriend at the time. 'This is Crash,' said Vonny, and the boy grinned at us. Bernadette and I looked at each other but we got in the back seat. As it turned out he drove very well and what happened next had nothing to do with him. Just as we approached the crematorium behind the hearse, a truck coming the other way signalled and turned into the crematorium. I don't know who was at fault, but the hearse and the truck banged into each other and the hearse had its front dented. I thought how Val would have enjoyed that, how we would have giggled about it and how no one ever talks about how sisters giggle when they get together.

Even Mugro and Lillibet in *Touch of the Sun*, who spend a lot of their time arguing, dredged up some memories of sisterly understanding and support. There's something about sisters, and yes, yes, I know I was lucky to have Valerie Rose for sixty-one years, but I wanted more, and I should have had more, okay?

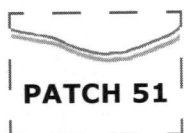

PATCH 51

From *Secrets* (Playmarket 1982, published with *Setting the Table* in Theatrescript series, editor David Carnegie), first performed at the Feminist Arts Festival, Auckland, 19 June 1982, with the following cast:

Emma ... Elizabeth McRae
Director ... Renée
Design ... Bernadette Doolan & Renée
Lighting ... Priscilla Pitts

EMMA Good morning urinal, washbasin, lavatory. Here is your friendly cleaner ready once again to do her stint. And as I am counted among your best friends, let me say, quite bluntly, you stink. To high heaven or at least the foyer. But I will put a stop to that, even if only for a few hours. Canute, eat your heart out. Today is spring cleaning day – every other day fifteen minutes of frenzy – but today da da dah – the real McCoy. Mr Foster, who thinks his shit doesn't stink, but I can vouch, on the Bible if necessary, that it does. Mr Foster says you need a Real Clean. So what Mr Foster says, goes. Mr Foster blames the cleaner but the cleaner, me, blames the clients. You see there are the small trickles, the large gushers, and the stream-line jetters and of course infinite variations on all three. I mean to say, someone can be a small trickle for years and overnight turn into a gusher. Yes, I know these are crude remarks I'm making – must be the job. You know what they say, touch muck and you become mucky yourself.

I wonder how that girl is. She was left right in it. That's one day I didn't clean every loo. I was too busy getting the ambulance and cleaning her up. She hung onto my hand. Said it reminded her of her mother's. I took that as a compliment. But I had to let go eventually, the hospital wouldn't have it, I wasn't her mother and I'd been cleaning lavatories. I felt like asking if the knitting needle was cleaner than my hands but I didn't. And when I got back Mr Foster said I'd acted irresponsibly, the theatre would be opening in half an hour. 'Why didn't you clean it yourself?' I said.

He said there was no need to add insolence to irresponsibility.

She was a little thing, only half my size. But I was half my size once.

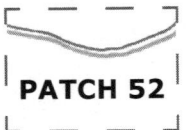

PATCH 52

I have always liked visiting cemeteries and I realised today that I don't do it anymore. I don't have to be looking for anyone in particular, although when we were in London in 1988 I visited Westminster Abbey to find Aphra Benn, and as usual I came across the names of other writers I admired. Staring at the plan of the abbey was useless. I have never been able to read maps, drawings, plans, and only when someone writes a list of directions starting with 1) Drive to roundabout, 2) Turn left (or right), and so on, do I have a chance of arriving at the planned destination. When people have done this I've usually found them first try, but there have been countless times when I've ended up in the wrong place.

The only time ever I got to a destination without a list of directions was when I asked Tim how to get from Ōtaki to Whanganui. 'Drive to Sanson and turn left,' he said, and to my pleased surprise, he was right. I had a lovely few days with him in Whanganui and then waved goodbye and drove back. I didn't get to the right place on the way home, however, because I forgot that if I turned left on the way there, I should turn right on the way back, which is how I ended up in a city, and when I asked a passer-by where I was, he took a wary step back and said, 'Palmerston North?' Then quickly walked away. Not to worry, another passer-by, much more helpful, showed me the way out of Palmerston North, even got in the car and directed me onto the road where I just had to drive straight to Sanson and turn right. 'Nah, no trouble,' he said when I thanked him. 'The other day my mum made a mistake at the lights and a woman passenger from another car got out and helped her.' I asked him if he'd like a ride somewhere. 'Nah, I like walking. Good luck.' He grinned and waved as I took off.

I caught a train from Paris once and visited Katherine Mansfield's grave at Fontainebleau. The gate was locked and when I rapped on it the caretaker came, took one look and began mumbling something I thought was probably 'bloody New Zealanders', but he went straight to the grave. I had a look around there at the same time because it was so pleasant to stand and stare. Then I saw all my favourites at Père Lachaise in Paris: Gertrude Stein, Oscar Wilde, Édith Piaf, Colette, lots of others, and like those in Westminster Abbey, many were illustrious.

When the kids were young, I used to take them for walks, pointing out various landmarks and items of historical interest. I have no idea why I thought this was a worthwhile thing to do. Perhaps it was something I read? Some advice on things to do with children in the holidays perhaps? Maybe I thought this was what good mothers who'd been to high school and university and who knew everything did. Now I wonder why the kids came along with so little complaint. They weren't that old. Chris might have been ten when we started these walks, so David would have been seven and Tim, five.

One such walk was over Bluff Hill in Napier to Ahuriri,

where I'd promised them fish and chips and a paddle if the tide was in. We walked around the old cemetery on Bluff Hill and we read the tombstones in the older part, stood and gazed at the one that said 'Here I Stay', and the ones with lists of children who'd died as babies. One time I took them to the hill at Westshore, which was an island before the 1931 earthquake transformed the landscape. I've forgotten most of the landmarks I showed them and I expect they have too, but I remember the fish and chips from the shop at Ahuriri and sitting on the sand in the sun eating and watching the kids paddle in the water. And I remember how good it is to stop and stare and think about the lives represented in a cemetery.

Stan and Rose are buried in Park Island Cemetery in Napier and up the path from them is Gertrude, my father's mother, ironic considering her opinion of Rose. Even the propitiating gesture of giving me her name as my second name didn't soften her outrage that her son had married a 'half-caste'. The path to their graves is now very old and very crumbly, and very scary when you're coming down.

When I had the Randell Cottage writers' residency in Thorndon, Wellington, some days I'd go for a walk in the Wellington Botanic Gardens and down among those graves whose owners were moved from their not-as-it-turned-out final resting place so the motorway could go through. I enjoyed walking around the Bolton Street Memorial Park and wondered yet again at the separation of Anglicans, Catholics, Presbyterians – as though, even in death, they had to be among people who thought the same way. I suppose their heaven is divided up with 'not in my neighbourhood' kind of lines. Probably why it seems so attractive to them as a last resting place.

I remember visiting a cemetery in the south of the South Island and seeing the graves of some Chinese gold miners. They were on the very edge of the cemetery, their headstones facing away from the respectable Anglicans, Catholics and Presbyterians of the town. I'm not sure but these might be the ones that were moved to Arrowtown, where you can take the walk along the various recreations of the life of the Chinese gold miners, who, of necessity, lived out their frugal, hardworking existence in little groups of their own people.

Walking around cemeteries is a way of learning stories. Stories of families, groups, places, times. Cemeteries are places that don't mind someone stopping and staring. If you do that on the street or walking round the neighbourhood, after a while people get edgy. Like the Welsh poet and tramp William Henry Davies, who died when I was ten, says in his poem 'Leisure':

What is this life if full of care
We have no time to stand and stare?

PATCH 53

February 2003, and for some while after, was a difficult time for me because Bernadette and I parted. Any parting is difficult, but I seemed to be the one whose number and email most people had, so it was to me that the questions, incredulity and disbelief were directed. We had been together for nearly twenty-two years, and much of that time we were engaged in stage shows presented to the public, and I did a lot of public things where Bernadette helped. We also knew people who had nothing to do with the theatre, and we were both hospitable, both good cooks. We held Christmas parties for our neighbours and joined Neighbourhood Watch.

My public response to any personal heartache is to dress up and act as though everything is okay and hope that in a little while it will be. Privately, it was a different matter and this is where family and friends shone, although it wasn't always easy for them. I wanted to remain on civil terms and so did Bernadette. There are too many break-ups where both parties allow bitterness and anger to surface, leading to positions from which it's difficult to retrieve anything good. We had parted but that didn't mean our relationship had been bad or a huge failure. On the contrary it had been a success for nearly twenty-two years.

This was a hard and unhappy time though. Dr Rose

suggested a psychologist so I went along. This one didn't work because, I realised later, I was too busy entertaining her. I tried another one a few weeks later at a friend's suggestion, but what I found most helpful was that his rooms were situated near the sea, and I could sit on a seat and stare at the water and be left alone for as long as I wanted.

Then one night a few months later, after I'd moved to a little apartment on The Terrace in Wellington, I woke up and felt terrible. I thought, I don't have to put up with this. I've got enough tablets in the drawer to end it all. *All I have to do is get out of bed, get a full glass of water and swallow the lot.* Thankfully I have a great deal of pride and common sense and – the one good thing to come out of my father killing himself – a strong conviction that one suicide in the family is enough. So I got up, but instead of filling a glass with water I made a cup of tea and thought, One of these nights, my girl, you're going to get so down, you'll end up doing it, so you have to do something.

The next morning, I rang a friend in Dunedin and asked her if she knew of any Jungian-trained therapists in Wellington, because I'd read they were good with arty-farties. She not only did, but she knew of one she could recommend. So I made an appointment and felt as soon as I entered her room that I'd made the right decision. These kinds of decisions need to be made at the right time and the failure of the two previous attempts to find a therapist had nothing to do with the people and everything to do with the time. You have to be ready.

So I went to her every Thursday afternoon for months and months, and when we knew it was time to stop, I stopped. She wrote me a letter, which I read every now and then because it's such a neat letter.

Dear Renée,

I'm wanting to take five more minutes on our session, especially as it might be some time before we meet again. Continuing on the theme of 'drama' and life and 'is this normal?' and a 'longing for tranquillity', I was left wondering if I'd missed a deeper level of pain/despair – and that this, too, is life (along with it being rich) but that it can be recognised and connected with from a healthier and older and more mature and wiser place of 'I can hold and contain this' (even though I don't want it) – as opposed to the, perhaps, never recognised despair of a little girl, who was precociously mature, but who was also 'secretly' depressed in her deprivation and anxiety – somewhere, very deeply, quietly despairing – amidst all of the surface 'drama' and 'bossy' responsibility.

Going back to Erikson's psychological tasks – I think I made them 'too simple' by splitting them – and that our more subtle and complex task is to be able to recognise and hold both stagnation/regeneration (ours and others) and our/other's despair/integration. Here's to yours …

Yes. And here's to yours …

PATCH 54

Tiger Country

You plunge off the cliff into Tiger Country –
sleek and smiling tigers play hide and seek
slope around abandoned chairs, sad tables.
Silk cushions call encouragement from the sofa
an old painting turns its face to the wall.

Tigers lurk in old cards, beneath yours forever
snooze under Christmas lights that never worked
lope ahead to a destination only they know.
Signposts are suspect; there is no tunnel, no light –
nobody pins a tail on these tigers.

Some nights after the sun has flamed
and seabirds search the pastures of the sea
tigers come and lean gentle over your chair –
wrap you in a striped shawl of sturdy warmth
fold their paws and purr soft in the silent room.

This is the danger time. Stand up. Walk slow.
Their eyes are on the game and you're it.

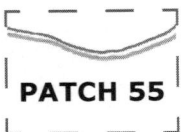

PATCH 55

On 19 April 2008, I moved to Ōtaki. The carrier arrived at the apartment on The Terrace bang on time. I watched the driver do a big U-turn up by the lights and then slide into a space outside the apartment building. They were cheerful, loaded the furniture, coped with the lift, no trouble. Then they left.

I didn't look back at the apartment. I never do. I don't seek or suffer from that kind of regret. Once I'm gone, that's it. I have made some great gardens and enjoyed living in a number of places. I don't mind going back and seeing that things have been changed. I seem to have been born with, or perhaps acquired, an in-built philosophical resilience about this sort of thing. There's always something exciting about a move to a new place.

I am attached to particular parts of places and to some rivers, but they remain places I can visit. Although the Tūtaekurī River I used to swim in as a child, the same river my sons swam in as children, is now unswimmable for their children, and the Wairoa River is suffering from a build-up of silt, so maybe no whitebait this year? And the rite of passage, which is the swim across the river — even though you've been warned not to or perhaps *because* you've been warned not to — will not be so attractive.

The streets or houses where I lived in all these places are not of great interest to me once I've left. It's like a door opens and I walk through, and then it closes and what is left behind is like, oh yes, I lived there once. There are no painful regrets or pining. Once they've gone, they're gone. I have a theory that this is because we moved so often when I was a kid, and I learned not to attach myself in any serious way to a particular house, place, furniture or books. I love them (or not) while I'm there and when I leave it's over. I'm glad of this.

Whānau and friendships are different. Like the river, they go on, sometimes changing shape or route, but always there. Sometimes friends remove themselves, like a number did when I left Laurie. I was told some years later at a function after a book launch that one friend had rung another and said they were to cross me off their Christmas card list. Three years ago I visited the Wairoa Museum when I saw that the Wairoa Little Theatre's history was included in an exhibition. None of the productions I'd directed were recorded – no photos, no reviews – nor was my presence on the committee, or even the times I'd scrubbed the dunnies. They'd wiped me off the Little Theatre memory. Well, fuck them, I decided. I'll write about those years myself sometime.

Last year on my birthday I got messages, sent via David, from people who were teenagers when I directed them in plays during those years, some for the college and some for Theatre Federation competitions. We rehearsed at the Little Theatre. Some of these people were in the production of *Charley's Aunt*, which I directed. I regret not keeping a diary back then, but there's my memory and their younger memories, which should be enough. I think often of the adult productions too.

For the move to Ōtaki, I'd made a few trips myself

already to move cartons of kitchen stuff, and on the day itself a team of helpers turned up. Sharon, Naomi, Abbie and Saskia came from Wellington, Tim from Whanganui, and Sunny Amey from Paekākāriki, who brought lunch. Sunny set the table, put out food for the two men on the truck who were keen to be on their way. They loved it – Sunny's a great cook and organiser and they particularly enjoyed her sandwiches. When the men left, she put more food on the table for us. Then she cleared everything up, whisked the dishes into the dishwasher, anything else into her bag, and left after hugs all round. Dear Sunny.

I've already mentioned that all the thanks she got was me ringing her a few months later while she was half asleep, saying, 'Sunny, Sunny, they're up,' about the broad beans. As I always plant broad beans on Anzac Day, this phone call must have been in late spring – some months later. That we remain friends is due more to her grace than my misplaced enthusiasm about the broad beans.

After lunch the others did all the work. They carted, carried, heaved, lifted. Abbie and Saskia put up the bookshelves, unpacked and shelved all the books, unpacked the groceries, crockery and pots, put them all away. Sharon, Naomi and Tim lugged beds and bed clothes, found sheets and pillow cases, made beds, moved chairs, tables ... and very soon it was four o'clock. Tim was staying but the others were going back to Wellington, so I said, 'I'll make a cup of tea and then you'd better be off.'

Sharon said, 'We're not leaving until all the pictures are up.' No wonder she was Dux of St Joseph's.

She and Naomi began discussing where the pictures should go. Tim grinned at me, sat down and waited till he was told what they wanted him to do. Naomi went next door and borrowed a power tool to put a hook in the kitchen wall to hang a painting, and she and Sharon had further consultations while they decided what should go where. By six o'clock everything was perfectly arranged, hung, made or placed. I was as fresh as an Ōtaki spring morning. 'The best shift I've ever had,' I said and poured them all a glass of bubbly. Then they went off, no doubt thankfully, to their own lives and beds.

There was a low wall in front of my new house, where I discovered that anyone who wanted a quiet smoke felt it was okay to sit and light up. The first few weeks I ran out many times, first asking nicely if they'd mind not sitting on my fence smoking, gradually going from the polite request to the firm order, 'Do not sit on my fence and smoke,' then the enraged bellow, '*Get off.*' I got sick of it, so I had a wooden rail put on the fence, then bought all the prickliest, scariest climbing roses I could find to grow over it. Gertrude Jekyll is a good example but I bought others. Fortunately it was end-of-season, so I got the roses much cheaper. My only direction when I placed the order at Pacific Roses was that they had to be prickly.

I wrote a letter to the CEO of Te Wānanga o Raukawa, which is just over the road, and she was fabulous. The sitting on the fence and smoking stopped. The wooden top was broken a couple of times afterwards, but it's been ages since that happened. The prickles haven't stopped the kids walking past from picking the occasional flower, and this year I've seen two or three picking off the prickles and remembered how we used to do that too – sticking them on our noses and chasing each other. I didn't know kids still did this until I saw a little girl sticking the prickle on her nose the other day.

Most passers-by are old acquaintances now, and we nod and smile at each other in the supermarket or up Main Street.

By coincidence, the week after I moved, *Wednesday To Come* – directed by Alec Gilchrist – began its season at the local Civic Theatre, an Ōtaki Players production. It was great to see *Wednesday* again and it seemed like a good omen. The boy playing Cliff put the mouth organ to his lips and, hallelujah, played a recognisable tune on it. Which was more than some of the young 'professionals' had done in the productions I'd seen. Sometimes Cliff just breathed in and out because the director had decided that breathing in and out would do. They didn't do their homework.

The mouth organ is the sound of the 1930s. It's the sound of someone sitting on a log playing around a camp fire. It's the sound of people queueing for charity, the kind of charity that's dished out like 'you don't really deserve this, it's your own fault you're in this mess'. It's the sound of people without hope, who still keep going because they have to do something to feed their kids. It's the sound of women who make scones with milk as that's the only fat they've got. Tony Simpson, who wrote *The Sugar-Bag Years*, told me and an audience in Dunedin's Globe Theatre that when he first saw the scene where Mary makes scones he didn't believe it. Renée's slipped up here, he thought. He didn't believe people back then made scones using only milk. He was corrected by someone who said, 'Tony, they couldn't afford butter or cheese.' Still disbelieving, Tony decided to try making the scones with only milk and sure enough they were scones. Not as good as they are with a bit of cream and cheese in the mix, or some butter and a few dates, but still *scones*. And if you were lucky like Mary and someone gave you some cream, you could make butter and spread the butter on the scones. If you didn't have butter (or even if you did) you could eat them with golden syrup, honey or jam.

The mouth organ is the sound of the Depression. A step-up from a piece of paper and a comb, it had the paper and comb's portability. It was relatively easy to learn. If you could breathe and you had the will, you could learn. Even I can still play 'When I Grow Too Old to Dream' (Sigmund Romberg and Oscar Hammerstein II wrote it in 1934) on the old mouth organ I have here. Nowhere near good enough to play to anyone but definitely recognisable. Maybe it's why I like Neil Young.

I was pleased with the Ōtaki production and that pleasure reminded me of a production by Massey High School in Auckland sometime in the 1980s. When the time came, I didn't want to go and see it. It was raining, I was tired, I had to get up early the next day etc etc … But I'd said I'd be there so off I went. I was pleased I did. Such a good production. Their Cliff had gone to a jazz player for lessons on the mouth organ so he could play melancholy blues and jazz. Perfect. And like the Ōtaki production, they'd gone to a lot of trouble to source genuine-looking furniture and set the scenes very carefully. I have a fondness for so-called 'amateur' companies. That's where I learned all my own practice and theory about theatre in the days before we had professional theatre. The standards were high and a lot of our directors were world class. A few years ago, I was an invited guest at a production of *Wednesday To Come* at Napier Repertory Theatre. It was a celebration of, I think, the fifty years the theatre had been in existence. The lights went out during one of the scenes and the young woman playing Jeannie staunchly continued with her lines.

A few years later, I directed a play-reading of *Wednesday To Come* at St Peter's Hall, Paekākāriki, part of a series Sunny and Jan and I did to raise funds for the renovation of the hall. The young guy in that play-reading had gone to a professional musician to get some tips on playing the mouth organ and he was perfect. Sarah Delahunty played Iris, and when she did the monologue over the coffin, Cliff played softly in the background, and the audience and I loved the whole scene all over again.

Back to the Ōtaki Players' production. I went off to supper with the director and cast after the play – a lovely end to an enjoyable night. What was even better was that I could just walk a little way down the road and I was home. What could be better? Life in Ōtaki had begun.

PATCH 56

In my lifetime, I must have made a million meat loaves ... well ... three hundred or so anyway. Meat loaves are not high on the list of culinary treats for most people. Mundane, mundane, mundane. Made only by the very poor or the very desperate.

I made one yesterday and thought how far my recipe had come since the first one. Like all my cooking when I first started, that first one was grey, held together by breadcrumbs and flour, one egg, high on onion, low on taste (apart from the onion and lots of salt), but Laurie, Val and Jim ate it without comment. I suppose after Rose's cooking, Val and Jim were inured to eating ill-tasting, sloppy food. Laurie's mother was a good cook, so in his case he was probably hungry after a hard day's work and prepared to eat anything, or perhaps, too much in love to notice what he ate.

How did I start to care about what I ate? I think it started with Laurie's mother. Rubina Bertha Taylor née Barr was a short, plump woman with a nice smile and an iron determination to win at five hundred. She only started to show she liked me when I had Chris, whom she adored. I don't mean she didn't like me before – I mean I don't know whether she did or not, but I do know that after I had Chris, I went up a notch or two in her estimation. When I showed that I was interested in cooking, she began talking about it to me.

My mother-in-law had been very kind to me when Rose died and she'd generously, with very little notice, put on that wonderful afternoon tea for us when we cancelled the wedding breakfast. There was no way anyone could have known Rose would suffer such a horrible brain haemorrhage a few weeks out from the wedding, but Ruby – as she was called – stepped up like the nice woman she was. She was a devout Christian, throughout her life attending first the Salvation Army, then the Church of Christ, and then the Baptist Church, because when she and Fred came to live in Napier there was no Church of Christ.

Frederick and Ruby Taylor were married in Christchurch and moved a lot because Fred worked as a guard on the railways and had lived all over New Zealand. But when it came to what he saw as his last move before he retired – a guard's job in Napier – they bought a house there, in Nelson Crescent. Fred had served in the First World War, one of the last of the soldiers to be sent to France, but the scar on his face came from when he was biking home from Salvation Army band practice carrying his euphonium and swerved to avoid something. The bike crashed on the ground and Fred's cheek crashed onto the sharp edge of the euphonium case.

They had five children. Laurie was third and the first boy, and his mother loved him dearly and he loved her. Laurie, it seemed to me, was Ruby's favourite so perhaps it was natural it spread to encompass Chris when he arrived. She died in 1954, before she really knew David, and Laurie was heartbroken. When he died on 16 June 2002, the kids asked me to speak at his funeral and I was happy to do this. I think I was very lucky to marry Laurie when I did. He was exactly right for me at the age and stage I was at. Neither of us is to blame for the fact that I grew into another kind of awareness and he didn't.

I learned to cook by watching Ruby. I learned about taste, I learned that slow cooking didn't mean cooking the life out of meat until it was grey and tasteless. I learned the value of tasting, of not overdoing the onions or sauces. I learned about heating the dripping or butter (now oil) before you put the meat into a pan, a pot or an oven. I learned some different ways of cooking potatoes, which didn't include boiling them so they were watery, tasteless slush. I learned that silver beet was better steamed. I hadn't seen a steamer until I saw Ruby's. The big thing was I learned to take time.

Ruby's meat loaf was a revelation. She was proud of it. She was right to be. What I noticed, though, was that Ruby took pride in serving tasty food, whether a roast meal, meat loaf, chops, a beef stew, a casseroled stew or simple mince stew over which she put a square of crisp and delicious pastry baked on its own on the oven tray. From her I learned to take pride in what I served too. Before it had just been a chore that I had to do to fill people's stomachs. Get it done, get it over, get someone to do the dishes, and then when all was finished I could sit down, listen to the radio and read.

Ruby taught me that food could be horrible or delicious and that the difference was in the cook. Good food had more to do with the cook's knowledge or willingness to try a new way than it did with her pocket. It takes time. A good cook begins by using her brain with recipes – trying new recipes, perfecting old ones and gradually building up her experience. Experience is the key. And that means time. Time spent reading, observing, cooking. Gradually I changed my attitude to food from regarding it as just something you shoved in your mouth to stay alive to taking care with it, tasting, trying out, making mistakes, many mistakes, and over time – a long time – became better. I don't think I've ever actually arrived at the 'good cook' stage but I'm getting closer. I can still produce a meal I'm not proud of and naturally remember these more clearly than the really good ones.

Laurie's sister, Phil, let me watch her make a shortcake topping for apple or rhubarb and I discovered why mine was so damn sodden and such a penance to eat. 'Just cut up the fruit, put it into the dish, sprinkle a bit of sugar over, then rub equal parts of butter, flour and sugar together until it's crumbly. Pat handfuls over the fruit making sure, with your hands, that it's spread evenly.'

'No water?'

'No water. If you put water in the topping it won't be shortcake, short means crisp. If you put it on the fruit it will go sloppy.'

'But won't it be dry?'

'No.'

She deigned to explain. 'The fruit provides enough juice. The sugar mixes with it and makes that juice just a little thicker. It doesn't need water.'

Back then I began to read recipes in magazines and borrow recipe books from the library. I started to take notice of the way others baked and what they baked. This was a great era for morning teas, and baking biscuits, fruit loaves and cakes. That's when I got into the habit of baking on Fridays, and on Sundays I often made a sponge, copying Ruby, whose sponges were the lightest, and had the tastiest jam, and whipped cream that was just right. Sometimes, oh bliss, she put real raspberries beneath the cream instead of jam. Sprinkled with sugar of course. She knew Laurie loved her sponges so although Sunday was a church day, she usually managed a sponge just in case we called.

This is Ruby's meat loaf with a few extras it's gathered along the way. I think she'd approve.

Ruby's Meat Loaf

Put 500 grams of best beef mince in a bowl. Add a grated carrot, a thinly sliced onion or spring onions, chopped herbs – whatever you've got in the garden or if you haven't got a garden, a pinch of dried herbs. If you want a kind of Middle Eastern taste forget the herbs and add tumeric and cumin.

Add:

handful of wholemeal breadcrumbs or rolled oats or mixture

salt and pepper

small glug of Worcester sauce

ditto tomato or plum sauce

handful sultanas or dried cranberries or apricots if you're adding spices (and in that case be sure the sauce is plum)

tablespoon of flour – maybe a bit more – but don't overdo it

one egg

With clean hands, mix all together, put into a greased bread baking tin and put in fridge for an hour. Or longer.

When you're ready bake in preheated oven (180–200 degrees Celsius) for an hour. Depends on your oven.

Take out and leave for ten minutes before slicing. Serve with steamed silver beet and potatoes boiled with mint and sprinkled with salt and a small knob of butter. I like the loaf with a spoonful of cooked apple, or rhubarb, but you can serve it with chutney or pickle or good old tomato sauce, whichever you prefer.

It all sounds very simple, and it is. Well, it is now.

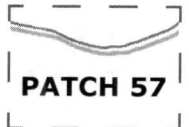

Dowsing

She lies on the bed,
a forked branch, held fast
over times and silences,
the touch of a hand.

She unpicks the feather and fan
of words, purposes, maps,
swollen buds on a dry stem,
the weight of tenderness.

She smiles into once upon a time,
darkness and light change places,
while here in this hospital room
water sings under the earth.

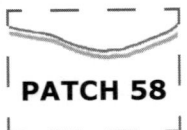
PATCH 58

It has come to this. This is where my long life has led me. Here I was at eighty-seven trying to scoop shit – actual instead of metaphorical for a change – into a sodding plastic container the size of a small pencil.

I'd had pain in the lower gut since November. A diverticulitis flare-up. With this condition you have to keep 'everything' (code for 'shit') soft, to make it easier for it to move along the way it's supposed to. I'd swallowed a variety of antibiotics (which give you thrush – but let's not go there), Panadol, codeine (which makes you constipated so you have to take lactulose syrup – yukko) and two Laxol tablets to 'keep things moving'. The doctor wanted me to have some tests and handed me forms for the lab. Faeces, said one. *Shit*, I thought.

It is bad enough trying to get urine samples – and you don't want to know the details of the times when it has failed. Needless to say I now dress for the job: plastic gloves, cape, boots, etc. Faecal samples are another thing altogether.

No one tells you how to do these things. They give you a little bowl and, if you're lucky, some rather sparse instructions or, in the case of the faeces, they give you a lab form and some small plastic containers – no instructions of course. Not even 'you poo into that and then transfer it to this'.

I need to sleep on this, I thought. I have never been good at algebra but I know X does not always equal Y. There was no utensil to do it with, so I had to improvise, as we say in theatre. After the first attempt ended in me having to scrub the entire toilet, then rinse everything with disinfectant, then have a shower, then wash every article of clothing I was wearing, I was a sadder and wiser woman.

No one talks about these things – you can babble on about menstruation, menopause, condoms, who does what during sex, but when it comes to scooping shit into a plastic container there's a deafening silence. In fact this silence covers most things connected with 'down there' as someone once described it to me. When I said to her, 'Do you mean the rectum, anus, vulva or vagina?', she looked at me like I'd committed a serious social crime and disappeared at a fast clip.

Doctors don't call it shit. They say stools or faeces. When ninety-nine per cent of the population call it shit or poo it's about time they got with the programme. And we're all in the same boat, whether you're a queen or the Queen, a doctor or a drainlayer, a parson or a panel beater. As someone once said to me when I was waiting offstage before walking on to give a talk to a bunch of doctors, psychologists and nurses, 'Don't worry about them, Renée, they all sit down to poo, just like you and me.'

After a number of attempts (let me count the ways), I managed to get a little bit of shit into the actual container instead of on the wall or the floor. By this time a few days had passed because you can't just poo to order. Then I discovered I still had to fill in the label on the tube. I had to put my name, date of birth, and date and time the sample was delivered into the tube. All this on an exceedingly small label. 'PM,' I wrote, and if there'd been room I would have added 'and you're bloody lucky to get it'.

So that was the first sample. I was asked to do three. I did one more then thought 'to hell with it'. If they can't find anything in either of the two samples, then so be it. This old worm had turned.

Next thing I knew, I was on my way to Palmerston North Hospital by ambulance. I did not want to go. My neighbour had rung them because I was in pain and I *was*, but as I pointed out to the ambulance officers, old people are not welcome at A&E. I understand why. They just don't have the beds there. I know how easy it is to become scared because of unusual pain, a faster than usual heartbeat or a higher than normal temperature, and I know that these fears become worse when you live on your own. We yearn for the feeling of reassurance that having a health professional in charge gives. At the same time a lot of this could be eased with more information about how bodies work or perhaps occasional visits from a medical professional, but no one's got the time, and the system doesn't provide the money to do this.

Anyway I sulked about this for half the trip then stopped because I realised the ambulance officer was only doing her job. At the hospital they did blood tests that showed the problem (are we surprised?) was in the bowel. I said, 'I know you don't do colonoscopies because I understand you have new priorities and old people with diverticulitis probably don't qualify.'

The doctor, who looked worn out, simply said, 'Shall

I book you a ride home on tomorrow's Ōtaki shuttle?'

The nurse, equally exhausted, said, 'Can you sleep on a La-Z-Boy?'

I thought probably not. But we walked down to an open area where there were other old people huddled on black La-Z-Boy chairs. Some had been lucky and scored a bed in a cubicle. But the rest of us passed an uncomfortable night coughing, sniffling, muttering, moaning and occasionally calling for the nurse, whose name I'll say was Charles because that's not what it was. Charles was kind and quick to respond.

We were a bunch of old ewes and rams put out in a back paddock to fend as best we could. One shepherd was detailed to keep order in case we jumped the fence. We had to accept that we had served our time and were now useless, unwanted and, to put it quite simply, a bloody drain on the health system. And some of us, me for one, were responsible for the 'cancer tax burden' as well, according to a woman interviewed once on RNZ. I spent the night trying to get comfortable, doing my best to shut out the sounds, ignore the lights and make it through the night.

I'm glad I had that experience. I'd had such a good one when I had the cancer op just over a year before that I'd begun to think the moans I heard about the health system were exaggerated. Now I know they're not. I think the medical and nursing professions start off with compassion and kindness, and it is gradually whittled away by the hordes of people wanting help and the lack of enough staff or space or money to give it to them. Not all the people seen at hospitals are sick enough to be admitted, but all of them need reassurance of some kind.

Many of this last group are old people who live on their own. We have to think of a better way of dealing with the fear of the unknown, a fear that happens to all of us whatever age, but which seems especially urgent when you're old.

When I got home, my neighbour listened to my story about scooping shit, and when she stopped laughing said, 'You cover the seat and the space between with plastic wrap. Much easier.'

Huh?

So January 2017 was quite dramatic and eventful and I'd learned one new thing. Glad Wrap. Must get some Glad Wrap.

PATCH 59

Mum and the bull
(a bit of doggerel but a true story)

One day a long time ago
Mum, Val, Jimmy and I
looked for mushrooms
in a likely paddock.

Mum, I said, there's a bull.
Don't be silly, she said.
Over there, I said, in the corner.
Godalmighty, said Mum.

Bugger off, she called
in the direction of the bull.
It lifted its head – grew larger.
You kids go, said Mum.

Mum, I said, I'm wearing
a red jersey. For Godssake,
said Mum, what's colour
got to do with anything?

I loved yellow but yellow
made me look too dark.

Red was better, Mum said.
The knitter makes the rules.

Mum was a little woman
dark hair and eyes that flashed,
were flashing now,
but the bull didn't see

the danger signals us kids
recognised a mile away.
Mum waved her purse
but the bull kept walking.

You heard me, shouted Mum,
now bugger off –
I won't tell you again.
She waved her purse. Menacingly …

The bull stopped. That's better,
said Mum, now hurry up
you kids. She held the wire –
we wrestled through the fence.

Mum waved her purse again,
climbed through the fence,
sat down on the newly cut grass.
Jesusbloodychrist, she said.

She opened her purse,
took out her tobacco and papers.
Her hand shook – bits of tobacco
flew everywhere.

PATCH 60

I went to a wonderful theatrical event last Sunday. It was Crows Feet Dance Collective's latest production, *Hakari: The Dinner Party*. It was inspired by Judy Chicago's famous 1970s feminist art installation, *The Dinner Party*, which showcases significant women from the Western world, while *Hakari* presents in music, song, dance and words, the stories of wonderful, strong, courageous women from Asia and the Pacific.

Hakari has been brilliantly conceived and choreographed by Jan Bolwell (who plays Kate Sheppard), a choreographer, playwright, actor, great gardener and teacher. It has two directors: Jan and Annie Ruth (simply fabulous in her role of Dame Whina Cooper), who has had an illustrious career in theatre and who headed Te Waka Toi for a long and successful time. Jan took care of the dance. Annie wrote the words. It's been a big ask for these dancers to take on the extra challenge of words, but they've done so with great energy and verve and achieved a truly professional production.

Crows Feet Dance Collective was founded in 1999 and is a mix of trained and untrained dancers. Anyone over the age of thirty-five who wants to dance can join Crows Feet. For example, Rachel McAlpine – in her seventies and in her other life a poet, playwright, writer and chorister – is one of the dancers. Crows Feet members meet once a week to rehearse and also attend two classes a week in Kāpiti, Lower Hutt and Wellington. They do this for love. After I came home from the performance, I thought of the many groups of people (unpaid) who present us with theatrical events we might never otherwise see.

The Globe Theatre in Dunedin became one of my favourite places after I arrived in Dunedin at the end of 1988 to be the 1989 Robert Burns fellow. Rosalie and Patric Carey had opened the Globe in their own house in the 1960s, and when they left in 1973 it continued as a theatre, run like all community theatres by a committee of volunteers. It's a mystery why and how community theatre continues to exist. In Ōtaki we have the Ōtaki Players, and in Levin to the north, and Kāpiti, Porirua, the Hutt and Wellington to the south, theatre companies continue their dogged and steadfast aim to amuse, enrage, awe, scare and enchant the locals.

Patric and Rosalie Carey, for example, encouraged everyone to experiment with then little known European writers such as Ionesco, Beckett, Sartre, Genet, and American playwrights like Albee, Williams and Miller, as well the staples of Shakespeare, Ibsen, Chekhov, Shaw and O'Casey. New Zealand writers like James K Baxter were encouraged to write plays for the Globe, and Ralph Hotere exhibited there, as well as designing sets and costumes for Baxter's *Temptations of Oedipus*.

The first Pinter play I saw, *The Caretaker*, was at the Napier Repertory Players theatre. I discovered I was sitting next to a priest, and we both, at the same moment, recognised each other as the school child we passed going to our respective schools each day, walking carefully on opposite sides of the road. Unlike other kids, we didn't shout insults at each other. I was glad to remember that. In those days I wasn't a great shouter anyway. I was a great glowerer though.

I began directing experimental plays with a group of Wairoa College students – N F Simpson's *The Hole* and Eugene Ionesco's *The Bald Prima Donna*. The students didn't seem to mind that a lot of it was incomprehensible. Some plays defy explanation but they work as a theatrical piece. On the other hand many reviewers and other theatre aficionados have attempted to explain the meaning of Beckett's *Waiting for Godot* to me, without success. I still think it's a giant joke at the expense of the same people who rave about it.

I acted once in *The House of Bernarda Alba*, and here was a playwright whose words, for once, I instantly understood, although in translation of course. Federico García Lorca. It was a production at Napier Rep and I played Martirio. Lorca has been a favourite of mine ever since.

Theatres like the Globe and the Ōtaki Players (and all the others) exist because their audiences want them to. If nobody came to their shows, they'd fold. It's as simple as that. And there are times when you just don't want to go. It's cold, pouring with rain, with gusts of wind that almost knock you over. Work has been a battle against time to get a job done. The house is a mess, and the kids have taken some chocolate they found in the fridge and given a bit of it to the dog, who is tearing around like a mad thing. The neighbour drives into her letterbox and has a panic attack about what she's going to say to her husband and you pour her a glass of sherry and hold her hand, sneaking surreptitious glances at your watch. Your partner, usually reliable and understanding and happy to look after the kids, has a bad cold and you just know you're all going to catch it. You simply do not want to go. You would give a hundred dollars from your holiday savings jar and leave it almost empty if you didn't have to go, BUT you go to rehearsal. Why? Because you can't let your mates down. Because you said you would. Because the show must go on.

In their other lives theatre people are professors and part-time nursing aides, teachers and electricians, shopkeepers and bus drivers, students and artists. In the theatre, they are all the same. The people who contrive wardrobes and build sets, and organise lighting, music and props, as well as doing every other job, are heroes. Front of house, suppers, ushering, music and sound, cleaning, you name it, there'll be someone who does it. And they do this work after a day of doing something else to earn a living.

Theatres run by a community are different from professional theatres. Sure, the level of talent will vary but the hearts and energy are there. A friend said to a group of us recently that Nola Miller, that inspirational director of Unity Theatre, Wellington, stressed that if someone is doing their very best then you can't expect them to give more.

Sure, community theatres are often rife with argument, resentments and irritations, but there's also warmth, support, love and lasting friendships. These are places where, if they didn't know it before, people learn to work hard, to work as part of a team and generally open their eyes and minds to new ways of thinking, reading, living and, while playing their individual roles, they know they can trust and be trusted.

Earlier this year I went to a performance of Shakespeare's *Much Ado About Nothing*, directed by Sarah Delahunty for a Paekākāriki community group. The performance I saw was staged in a barn in Ōtaki. The audience was composed of old (me and another woman who were provided with especially comfortable chairs), young (the youngest looked about three) sitting on stools, and every age in between. It was an inventive, funny, lovely and lively production and the performers were great. After the show, I heard a young guy, sixteen or so, say, 'That was *mean*, really *mean*,' as he and his friends moved out, all smiles.

Now, after Sunday's performance of *Hakari*, I have come to the conclusion that there is only one thing that sets amateur and professional productions apart. *Hakari* was professional in every sense of the word, the people who presented it just didn't get paid. Professionals do it for love and money; so-called amateurs do it for love. And they have mine.

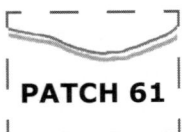

PATCH 61

When we first arrived in Dunedin we wanted to rent a flat. 'Looked at flat in Maitland Street. Some of the paintwork sure is dirty,' I recorded in my diary. Later we were to discover that it wasn't just the paintwork.

I had time before my year as a Robert Burns fellow started and before teaching a course at the summer school, so the next day we took a bus trip to see some ancient Māori rock art in the Waitaki Valley. It's looked after properly now, but previously the drawings were hosed or dampened before people came to see them so that they stood out more. The consequences were that some of them were wrecked forever or damaged very badly. All have suffered the effects of time. Any tampering with the rock art was banned some time ago.

Looking at the drawings was one of those moments when you stand still and stare in awe at the sight before you and try to imagine the artists and puzzle over what they were telling you from that time. In a more mundane sort of way I feel a bit like that when I'm looking at the entries in my diaries. Only I know what those mysterious names and events refer to, and I shudder at the thought of someone picking through them one day looking for clues to this or that. Often when I'd felt things deeply or had been hurt by malicious media, theatre or other gossip, I made no written record of it at all. There might be a cryptic note or, in the case of the Mervyn Thompson assault in February 1984, no note at all. However, I wrote a short article for *Broadsheet* about it later because I was so angry at the way I was treated both by the media and some of the people in theatre, but mainly because I was angry and hurt at the way I'd been dumped in it by the women who were responsible for the attack.

In February 1984, Mervyn Thompson – playwright, university lecturer, co-founder of Court Theatre in Christchurch and one-time artistic director of Downstage in Wellington – was attacked by a group of women who tied him to a tree or a post and hung a sign around his neck that accused him of being a rapist. This was a direct copy of a scene from my play *Setting the Table*. Because the attackers kept very quiet – as did everyone else who knew who they were – all the media, police and theatre people had to go on was me and my play. I had written the play, they argued, so I must have been involved in the attack. I had done it because I was a vicious lesbian feminist. I had done it because I was jealous of Mervyn's career and place in theatre. I had done it because I hated all men.

Mervyn, too, came to believe I had been involved and took to haunting our place in Richmond Road, Ponsonby, leaving notes in the letterbox and occasionally poems. He wrote an article where he compared me to Salome with his head on a platter. The morning after the attack I'd received a call from him asking me to go round to his flat because something hideous had happened. Bernadette and I went, and his partner at the time was there. Mervyn looked terrible. He told me what had happened and asked if I'd had anything to do with it or had any knowledge of it, and I said I hadn't and he seemed to accept that. I think we even had a cup of tea.

There were some similarities between Mervyn's life and mine. We knew what it was like to live with the fact that a parent had committed suicide, we knew poverty and hardship as kids, and he was a playwright like me, writing some very good plays. We both loved theatre and belonged to a group called Working Title Theatre.

I went to work at *Broadsheet* and the office was buzzing with the news. I said straight up, 'I don't hold with this sort of vigilante justice – I think it's wrong, and you all should know that.' I was steaming and they could see it. I knew instantly that my play would be seen, at the very least, as the template for the attack. *Setting the Table* is really an argument between four feminists, two of whom reckon they should use the same weapon that men use, violence, and two who say it's not the answer. The resolution is that the two who say violence is not the answer are right. Mervyn had directed a week-long workshop on the play two to three years before and liked it.

Of course a few words said in an office had nothing to do with anything. Those who were gleeful about the attack went on being so, and how the rest of the world saw it wasn't their concern. To the rest of the world I was that terrible creature, a lesbian feminist – I wrote plays about such women. I must be guilty. In any case, there was no one else to blame. The women who did it kept very quiet and had absolutely no compunction about dropping me in the shit and walking away.

'Sisterhood rules – okay?' was how I finished the

Broadsheet article on the incident, and that's how I still feel. *Sisterhood rules?* You're joking, right? I was angry with myself too because I had been naïve enough to think that sisterhood meant something. Now I saw it meant nothing. Maybe I needed to lose that illusion? I don't know. What I do know is that I was very angry and very hurt and remained so for years. I suppose it was the feeling of being unjustly accused and being unable to do anything about it. If I'd actually done something, maybe the anger wouldn't have lasted so long?

The notes in the letterbox from Mervyn, the vicious theatre gossip that someone always 'thought I should know', the police detective calls at the house, and the two men who knocked on the door in the middle of the night and – as I saw when I sneaked a look out the window – were close enough to the door to barge in if I'd been silly enough to open it. When I shouted, 'Get the hell out of here, I've called the police,' they scarpered instantly. The phone rang constantly – media, callers who wanted to know what colour panties I was wearing. Work calls, even what seemed like friendly calls, were suspect because who knew if they were friendly or not? I started to jump every time the phone rang and it began to get me down. Bernadette was worried, so she consulted with some friends in Tauranga, and between them they decided I needed a break. Bernadette would stay behind and answer the phone and deal with anything else.

Off I went to Tauranga, and there, in the house of two friends – having, like my horoscope sign, the Crab, scuttled back inside my shell and suffered it out in silence – I was able to slowly open up again, find some peace and eventually some sleep. Even then I knew I couldn't be the only one the police approached or were suspicious of and, I found out later, I wasn't. At the time, though, it sure felt like it.

This was the year that *Wednesday To Come* was chosen by Playmarket as one of the plays to workshop in May, and dear George Webby directed this. He said people had warned him, 'Watch out George, you might get tied to a tree.'

Five years on, I was thinking about rock drawings as I sat in a large room at Otago University full of people, while Helen White made the introductory speech to open the summer school. When she said my name, one male writer there, an alcoholic I was told later and already boozed to the eyeballs at 10am on this particular morning, shouted something in which the words 'bloody Renée' featured in every sentence. Everyone pretended to ignore him. My note in the 1999 diary says: 'Helen handled it very well.'

By this time, we'd taken the flat in Maitland Street and spent most of our spare time cleaning the place. I didn't have much time to worry about a drunk's stupidity and besides, there was this new city to explore, new and old friends to link up with. I started to get to know Dunedin.

PATCH 62

From *Tiggy Tiggy Touch Wood* (Otago University Press 1996, in *Playlunch* – five short plays – editors Christine Prentice and Lisa Warrington; Brito & Lair 1997, New York, in *Intimate Acts*, eight lesbian plays), first performed on 2 July 1992, in the Lunchtime Theatre series at Allen Hall Theatre, University of Otago, with the following cast:

Missy ... Anna Samways
Tig ... Anna Cameron
Helen ... Lee-Anne Duncan
David ... Richard House
Director ... Lisa Warrington

Missy has Tig tied to her with a rope. Helen, a social worker and David, a doctor and board visitor. All are in their forties or fifties.

TIG: (*tied to* MISSY *with a longish rope*) One two three I'll go He. Don't leave me, Missy, don't leave me.

MISSY: I guess I'm stuck with you.

TIG: I'll be good when you go shopping.

MISSY: Be quiet, Tig.

TIG: Helen says I'm just a bloody nuisance.

MISSY:	She's right.
TIG:	I'll be good, Missy, I'll be good.
MISSY:	I think we'll have to pack our little spotted hankies and take off.
TIG:	Take off. 'Hurry up, hurry up and taken them off or we'll take them off for you.'
MISSY:	Who were they, Jess, who were they?
TIG:	Who, Missy?
MISSY:	Tomorrow. We'll go tomorrow.
TIG:	Oh, Missy, and we'll live in the bush and eat roast bloody possums and I'll hide and you'll come and find me, eh, Missy.

DAVID and HELEN enter

HELEN:	Melissa, this is David Morse, he's the Board Visitor.
MISSY:	Bitch.
DAVID:	Miss Denham?

MISSY doesn't answer

DAVID:	And this is Jess Mackie.
MISSY:	She likes to be called Tig these days.
DAVID:	Hello, Tig.
TIG:	Don't you bloody come near me.
HELEN:	Shall I take her outside?

MISSY: Don't touch her.

DAVID: I understand there's been some problems.

MISSY: Tig's okay most times. Just occasionally she gets ... restless.

DAVID: Restless.

MISSY: She likes attention. She likes to play.

DAVID: I looked up her file. She was given into your care on the understanding you would let us know if her condition worsened.

MISSY: It's not her fault.

DAVID: I'm aware of the background.

MISSY: Why can't you leave us alone? We're all right. She just gets bored.

HELEN: The kids like to walk this way to the City School. She jumps out on them, grabs their bags, tears up their books. She even made one of them give her their shoes.

MISSY: Just keep out of it. We'd be okay if you didn't interfere.

DAVID: Is it true that children have been frightened?

MISSY: They tease her. They bloody tease her.

TIG: Go away you dirty old witch, ugly old bugger, get away.

DAVID: Do they tease her, Helen?

HELEN:	They don't understand. They're only young.
MISSY:	Their parents haven't got that excuse.
TIG:	Do you want a game?
MISSY:	Be quiet, Tig.
TIG:	Tiggy tiggy touch wood.
HELEN:	She's very strong. She gets hold of the kids and won't let go.
MISSY:	I keep her tied to me now.
DAVID:	Isn't that inconvenient?
MISSY:	I don't want her put into a home.
DAVID:	I've received a number of complaints. I'm sorry.
MISSY:	Listen to me. That woman you abandon so lightly to strangers, this woman worked herself to the bone for kids in this neighbourhood. Is it too much to ask that she should have some dignity in circumstances beyond her control?
TIG:	Do you want to see my cunt? *(laughs)*
MISSY:	She wants to be good. And she is lots of the time. It's not her fault.
TIG:	He wants to see my cunt, eh, Missy.
DAVID:	It's not the children's fault either, Miss Denham. They have a right to walk to school without being frightened.

TIG:	Bloody bugger, bloody bugger.
MISSY:	They're frightened because their parents make them frightened. They've always hated us round here. We don't fit in. This is a golden opportunity to get rid of us.
HELEN:	It's not like that at all.
MISSY:	Because it might have been their sons or brothers or even their fathers or uncles who attacked her and left her like this. Whoever it was made absolutely sure she'd never testify against them and for a while they felt safe. But that wasn't enough. They can't stand having her around because she reminds them of something they don't want to face.
HELEN:	All you say might be true. But she does frighten the kids and she does steal and she can't be trusted …
DAVID:	Are you a relative?
MISSY:	No I'm not a bloody relative.
DAVID:	Her file says she has no next of kin.
MISSY:	She has me.
DAVID:	I've talked to your neighbours and people in the area. There's a lot of concern.
TIG:	Gonna get you. Gonna get you.
MISSY:	I'll look after her. I'll take her away and you'll never see us again.

TIG: *(she has the knife)* I'm gonna cut you, I'm gonna burn you. Whoo-oo-oo *(jabs knife in table)*.

MISSY: Tig, give me the knife, Tig. Tig, give me the knife.

A battle of wills but TIG eventually gives up the knife

DAVID: You can't go on like this. Forgive me, Miss Denham, but you're not getting any younger. What if you get sick? What if one day she won't give you the knife?

MISSY: Nothing's going to happen to me.

TIG: Are you okay, Missy, are you okay?

MISSY: Ssh, Tig.

DAVID: People have a right to live in peace.

MISSY: So leave us alone.

DAVID: You're part of this community. Surely you want what's best for it?

TIG: Are you all right, Missy, are you all right?

MISSY: Do you really expect me to care what this community wants? This community wants her out of sight and off their doorsteps and they'll be happy. Everything nice and neat.

RIG: Tiggy tiggy touch wood.

DAVID: Why does she keep saying that?

MISSY: It was a 'game' those bastards played with her.

TIG: One two three I'll go He.

DAVID: Miss Denham, I'm sorry. I have to agree with Helen. She needs professional care. Now, I don't want to have to restrain her.

Pause

MISSY: All right then. We'll go together. Stand up Tig. Stand up straight, there's a good girl.

TIG: Is he going to prick us, Missy? *(jumps about)*

MISSY: Stand still, Tig.

TIG: I won't say bloody anymore, Missy.

MISSY: Good girl.

HELEN: Shall I untie the rope?

MISSY: Why would you do that?

DAVID: Please, Miss Denham, don't make it any more difficult for yourself than it already is.

MISSY: Now listen, Mr Morse, she's terrified. And I think she's been frightened enough don't you? Give me your arm, Tig, go on, there's a good girl. We're moving house.

HELEN: Melissa, you can't.

MISSY: Come along, Tig. Come on. There might be roast chicken for tea.

TIG: No more bloody apples, eh, Missy.

DAVID: Visiting hours are very flexible and your help would be appreciated but you won't be allowed to stay with her outside those hours.

MISSY: I'm not leaving her.

DAVID: You must see this is for the best.

MISSY: You'll drive her really crazy, you know that don't you.

HELEN: Please, Melissa. Untie the rope.

DAVID: Believe me, you'll be a lot better off.

MISSY unties the rope

MISSY: Run, Tig.

HELEN: Come on, Tig.

TIG: *(excited, ready to play chasing)* Tiggy tiggy touch wood, I'll go He.

There's a scuffle and TIG is caught.

DAVID: Miss Denham, I think it's better if you don't come. Patients are often upset by the formalities of reception, it's just the strangeness, the unfamiliarity, and we understand that, but they accept the situation more readily if they have time to readjust.

TIG: Are we going now, Missy?

MISSY: She doesn't like needles.

DAVID: I'll tell them. I'm sorry.

HELEN: You want to go for a ride, Tig?

TIG: In your flash car?

HELEN: Better than that. A big white and red ambulance. You like sirens don't you. We'll play the sirens for you if you're a good girl. Would you like that?

TIG: You coming for a ride, Missy?

MISSY: I'll see you soon.

TIG: I don't want to go without you, Missy *(ties herself back to MISSY)*. I won't go without you. Bloody buggers, bloody buggers.

HELEN: Missy's going shopping. It's Thursday today. Thursday's shopping day. Remember, Tig?

TIG: What are you going to buy, Missy?

MISSY: What would you like, Tig?

TIG: Roast chicken. And peas. And gravy and ice cream and cake and lemonade and chocolate.

MISSY: All right, Tig *(begins untying TIG)*. And while I'm away at the shops, Helen's going to take you to a lovely new house with a beautiful bathroom for you to wash in.

TIG: Does it have gold taps?

MISSY: Maybe *(unties* TIG*)*.

TIG: And red towels?

MISSY: Be a good girl, Jess. I'll see you soon.

HELEN, DAVID and TIGGY go and MISSY is left. She rolls up the rope as the lights dim. End of play.

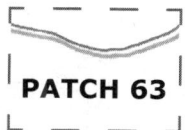

PATCH 63

Recently I was told about how an old pop song got through to someone who was suffering from dementia and who, before the song was sung in her hearing, had not responded to any other stimuli. Her eyes lit up, she smiled and, to the surprise of the singer, the old woman began to sing along. Suddenly she was back.

This didn't surprise me. When I was quite young, I said to all and sundry, 'When I'm dying, if you want to bring me back, play Louis Armstrong.'

There are a lot more pop and jazz contenders for the job now, but when I was listening to RNZ's *Music 101* last Saturday, Moana Maniapoto was being interviewed and had been asked to choose particular songs that had memories for her. Her first request was Prince Tui Teka singing 'For the Life of Me', and *whoosh*, there I was, back in the seventies in Wairoa. There were a few things I didn't like about Wairoa and lots of things I did, and one thing I liked a lot was the singing.

Everyone – any age, gender or culture – sang. There were very few theatre last-night parties in the seventies where at some late stage of the evening someone (probably me) didn't start singing. We hammed up the songs of course but nevertheless sang our hearts out. A little bit of encouragement and a couple of red wines and

I could probably still belt out a few old pop songs. Ha.

Over the last few months I have been engaged in finding old and new pop songs for this play I'm writing. I'm calling it a tapestry play (although its more of a revue format I suppose), and it spans about eighty years, following the ups and downs of a family trying to keep a country newspaper going. I decided that some of the best cues to indicate the passing of time are pop songs. So those, a few hymns and some waiata do the job. Beautifully. But I would say that wouldn't I?

It has been a lot of hard work, hours of time and much fun, searching back though my own mind at first, then through some charts, and finally other people's memories. At one stage I texted Chris and said, 'What song speaks to you of the sixties?' and he replied that he couldn't make up his mind from three contenders, so I texted, 'What about "The Times They Are A-Changin'"?' and he replied, 'That's near the top.'

Then last Saturday when I was listening to Moana in 'For the Life of Me', I thought, Renée, you might have used a few songs already but there are dozens more out there which, for one reason or another, mean something significant to someone.

We might moan about some of them, hate some and wonder how the hell anyone made up such drivel, but somewhere, someone is listening and moving and singing and dancing and loving that particular song, and good on them. To prove my thesis, I did a very scientific survey and texted whānau, a friend or two, and some ring-ins, who were actually the poor unsuspecting emailers who'd sent me the first four emails that morning. Life's not meant to be easy, guys.

Saskia says: '"Gangsta's Paradise" by Coolio takes me back to being in form one, sitting in a classroom during a wet lunchtime reading *Girlfriend* magazine, which I wasn't allowed at home. Anyway, "Gangsta's Paradise" was playing as I was reading a story about a young girl, a "good girl", who took ecstasy just once and died. Every time I hear that song I think of her and that lunchtime. And Rihanna's "Umbrella" takes me back to when Abbie and I first got together and we used to turn it up on a Sunday morning while lazing around in bed. Eventually we'd want to start moving and dancing to the song, so we'd get out of bed.'

Sharon says: '"In The Midnight Hour" by Bryan Ferry takes me back to Wairoa.'

Chris says: '"The Happening" by The Supremes takes me back to Kabul Street and Wairoa College.'

Tim says: 'It's more an album rather than any one song,' and nominates David Bowie's *Aladdin Sane*.

David texts: 'Okay, "Baker Street" by Gerry Rafferty always reminds me of my time in London. The song came out when I was working in Hanover Square just around the corner, 1978.'

Sarah heard 'Penny Lane' by The Beatles at a friend's house, where the sun was shining and life was suddenly full of possibilities. Aneta's 'fave of all time' is Booker T and the MG's with 'Time is Tight'. Ann goes for 'A Whiter Shade of Pale' by Procol Harum, which was played at her wedding in England in 1969 when the band was, as Ann says, *hot*. Steve remembers a day in 1966, sitting under a sun umbrella on a porch in Mt Maunganui listening to The Lemon Pipers' 'Green Tambourine'.

Naomi says: '"The Gambler" by Kenny Rogers takes me back to when I first started high school and was boarding at the hostel. I worked with Mum and Abbie at the Baxters van selling hot chips when Kenny Rogers played at the Mission. "Heaven Is a Place on Earth", Belinda Carlisle, was the first tape I got, so reminds me of Lucknow Street in Wairoa, dancing in the living room. Pet Shop Boys and "West End Girls" – Wairoa Primary School and dance lessons. UB40's "(I Can't Help) Falling in Love With You" – Lucknow Street and having a sleepover with friends; we listened to it while falling asleep in the lounge. All of Tracy Chapman's music. Trying to learn the words, stopping and starting the tape to write the lyrics, then finding them on the cassette cover.'

Abbie Marie emails from somewhere in the world: '"Like a Prayer" by Madonna – so many memories. I played and danced to it so much. I used to wake up to it on phone messages from friends thinking of me. I played it at pretty much every birthday party in my twenties and it always reminds me of one of my best friends at uni, Emily. We were trouble.' And in a following email: 'One that reminds me of Naomi – Bon Jovi's "Livin' on a Prayer" is her song. Anytime I hear it I think of her. I went to Luke's wedding and did a speech for her because she was pregnant with Tui and couldn't travel to Perth. At her request, I sang "Livin' on a Prayer" in front of about one hundred people, none of whom I knew.'

You see? And there are lots of others: Joan Armatrading singing 'Down to Zero', Kris Kristofferson's 'Help Me Make It Through the Night', Billie Holliday and 'Strange Fruit', 'Poi e' by the Pātea Māori Club, Phoebe Snow singing The Beatles' song 'Don't Let Me Down', Chuck Berry's 'You Never Can Tell', Moana Maniopoto's 'Tihore Mai', that fabulous song 'Bread and Roses' – I've heard it sung in all sorts of places: marches, concerts, and Sonja Davies' funeral, where I guarantee everyone there was singing through tears – and oh, yes please, Peggy Lee's plea to keep on dancing (if that's all there is, my friends).

I like what Nick Bollinger has to say in his book *How to Listen to Pop Music*:

> Pop is a fast moving river. Stand in one spot and the music that flows past you will be different from day to day. The genre is continually being refreshed as new sounds are discovered, new instruments invented. Even old styles take on new meanings when they are received in an unfamiliar context. Some listeners let the mainstream carry them where it will. Others hurl themselves into the rapids. Still others prefer to find ponds or slow-moving tributaries, where traditions remain relatively undisturbed. Somewhere in the river is the sound that sings to you …

And somewhere in that river, there we all are.

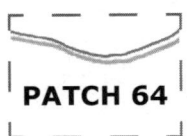

PATCH 64

More from *Wednesday To Come* (Victoria University Press 1985):

IRIS has got a hammer from Ted and has wrenched the nails from the top of the coffin, taken it off, and now speaks to the dead Ben in the coffin.

IRIS: Well, Ben. So there you are. There's some things I have to say – oh look at your poor shoulders then. Rubbed raw, were they? You found the rough side, didn't you? There were some things you never understood. Wonder if you do now. See, you're going to miss out on a lot of things. Cliff and Jeannie growing up. You taught Cliff well – he's going to be the best, and he won't forget you – neither will Jeannie, she's going to be the best too. They've got their ways to go. We did well with them, didn't we? Not so well with each other – could never understand why, you said. But you did really. And fooling around with Molly, your one last effort to make life do what you wanted it to do. And you knew all the time it was just – playing. I know you did. Oh, Ben. *(She sees the mouth organ)* What's that in your hands? So that's where they put it. Did them an injustice, didn't I? I grew up when I was twelve. Took me six months. And nothing was ever quite the same again. It's going to be the same with Cliff and Jeannie, only for them it's a few days. I suppose I should thank you. But I'm not grateful. You see, what you don't understand is that we all have harnesses. And most of us survive somehow. But not you – you couldn't take it. Not supposed to say that to the dead I know, but it's true. Oh it's a shame. You see, what you did will be remembered by some, but they'll forget that it takes a whole lot more to go on living. Who'll remember us? We need someone, Ben – because it seems to me that everyone's forgotten about us. We're the ones they leave out when they write the history books. Still, no use going on is it? I'm going to miss you ... in spite of all ... I'll miss you ...

PATCH 65

My first weeks as the Robert Burns fellow were a bit fraught. Our flat on Maitland Street needed a lot of cleaning, and the rent was still a hundred and ten dollars plus fifteen for the garage, which doesn't sound so much these days but was a lot then. Bernadette and I had got back from our trip to the US and Europe almost broke and flown straight down to Dunedin.

Living in this flat proved to be a fraught experience. The tenants upstairs were very noisy. At first I thought maybe they hadn't realised we'd moved in, but as time went on, and in spite of two requests, they didn't turn the music down. The cleaning was really hard work too. Every inch of the damn place had to be cleaned, and we spent over eighty dollars on cleaning gear.

As I scrubbed the walls I worried about the non-arrival of my monthly cheque for the Robert Burns Fellowship. I decided to ring the office but when I did there was no answer. The cheque eventually arrived days after the date it was supposed to. I wondered how many other Robert Burns fellows had arrived in Dunedin broke. I couldn't be the only one, could I? I thought of those comfortable salaried people running the fellowship and wished I could stop their wages and see how they liked it. Perhaps they had minds above money?

Bernadette knocked on the upstairs door, and the

woman there said she had to have the radio on loud or she couldn't wake up. We tried sleeping in the front room but were woken by loud radio at seven. An hour later it switched off. Maybe she was awake by then.

There was a loud party next door. Lots of car noise. So we agreed we'd have to move. The noise continued. When I went to have a shower one day, there was no hot water. An SOS from us and an inspector called. I'd directed *An Inspector Calls* by J B Priestley in the seventies in Wairoa. This inspector was on different business – he said we needed a new switch in the hot-water cupboard, so an electrician came and put in a new switch. More money. I didn't think to ask the landlord to pay.

My work was not going well. But sometimes it doesn't. That's why it's called work I suppose. The good news was that there would be a room (5C/13) at the Hocken Library for me to write in. They didn't have room in the English department apparently, but they would put on an afternoon tea so I could meet people.

A student rang from Rome regarding her thesis, which she wanted to do on my work and me. I wrote a letter to her and said no to everything because if I did all she asked of me I'd be writing the damn thesis myself. I'd just finished writing it when there was a knock at the door. The people from upstairs. They'd received a letter threatening eviction. I didn't feel all that sorry for them but got their phone number so we could ring if the noise got too much. It crossed my mind that they probably wouldn't hear the phone when they had the music on full blast, but ho hum – I simply couldn't be bothered saying anything.

There was no afternoon tea at the English department.

The guy forgot. I wasn't too worried. When I first arrived and was being introduced, a male lecturer had said to me, 'We must have a discussion about feminism some time.'

'What's to discuss?' I said.

Not to worry, there were welcoming smiles from John and Helen, and Jocelyn and a couple of others were lovely. And there was a welcome hui for me at, I think, the education department. At the supper afterwards, Anna Marsich – who put on that wonderful supper in 1983 after the performance of *What Did You Do in the War, Mummy?* – said she had a house to let.

A house?

I nearly cried with relief. So after supper Bernadette and I went and had a look and said yes immediately to 23 Montgomery Ave. It had a night store heater and no one living upstairs – it was a dear little self-contained house. The next day I rang Anna to check it wasn't a dream and she said she'd been feeling the same way.

We were so happy as we packed and moved our gear to Montgomery Ave. And there we were, surrounded by boxes and cartons, still thinking this was too good to be true, when someone arrived with two kittens as a housewarming present. *They'd heard we'd like a kitten.* We went into shock. Yes, we were going to get a kitten at some stage, but we had planned to settle in first. Now we were faced with two – a ginger kitten and a black kitten. Naturally our intention to refuse to take them weakened when the little dots gazed up at us big-eyed with fear. We caved. Decided to call the ginger one Robert and the black one Burns.

PATCH 66

June 2016, and in Orlando, Florida, the Pulse night club's patrons are targets of a hate-filled crime that kills forty-nine people and wounds at least fifty more. The queue to give blood to help the wounded reaches nearly a kilometre down the road. Others carry friends that distance to the hospital.

June 2016. In Ōtaki something tugs at my memory as it has done ever since I heard the first reports. I think I said in another patch that I only started keeping diaries in 1979, so I have to rely on my memory, helped out sometimes by the kids (I should get out of the habit of calling them 'the kids').

Remembering works better if you just let your mind go where it will and trust that. Like a cat going round and round in circles until it gets comfortable, your memory will finally find the right spot and settle down with a smile on its face. So I let it circle … and the first place I land is …

I'm directing a play at the moment, or I should say 'starting to'. We had the first audition on Saturday afternoon and a lot of people came, and Thursday night we'll have the second audition. I have two assistants, one doing all the organisational work and the other one, having worked in theatre before and giving me the benefit of her experience, is being my legs.

The play has songs in it, and there's nothing more heart-warming than seeing a group of strangers become friends through singing. I used to think that every week when my ukulele group met. There's something about singing together that makes everyone feel good.

We've had a keyboard loaned to us for two or three months. I've never actually met the donor. He rang me to ask what the play was about and what songs I wanted, and just before we said goodbye I asked what I ask everyone who contacts me for any reason on the basis that if you don't ask, you don't get, 'Do you know anyone who would lend us a keyboard for two to three months?' He said, 'I think I might,' and lo, although it turns out he's not able to be in the play, he left his keyboard with Ann, the one who asked me to write the play (so it's all her fault).

At first only a straggle of people arrived at the audition, then after a few minutes a crowd surged in. They'd gone to the library by mistake. I wanted to start off with a song, but there was no pianist because the one who was going to do it couldn't be there for the Saturday audition. However, a guy in the crowd said rather diffidently that he hadn't played for a while but he'd give it a go. And, after getting the right chord, he tried out the first line of the song from memory and we were away. Later he was asked to read against someone else auditioning, just to fill in, and he did it so well, everyone shouted, 'Go for Joe.' So we did.

I let my mind continue to circle …

When I directed *Charley's Aunt* for Wairoa College, both teachers and students were in the cast and helping out backstage. The play by Brandon Thomas was first performed in London in 1892. It's about two Oxford undergraduates, one of them called Charley, who want to impress a young lady, so they persuade another young man to play the part of Charley's rich aunt from Brazil.

There was a lot of help needed to move some large bushes in pots onstage for an exterior scene. I wanted it done quickly. I remember the history and social studies teacher saying ruefully, 'Not easy being a colleague of yours, Renée,' as he lifted, for the hundredth time, a large pot with a good-sized tree in it and lugged it on for the scene. Then he had to wait offstage to heave it off when the scene ended because the next scene was an interior. 'They said nothing about this at teachers' college,' he puffed.

Both kids and teachers were changed by the enforced merging as they worked together for the good of the production. In fact, a couple of teachers who'd had a lot of problems with one particular boy told me being in the play had transformed him from the lout he was on the way to becoming to the good-natured and obliging kid he was meant to be.

More plays surface as I circle ...

O Temperance! by Mervyn Thompson is a good play and I loved the temperance choruses; one was 'Won't you sign the pledge dear friends today', which we all sang with great gusto at the last-night party while glugging down a glass of wine or, in one case, gin and icing sugar. (Yes, I'd never heard of such a mixture before either.) David played Reverend Taylor in that production, and Laurie banged the big drum a friend had 'borrowed' from the music department at the school where she taught music.

The last of about seven plays I directed for the Little Theatre was *Sweetie Pie*, written by a feminist theatre collective in Britain whose name I've forgotten and been unable to trace. Apologies. It was a fabulous show that the cast and I enjoyed. It had unfortunate repercussions, though, when a few days after the show ended, a male teacher approached me in the college staffroom and accused me of doing a play that encouraged his wife to leave him. It was the first I'd heard of this and I stared at him without, for once, saying anything. A few days later he knocked on the front door at Kabul Street and said, 'Mea culpa.' I wasn't impressed, so I wasn't all that gracious and just said, 'Yes, okay.' Good way to go. Accuse in public and apologise in private.

I hear another report from Orlando and then in the middle of it – *bingo*, I remember. The first play I directed for Wairoa Little Theatre was *Butterflies are Free* by Leonard Gersche. It's about a blind boy, Donny, who persuades his over-protective mother to let him rent a flat and leave him to manage on his own for two months. He meets one of the other flat dwellers, who seems to be a bit of a ditz at first, but who encourages him in his dream for autonomy by quoting from Charles Dickens' *Hard Times*. It's this quote I was seeking after the Orlando reports:

> I only ask to be free. The butterflies are free. Mankind will surely not deny to Harold Skimpole what it concedes to the butterflies?

Now that my memory's redeemed itself, I don't know that it's much consolation.

PATCH 67

From *Yin & Tonic*, a collection of articles and stories, (Vintage 1988).

Dear Publisher,
I wish to apply for an advance to enable me to write a novel. I haven't started it yet but I read a book that won the 1997 Brilliant Book Awards and I know I can do just as well. My life has been filled with crisis and drama, twists and turns of fate, so I feel a book based on my life would be very successful. It's not just me. Many times my friends have said, why don't you write about it, Liz, instead of talking about it and ruining the five hundred? Just so you get the idea, here are a few highlights from my life.

HIGHLIGHTS FROM MY LIFE
I'm the second of five girls. Our parents had very little money. My father inherited this place when his uncle died and we all knew that when he died it would go to a cousin, so it was up to us to do what we could for ourselves. My older sister, Janie, was a nice girl, everyone said so, but my three younger sisters were real bad news. The two youngest, Kitty and Lydia, were absolute dillbrains – anything in trousers (sorry to be crude but

that's how it was), and Mary, the middle sister, was an absolute pain in the arse (sorry) who was always reading the Bible and maundering on about God and duty and that. Not that I'm knocking people who believe in that sort of thing but a little goes a long way.

One day a rich young man, Bingo, came to live in the same village, and he and Jane took a shine to each other. His sisters and his best mate weren't so keen on us. I have to admit that when Mum gets wound up she does talk a bit loud and my father always has his head in a book, but nobody's perfect are they? And as I always say, you can choose your friends but not your relations, ha ha. Bingo's best mate was called Darce, a bit poncy I know but some parents never think, do they? The word was he had a big property down south, been in the family for generations apparently. Some people have all the luck, eh.

Things went from bad to worse. Bingo's sisters and Darce worked on Bingo, and he left the district and my sister high and dry. Meanwhile Lydia and Kitty were making fools of themselves with some soldiers, although I admit they didn't have to try too hard. I talked to Mum and Dad about it but it was like talking to a brick wall.

Anyway the upshot was that Lydia, when she was away on a holiday with the colonel's wife, ran off with this guy called Wick for short. Well named as it turned out, because he was a stinko of the first water.

But I'm getting ahead of myself. I was staying at my cuzzie's (a nerd but his wife was a friend of mine) when who should appear but Darce. He got all white and trembly, said he shouldn't be doing what he was doing, I was from a fairly dicey family, but he couldn't help himself – and then he *popped the question.*

Talk about flabbergasted, I was speechless. But only for a second. I wasn't going to have some wanker like Darce slagging off my family. I mean for me to do it is one thing, but he hardly knew them. Well, the long and short of it was that I told him to shove his hook …

Anyway this is probably enough to give you an idea of how it would fit into a novel. I think it would be a bestseller and make a really good film. It has huge potential.

Yours faithfully,
Liz Darcy

PATCH 68

Old people are

One. Boozers, losers, out-of-jail bruisers. Jockeys, cockies, once were great soccies. Litterers, knitters, reliable house sitters. Miners, diners, intelligent signers. Gardeners, cooks, some who write books. Piano and guitar players, definitely some gays. Singers, clingers, ringers and wingers. Wealthy, stealthy, against-all-odds healthy. Runners, gunners, dedicated punners. Winners and players, sinners and swayers. Well-off, poor, curious, bored. Patient, walker, creepy grey stalker. Painters, fainters, always some ranters. Fat, skinny, tall, short. New, old, borrowed, bought. Fraught, taught, occasionally sought. Preachers, teachers, some who make features. Bad-tempered, kind, clear-sighted, blind. Some bold, some rolled, some polled, some sold. Doctors, nurses, lecturers, bursars. Bouncers, prancers, dedicated dancers. Rich bitches, old hitchers sleeping in deep ditches. Happy, sad, conniving, bad. Lout, devout, chock-full of doubt. Whingers, Ginjas, society's fringes. Packers, actors, surprisingly good hackers. Loving, hating, dating, waiting.

Two. Old people are selfish, loaded with money and investments, deliberately hanging on in their five-bedroom house in Remuera or Parnell, grabbing the government superannuation when they could well afford to live without it. They stuff up the health system, clog the footpaths, get in the way of cyclists by walking across pedestrian crossings. They dodder, they're slow, they peer at things and they can't hear properly, and when you shout at them they prod you with their umbrella. When you suggest they get a hearing aid they say they can't afford them. *I mean what do they do with the government super?* They don't need a lot to eat. So why do they take so long in the supermarket? They dawdle, pick up things, put them down, complain they can't reach the top shelf. They *tut-tut* at the price of things and ask the man at the meat freezer if they can have two soup bones instead of six or a smaller slice of lamb's fry. *Ugh. Lamb's fry?* Only old people would even dream of eating that wet, slimy, dark stuff that's got a horrible little skin all over it and you have to peel off before you cook it. I suggested to one old woman that she try quinoa instead of meat and you'd think I'd told her to drink disinfectant. Actually I've only tried it once myself but I'll use it again at some stage. Got lots of vitamins in it apparently. Old people don't mind waiting. Why should they? They've got nothing to do. They can wait while you serve someone younger. They adore being called 'love' and why the hell should they mind when you call them Mrs? They're all married, aren't they? And what does it matter anyway? They limp and they whine about ramps and put on a drama when they have to walk up stairs. I mean if they can't climb up a few stairs then they should stay home.

They should hold their shoulders back, walk quicker, get their heart rate up and stop complaining about uneven footpaths. They're the same footpaths that were there when they were young and they were okay then, weren't they? It's all in the mind. All this hooha about home help. I mean, dusting a room's not going to kill them is it? If they can't see properly then they just need to take it slower. Take all day if they want. What else have they got to do? It's simply a matter of using their brains. All this bitching and carping, fussing and fretting about being old is simply a waste of time. It's all in the mind. If you don't think you're old then you won't be. I have made up my mind. I'm never going to be old.

PATCH 69

I realise I haven't included much so far – or even anything – about the 1990s so I shut my eyes and take up a diary and there it is, 1995. Before the entries actually start, there are four carefully handwritten recipes: Onion & Anchovy Tart, Mt Cook Coffee Toffee Pie, Jazz Bar Brownies and Divine Chocolate Cake. The Onion & Anchovy Tart is the only one I'm tempted to try. I'll start with the last few days of 1994. I'm in Napier.

> **30 December 1994.** Walked around the centre city then went to Park Island Cemetery, where I swept Rose and Stan's grave, then Gertrude's, and put some Abraham Darby and Heritage roses on them.

I was very keen on David Austin roses at that time. I still like them but I'm not besotted with them like I was then. We were on holiday from Hamilton and I had cut these roses as tight buds and hoped they'd last. Plastic flowers work in their own way, I suppose, but give me real flowers any time. Yes, they die and droop, but for a few days they look wonderful and you know someone has visited.

My grandmother Gertrude died in 1931, Stan in 1934 and Rose in 1949, so there's a whole swathe of feelings and memories when I visit them. I leave flowers because

I wish I'd met Gertrude, although I'm not sure I'd have liked her or she me. I met my father of course but I don't remember him, and for half my life I hated him, so taking him flowers is a kind of philosophical gesture towards growing up. And I'm still so bound up with Rose that if I didn't take her real flowers I think she'd probably rise up and take me out in a whirl of smoke – so real flowers it has to be.

31 December 1994. Napier has changed since VJ Day, 15 August 1945, when we laughed and danced and shouted our way up Emerson Street. American servicemen sitting on the backs of trucks cheered and threw packets of cigarettes to the crowd. I must have just turned sixteen and when I looked at those servicemen sitting on the back of the truck, I remember thinking they didn't look much older than me. Did some of them even shave? I bet their mothers were relieved they would soon be home, but as the full story of the effects of the atomic bomb dropped on Hiroshima began to be known, the celebrations became more subdued. We all wanted the war to be over. The horror stories of the POWs' treatment at Changi were beginning to trickle through, too, and although the terrible extent of the atrocities committed by both Germany and Japan will live forever in my memory, I was appalled also at the long-lasting effects of that bomb on Japanese civilians. Wairoa looks extremely dry. *Fire risk acute*, the notice says. Found Sharon's place, Naomi and Abbie were waiting on the road to make sure we didn't get lost.

1 January 1995. To David and Hoot's. Tim there. Went for a ride to the Wairoa bar [no not that bar, the one at the end of Kopu Road, the scene of many shipping accidents and wrecks in earlier times], then to Kihitū and Te Uhi. At Kihitū we saw Rauhina, the marae built in honour of a group of chiefly women (or just one). Very depressed, poor-looking area. Hoot's mother's unveiling had gone well and Hoot was feeling 'very light'. Back at Sharon's on this first day of January 1995. We all cast runes to see what came up. Rune cast – 24, 21, 19. [I have no idea what this means.]

2 January 1995. Went for a drive to Māhia. Called in at Bremdale Gardens on the way. This garden is worked bio-dynamically. The gardens were not impressive. Seas of deadheads everywhere. [I didn't know what bio-dynamic meant then, but in 2017 I still hate 'seas of deadheads'.] Good ideas for arches and frames using mānuka and silver birch. Wonderful idea for flowing water down through several gardens shaped like nasturtium leaves and finally into a big round container where herbs are mixed to make fertiliser for farm and garden. Water moves down in figures of eight. The owner said five years ago he was a Lincoln-trained conservative. Then he went to a workshop on bio-dynamics and his whole life/perspective changed. As I listened to him I thought, well I know about life-changing moments, and when he finished his story, I wished him luck.

4 January 1995. Saw David, Hoot, and picked up Sula, who was just recovering from mumps, and took her with us back to Hamilton. We planned to go to Raglan for a few days once we got home.

5 January 1995. Home. Bathed Willy. Packed car for Raglan.

Travelling in those days was a bit of a drama. I always had Pekinese dogs and the latest was called Willy. He was the second Pekinese I had called Willy. The first one was one of a pair of mistreated little animals that a vet, who knew I was looking for a dog, asked me to give a home to. Missy and Willy were the first Pekinese dogs I'd ever known. Their owner had died on the bed under which they were huddled among fifty or so empty gin bottles. By the time the police were called, the dogs were starving, had sores all over their little bodies and were near death. Thanks to that vet and his wife, they survived. After a week or two, when the sores were looking much better and their hair had started to grow back, I took them. Missy was highly intelligent but Willy was, as one of the kids said, an egg short of an egg sandwich. Willy always had a bit of his tongue hanging out of his mouth. It used to get paler and paler until someone would say, 'Willy – open your mouth,' and he would, and then five minutes later the piece of tongue would be slowly petrifying again. The second Willy was different. Bright, brave and occasionally belligerent, he was a lot of fun.

> Willy's gear – food, tablets, treats, bed, leads etc.
> Burns' [cat] gear – food.
>
> Us (including Sula) – clothes, toilet gear, jackets, umbrellas, hats.
>
> Food in chilly bin – ham, orange juice, cheese, tomatoes, bread, butter, jam, Sustain, milk, cream, Christmas cake, coffee, sugar, tea, lemon, marrows, lettuce, chives, chocolate.

Reading this I wonder how there was room left for us in the car.

6 January 1995. Raglan. Wakeful night, maybe possum is playing about? To beach at midday. Tide comes in quickly here. Sula feeling very much better after a long sleep. Plan a picnic tomorrow. Listened to tapes. Holly Near & Ronnie Gilbert's 'Lifeline'. And 'Two Good Arms' one of my very, very all-time favourites.

'Two Good Arms' is a folk song that remembers Ferdinand Nicco Sacco and Bartolomeo Vanzetti, anarchists who were sent to the electric chair in August 1927 in USA for a crime they didn't commit. They were charged with the murder of a guard and a paymaster in a robbery at a shoe company. In spite of a series of pleas based on recanted testimony, conflicting ballistics evidence, a prejudicial statement by the jury foreman, a confession, and campaigns led by prominent academics, writers, artists and musicians, Sacco and Vanzetti were judged guilty and sent to the electric chair purely because – in my opinion – they were anarchists. No one on the bench really knew what that meant but it had to be bad. It was used like the word 'communist' was used in witch hunts of writers, musicians and artists in 1950s America.

The writer Maxwell Anderson wrote a play, *Winterset*, based on the Sacco/Vanzetti case. I like the play very much and it was part of the programme of play readings we (Sunny, Jan and I) presented to raise funds for the refurbishment of St Peter's Hall in Paekākāriki. The reading of *Winterset* was directed with love by Ralph McAllister and it was wonderful to hear the words again.

No doubt there have been numerous other songs written about this terrible injustice but I love the simplicity of 'Two Good Arms'. A good friend of mine Rona Bailey gave me a tape of Holly Near songs and I just about wore the tape out playing this one.

7 January 1995. Finished Art Deco book. Good story about the *Jazz Bowl*. Read *Owls Do Cry* again. First published 1961, it says, but I thought it was published before that? [It was. Pegasus Press, 1957.]

8 January 1995. Tempted to stay on. Raglan is lovely but we decided that because trips had been planned to Rotorua and Auckland, plus I wanted to spread compost and fertiliser on the garden, we went home. A nice letter and books from Chris – *Akhenaten*, poems by Dorothy Porter, and *White Eye* by Blanche d'Alpuget.

9 January 1995. Monday. Gardened. Tidied back. Composted and fertilised. B adjusted water system. Looks really good now. Corners that weren't being reached, now are.

So that's the first nine days of 1995. I'll write about the other 356 another time.

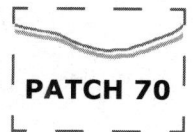

Old songs

Early light angles
glimmers above the stones
sea birds high and tremulous.
Through a hole
in a white bone a lone voice
sings up green and hesitant girls.
Old women on the banks
lift their heads smile smile
giggle nudge sigh.
Sea birds lift, turn toward the sea.

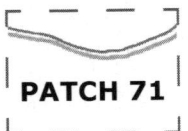

PATCH 71

A House To Let was performed at 7.30pm on Thursday, 4 August 2016, to an audience of over three hundred, some standing. That'll teach them to be on time.

The response — judging by those who came up to me, and not counting friends who might have felt they should say something complimentary whatever their private thoughts — was wonderfully approving. In any case *A House To Let* seems to have struck a chord with people who go to theatre, people who hardly ever go to theatre, friends and family of the cast, and complete strangers. 'A trip down memory lane,' someone said.

A House To Let traces the influence, actions and events of the ten Labour prime ministers. At the same time it marks the major events that happened in Aotearoa New Zealand during those years. It begins in 1934 and ends in 2008. In between the scenes dramatising events around those prime ministers, I used the linking device of two paper girls calling out headlines or reading a news report, and the cast sang popular songs or hymns.

After the performance, party leader Andrew Little made a speech and said some very nice things. He remembered seeing *Wednesday To Come* and *Pass It On*, and said how much he loved them. He came up to me at the supper and said, 'What I said was true. I did love those plays and I haven't forgotten them.'

So the play was successful but let me say here that I didn't do it on my own. I wrote a script, then wrote another one because we couldn't cast the first one, and off we went. The musicians (piano, guitar, harmonica) had been onstage before, but in the cast of around thirty I'm not sure more than three or four from the cast had ever been in a play before. I was assisted, nobly, by Merle Metekingi, who was also prompt, and Sarah Delahunty came up once a week to do some acting coaching and was there all weekend the week before we opened. She did some great work with grouping and made the play move a lot better. Ōtaki College students Andy and Michael were on sound and lighting. When I met their teacher, Steve, he said he was in the audience at Downstage on the first night of the 1984 production of *Wednesday To Come* and had never forgotten it. This is the way to win the heart of a playwright.

We had a mixture of ages in the cast: kids, grown-ups, young and old – the oldest actor was eighty-three but that's okay because the playwright was eighty-seven. At the beginning before we got under way, it was implied a couple of times that I was too old to be doing this.

'I got a surprise,' said one smiler, 'I thought it can't be true – you're not directing a play are you?'

'Yes, why?' I said – possibly a little belligerently.

'Oh, nothing, I knew you'd been sick and –' laugh, laugh, laugh '– none of us are getting any younger are we?'

The one who did all the organising and was responsible for the entire thing because she asked me to do it – Ann Chapman – ended up playing storyteller, so that'll teach her. The young woman who offered to do props found herself playing the Queen, perky little hat, cream gloves, perfect blue ensemble, Cuban-heeled shoes and all, and got a special clap from everyone, even the republicans there. Fatal to offer help of any kind really. If anyone even approached me to ask the time, I told them they were in the play.

Andrew Little said he really liked the journey of it. He has to be nice, say nice things, but he sounded like he meant it. I decided to believe he did. I'd told Ann after she asked me to do the play that it wouldn't be a paean of praise and it wasn't, and in the supper room a woman thanked me for this. 'These things shouldn't be glossed over,' she said.

Those at the supper all commented on their enjoyment of the songs, and it is true, there is something magic about listening to and singing the songs of a particular era. Hymns and songs like 'Bread and Roses' carry a wealth of memories for all of us, and after the Thursday night performance they made some new ones. We all owed a lot to the talent of Ann-Marie Stapp, musical director, who not only coaxed, coerced and charmed everyone into singing their hearts out, but also played the trumpet for a particular 1960s memory in the show and is, alas, the only one not in the cast photo, because she took it.

Friends painted placards – *Support a Woman's Right to Choose, Stop the War in Vietnam* – and Adrienne Jansen, Sarah Delahunty and Glenn Colquhoun gave permission for their poems to be used. And, woohoo, everyone except for three of us had to learn the words of *The Red Flag*. The three who knew the words were: Sarah, a union guy who was playing Savage, and me. Sarah said she and her siblings were taught to stand up for it.

I moaned a bit, got irritated, growled, smiled a lot,

and I had doubts, doubts, doubts. But I'd forgotten that this is where theatre began. I'd forgotten theatre began with a bunch of people from a community telling or re-telling the rest of the community their own stories in a mix of music, song and poetry, and by acting out past events. They didn't have fancy lighting, sounds or drama diplomas to do it, all they had was a love of words and for telling stories by acting them out and for the effect this has on people.

That's what this cast had. They enjoyed being in the show, relished the play, the songs, the company they were in, the whole experience. On Sunday I got an email from one of them, which said, 'I wish we could start all over again, I just loved it.' I think that might be a wish too far, but we're all going to keep in touch. Someone is putting on a pot-luck and we're going to do something about National Poetry Day – it might not be on the actual day but, hey, here in Ōtaki, we make our own rules okay? So one day ... you never know. You throw a pebble into the water ...

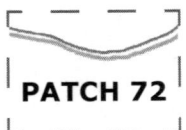

PATCH 72

I first became interested in Asbestos Cottage in the Cobb Valley after reading *The Exiles of Asbestos Cottage* by Jim Henderson. I knew Jim's work. This was his eighteenth book, he was a well-known voice on radio and he was a friend of my uncle Orm's. An earlier book, *Gunner Inglorious*, tells of their experiences as gunners in Egypt during the Second World War. Jim was left for dead in Sidi Rezegh in 1941 and lay for two days before the Germans arrived and took him prisoner. His worst injury was his shattered leg. He was an amputee prisoner of war in Italy and came back with a wooden leg.

Back home Jim became known as a historian and collector of country lore and stories, produced *Open Country* for National Radio for fourteen years, and became so fascinated with the story of Henry and Annie, who lived in Asbestos Cottage, that he spent years researching and writing it.

The cottage is situated in Kahurangi National Park and today it is only a few hours walk in to get to it. When Henry Chaffey took Annie there, it was a much more challenging climb. Annie was in her mid-thirties and he was in his mid-forties. Her husband had abused her and threatened to kill them both with a .22 rifle, so she'd fled, leaving her two young sons behind. Here's Jim on what it was like for Annie:

She would not see another woman for seven years. Even when she broke her leg she refused to budge and she only came out to civilisation once, compelled by an internal trouble; it was a 'hospital job' bitterly resented. When the Murchison quake shook the entire valley, Annie was there on her own while rocks and boulders made giant cracking noises as they rolled down the hillsides with the occasional one banging into the cottage. She loved the cottage and the area, although Henry may not have been a comfortable companion in bed because it is said that occasionally he slept with imperfect explosives under his armpits.

After Annie's husband died, and twenty years after she went up the track, Annie and Henry were married at Asbestos Cottage. At the age of eighty-three, Henry died on the track he'd walked up and down for forty years, carrying everything they needed from the store on his back. Annie could not manage living there on her own, so reluctantly she went to live with a relative in Timaru. There, she could not settle, became more and more unhappy and eventually ended her own life.

Something about this story gave me a hankering to visit the place. Anyone who knows me knows I'm not a sports-minded woman. I like walking, but I walk because I like it and not because it's good for me. Tramping or camping? Oh no. Done my time at living hard, leave that to those who do it for fun and want a definite beginning and end to their adventure. So it was a surprise, to me anyway, that I had this desire to tramp up to Asbestos Cottage. Even more of a surprise, I suppose, that three friends who'd also wanted to climb up to the cottage decided to come too – or maybe they were going anyway and decided they would let me come with them. Which is how Sunny, Jan, Anna and I ended up in a DOC hut in the Cobb Valley with a little man-made river shushing away over the road. My diary moans:

> **24 March 2005.** Packing a pain and a problem. I've never packed for a few days in a DOC hut before. Towels etc, things you don't usually take, have to be taken. Pillows. At the last moment I bought a pair of jeans from Farmers and tried to take them up, gave up and just cut them. Aue. But they will be fine. Cut raw edges are in. Or will be. This is all harder but perhaps more exciting because of that.

> **25 March 2005.** Rose's birthday. To Nelson on ferry then to Cobb Valley and Asbestos Cottage. Jan and Sunny have organised this and I'm so grateful. No problems on ferry trip. The sea-sickness pills, recommended by an assistant in the pharmacy on Lambton Quay, were great. Jan drove the hired 4WD from Picton to Nelson where we picked up Anna. Said hello to Synevre and Kerry, haven't seen them for ages. Met Olivia and Tahi, two beautiful children.

The drive to Cobb Valley was exciting. It was pouring with rain and very cold, and there in front of us was a cave-in, a split in the road and water gushing down from above so you couldn't see the other side.

'Hang on,' said Jan, and drove straight at it. I shut my eyes and opened them when we were through. I noted in my diary later, 'Jan is a superb driver,' and this about the walk itself:

> Long walk, much longer than I anticipated, and of course it rained. Rock-climbing/slithering, you name it. Some of the parts had been washed away and had to be done on

my bum, all was difficult. However, with Jan acting as my 'buddy' for the day, I did it. I have a lovely sense of achievement. Sunny's sandwiches were just delicious.

It was wonderful to get there and see the cottage and it was equally enjoyable being with Jan, Sunny and Anna. I would never have done it without them. There was still some of Annie's mint growing wild. She and Henry had a great garden.

Asbestos Cottage is small and you have to wonder how Annie survived the lonely times. She baked, cooked, made bread and jams, preserved fruit from their orchards, dried apricots and peaches, roasted goat, made stews chock-full of vegetables and whatever meat she had – all cooking done on the camp cooker, which you can still see. She sewed all her own clothes and only wore what had been fashionable when she was young. Maybe she thought, as she did about Henry, that if you find something good, stick with it. Maybe wearing dresses that went from neck to ankle was warmer?

Annie and Henry were hospitable but you had to let them know you were coming. Neither of them welcomed unexpected callers. You had to stop at the sign and shout, then wait for an answering call. If it was 'no visitors today', you turned around and went back down the track. They were generous hosts once you were inside, but they didn't welcome surprises. I suppose that's understandable if you lived for twenty years expecting an angry man armed with a .22 rifle – and after that maybe it becomes a habit.

I thought of all these things as we looked around the small dark interior. Imagined Annie and Henry settled comfortably in the warm after the day's work. Did they talk much? They probably understood each other without too many words being involved. Did she knit? Did they read?

Walking out from the cottage was hard, and by the time we got to our hut I grabbed the whisky Jan gave me and downed it in one swallow.

Jim Henderson had a way with similes. I've always remembered 'as patient as a limbfitter' as a good description of the character he was writing about, but also, given his wooden leg, as a telling comment on a situation he must have experienced a few times. 'As dull as a shingleslide,' he said of a man he met. He also had some things to say about how the isolation might have affected Annie:

> Did loneliness creep aching like a chill marrowbone fog? Certainly. Loneliness and longing for a woman's company and affinity, a sharing of little things instinctively, come from time to time to every housewife on a lonely station. The story of a host of New Zealand women must and will be told one day, but meanwhile we must endure learned ones obsessed with *Man Alone*.

The book was published in 1981 so maybe the author had been influenced by feminist voices. He certainly had by his 'companion and soul-mate', Peggy. He dedicates the book to her and to Annie.

When I got back to my snug little apartment on The Terrace in Wellington, I wondered how long I'd have lasted in a winter in Cobb Valley. No real answer to that, of course, but I'd like to think I might have stuck it out. I'm pretty sure I'd have objected to sleeping next to someone who had imperfect explosives under his armpits.

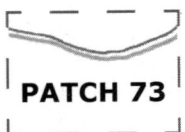

Open home

Tread slow around the old house,
let the bones of this moment stir, settle,
see the irises turn – the lavenders freeze,
see how the grey gate waits for the touch.
Watch how you go down the knobbly path,
remember the day the bricks were set there?
Piled in barrows from two streets away.
Wheeled among walkers, bikes, chairs.
Finally laid to rest on the path to the chook
house. And there still, quiet as a watchful nun,
the black cat under the observant sun.

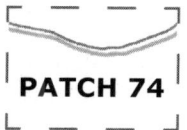

PATCH 74

I'm fascinated to read the me of 2004 when I'm still getting over the break-up with Bernadette. Unlike most of my other diaries, each page of 2004 seems full of how I'm feeling – at least for a while. I'd got over my tendency to stay silent on the page about things that upset me. Here's an example:

> Trust is temporary, love is a lie, loyalty a joke, betrayal a certainty – so happiness – the possibility of it is a fairy tale for children, the lucky ones who have stories read to them – or perhaps not so lucky – they might believe there is a happy ending.

And I quote from P D James' memoir, *Time to Be in Earnest*:

> There is much that I remember but which is painful to dwell upon. I see no need to write about these things. They are over and must be accepted, made sense of and forgiven, afforded no more than their proper glance in a long life in which I have always known that happiness is a gift, not a right.

I agree with her. I think I needed to put the words on a page just once, toss my toys out of the cot just once.

That I didn't feel like that for long reinforces my feeling about our need to taihoa – take a break – for a while, and know that everything passes. I've come to see I've been very lucky in my two long-term relationships.

In 2004 I went to a hip-hop lyric writing course taught by Anton Carter and really enjoyed it. My lyrics were pathetic and I was hopeless at delivering them out loud, but the other participants (all of them a hundred years younger) were extra special and I enjoyed them and Anton. A good teacher.

My neck problem got worse and is still there. I was working on *Kissing Shadows* and I began to meditate, and I keep that up but in a desultory fashion. I got a call from Pip Byrne about teaching a writing class at Whitireia Polytechnic. Chris cleaned the windows from time to time. Tim popped over for an occasional weekend. David wrote me a letter enclosed in a card.

Then David came and stayed. He was going to a wedding of a school friend. It seems old Wairoa College friendships are being kept alive these days by texts or emails and occasional meetings. Tim keeps in touch with some of his school friends in the same way. David brought me a cup of tea in bed and then went off to organise ferry tickets. After that he came back and ironed his clothes. I drove him to Houghton Bay where the wedding was to be held.

My friend Anna, from Warrington near Dunedin, rang to say she'd got to page 140 of the draft of *Kissing Shadows* I'd sent her and it was 'exceedingly good'. I write, 'The relief is extraordinary.'

It was Anna who told me about what she called 'messages from the bones'. These are the unspoken connections with both living and dead whānau, connections that we understand but are unspoken. *Kissing Shadows* is a novel that a lot of readers mistake for a real life account of Rose and Stan, with just the names changed. They couldn't be more wrong. There are some factual things in the story, the suicide for example, Gus's stutter, but most of it is surmise, fictional inventions and some, as Anna says, 'messages from the bones'. I had to be creative, in other words make a lot of it up, because, apart from telling me what Stan had done, Rose never spoke of it.

I enjoyed a panel of writers consisting of Peter Bland, Sunny Amey, Jacquie Sturm, Bill Oliver. Jacquie commented that she came 'out of the closet' as a Māori writer in the fifties and moved between hui at Ngāti Poneke as Jacquie Sturm and PEN cocktail parties as Jim Baxter's wife.

On 13 April at Downstage, I saw *Niu Sila* by Oscar Kightley and Dave Armstrong for the first time. I didn't want to move after it finished. I wanted to stay sitting and let the play settle in my consciousness. It was something I already knew, but here it was onstage and becoming new all over again in the telling. The play was absolutely lovely. Great script and wonderfully well acted. I finally roused myself and walked away in a state of high exhilaration; this was exactly the kind of play I wanted to see.

I met Elspeth Sandys and we went to Michael King's memorial service on the fourth floor at Te Papa. A most extraordinary lineup of good speakers made the service memorable. All spoke of the different aspects of Michael's work, career and character. Pat Rosier called and we had a cup of tea. It was great to see her and hear what she was up to. Her second book is about to be published [2017].

The Boa Club is formed. Rosemary, Shelley and me. Rosemary has an orange boa. I tried to get one too but could only find a pink one. We plan to have Boa Ladies' Lunches every now and then. It good to renew the friendship with Shelley, who played Kate Sheppard in the Wairoa Little Theatre production of Mervyn Thompson's *O Temperance!* that I directed.

Appointments for mammograms, classes for te reo … Anna wrote to me about Plato's Cave and the illusion of reality and allegory. Then later I wrote in my diary, 'In search of Plato, caves and quotes – have found some – not particularly related to caves or light but lines that appealed strongly to me.'

> **5 May 2004.** Just home from Hikoi. Rang Rona and she was tired but happy she marched. Another mammogram. Unsettling. Same old dance. Second lot had to be done. It's the staples I think. To lunch with Marilyn. Totally enjoyable. She had bought the most beautiful pair of ankle boots – so stylish – she's got a very good eye.
>
> Had a great email from Chris. He got an A+ for the final history grade and some wonderful comments. Most impressive essay. Hopes he'll do honours. Chris says he's stoked with the mark and so am I on his behalf. When he went back to university he was a little anxious about how he'd keep up with the younger students, but I told him his brain would be just as good, possibly better.

I was invited to participate in *On The Bus: Flat Out Brown Contemporary Māori Writers on Tour*. The other writers were Briar Grace-Smith, Mere Whaanga, Phil Kanawa and Kingi McKinnon, and we toured the country. Some of the schools were not all that well prepared but others were great and the kids had good questions. Tours are always interesting. Every day a new group to read and talk to, a variety of ages, and after a while you get used to being in a different place every night. It's tiring and you're never sure whether you've done well or not, but the other writers make it work and they make it worthwhile.

> **8 July 2004.** David rang to say my granddaughter Kokotui had given birth to a daughter by caesarean section. She and baby, Alitalyia, are well. So now I'm a great-grandmother.

I celebrated my seventy-fifth birthday in 2004 with a party in my small apartment in Atrium Apartments, and everyone I wanted to come came. I warned everyone on the floor beforehand that there might be a bit of noise and people would spill into the hall. Rosemary brought balloons and other decorations. Bernadette and Jill generously provided the food. Rapai played the guitar and sang. Tim said when he was coming up in the lift he could hear 'Blue Smoke'. Naomi was in Korea but sent me a tea set that arrived on the day. People crammed in everywhere, all smiling. A great memory.

I think that's probably enough of 2004 except to say it was a very full year and I learned a lot, and by the end of it I had come back round to a position something like this passage I wrote for Daisy in *Daisy and Lily*.

> What puzzles me is why our parents, or teachers, if our parents are loath or careless, don't teach us the probability of this decadal happening. Surely if we knew we were

going to suffer one or even two bad things every ten years we'd be able to endure them while they were happening? We wouldn't go around asking why me because we'd know the answer was it was our turn and it would pass until the next decade. And we'd be more understanding of other people's bad episodes because we'd know they were merely going through their bad patch ... I am convinced that belief in God is nothing more than a crutch, like smoking or drinking, to help face the next hour, the next week or in the case of Christians, the next life. Like Lily, I believe in love. That is my crutch. In spite of all evidence to the contrary I believe it's the most important thing in the world ... just plain, ordinary old love. Except it is never plain nor ordinary ...'

'You can't unknow the known,' a friend said to me once and that's true. You can't unknow love, you can't unknow betrayal, but you can choose – and you have to in the end – which one to remember. Like Daisy, I choose love.

PATCH 75

I wrote a poem addressed to Grace Josephine, my grandmother, daughter of Puti Mary and Charles Harmer. It's a bit cheeky. I don't know a lot about this Grace and most of what I do know is from gossip a long time after she died. I knew her youngest daughter, my auntie Grace, much better, especially after I had Christopher. This younger Grace took a proprietorial interest in my eldest. Like a lot of people in her position as a senior midwife, she had the theory but not the practice, but I suppose that was an improvement on me who had no theory and, before Chris, no practice. Before David, I thought Chris was my learning experience; after David and then Timothy, I realised *each* child is a learning experience. Later, when Grace had her daughter, Maree, it was interesting to see her grapple with the difference between theory and practice.

Grace senior's story has always intrigued me, probably because all I have are hints and suppositions. Val and I were sent to stay with her and Walter in Taihape after we three kids had caught measles, chicken pox and whooping cough in quick succession and, unsurprisingly, Rose was exhausted. As far as I know it's the one and only time she ever asked her mother for anything. Grace senior only visited us once. This was probably more due to not being able to be spared at home than that she didn't want to. I suspect that Grace and Walter might have paid the service car fares for us but don't know for sure.

So we two were put on the service car and told that the driver would put us off at Taihape, where someone would meet us. I might have been seven. I wasn't feeling too good about being sent off to this place I'd never heard of with people I didn't know, and I soon felt worse because I got carsick. In my memory, there is no recollection of annoyance or impatience from the driver; maybe I wiped it from my mind, but I think he must have had kids of his own because he just handed me brown-paper bags and opened the window by my seat. The drive took forever and when I think of it now, I feel sorry for the other passengers. Val slept most of the way.

I remember being scared. There were two or three big boys; a man called Pop Martin, who was married to my grandmother; Uncle Jimmy, my mother's brother; and this grandmother I didn't know. But it was fine. I learned that some people put salt on their porridge – but now wonder if they were playing a joke on this little girl who didn't say much and frowned a lot at their antics and attempts to amuse us.

It was very strange living in a house with the big boys. David, the youngest, wasn't that much older than me, but he was big and fair with a cheeky grin. He was his mother's pride and joy. He showed us how to steal apples from the tree and to roll down the sloping lawn in the front without rolling onto the road. We got growled at for eating the green apples but it didn't worry David.

By this time I think, Pop Martin – real name Walter – had left butchering and started up his transport business. There were two links to Walter other than that he married my grandmother. He too had gone to Taradale School, and then learned the butchery trade in the same premises where my brother, Jimmy, was to work after school and on Saturdays when he got a bit older. I've never been sure where or when Grace and Walter got together, but the whisper was that she and Walter had been close for a few years before they actually married, and that once Grace's husband Bill died of cancer from lead poisoning (he was a linotype operator and many of them died from this) she and Walter married and moved to Taihape. But who knows? However, it gave me an idea for this joke with my grandmother.

Dear Grandmother

Husbands are a necessary part of the design
God drew on his sketch pad, Sister Joseph tells you,
if he hit you for flirting with a man you wouldn't
be seen dead with – it's the drink, the devil drink –
he's a good man really, always money in the plate
and I've told you about that smile before.

So here is handsome Walter on the butcher's cart –
he's looked at you over the minced beef for months.
You smile that smile and he smiles back.
'A pound of the best fillet,' you say.
'Coming up,' says Walter, a man
it turns out, you are happy to be seen dead with.

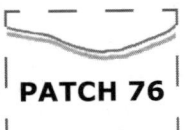

PATCH 76

Red moon time

I say, How are you?
She says, Good thanks.
I say, Shall we now tell each other the truth?
We grin. I make tea. Put out Anzac biscuits.
She says, When they ask me why I'm crying, I say I don't know, but of course I do. I'm crying because it's the beginning of the end and I just wish it didn't have to be so hard. I'm crumbling – little pieces are going wrong bit by bit. Why didn't someone tell me it was like this?
I say, It's like before the eclipse – the moon goes red …
She says, Tears have never come easy but it's true they're easier now. Is there a female version of curmudgeon?
I say, And then the moon goes dark.
She says, I'm depressed but I don't want pills. I just want someone to tell me it'll be all right, that it'll be like listening to a story with a happy ending.
I say, Did you have stories read to you as a child?
She says, No. They were too busy.
I say, So we're looking for a story with a happy ending?
She says, I don't want to be cheered up, I just want someone to say it will be all right. I'll hold your hand, it will be all right.
I say, It will be all right. I'll hold your hand. It will be all right.

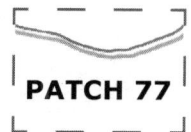

PATCH 77

From *Kissing Shadows* (Huia 2005).

I woke later to a sound from Gus. 'What?' I said. 'What?' Then in the brighter though still bleak light I saw them. A raggle-taggle herd of people walking along the side of the road. They stretched for a couple of hundred yards, in twos and threes, bigger groupings and some lone individuals. I saw a girl and a man. They had their arms linked around the arms of a woman who was hopping along the grassy verge.

I felt rather than saw Nanny struggling out of her seat to stand by the window and have a look. Other travellers crowded the windows to stare at the marchers.

'Must have hurt her ankle,' someone said.

'Won't get far like that.'

Were they having a competition in stating the obvious?

As the marchers saw our faces at the windows, some of them waved and a few passengers waved back. Frankie had told me about the marchers going through Porohiwi a couple of days before.

'Where did they sleep?'

'Town Hall,' he said. 'The mayor came and made a speech,' he grinned at my disbelieving face, 'and people brought bits of food, mattresses, blankets, from all round. Most of them didn't have much but what they had they gave.'

I looked over and Nanny was smiling, even her pāua eyes were smiling. It was catching. For a second my own lips curved. I nudged Nanny to show I understood she'd enjoyed seeing them and heard, 'Wh-wh-wh.'

Did she just admire their determination or did it remind her of something else? Sixty-five years was a long time. I wasn't even halfway. God, I thought, not even halfway and look what you've crammed into it. Wonder what Nanny had done by twenty-seven? How old was she when those animals attacked her and my mother? Forty-seven years ago her husband died. A long time to be on your own. Perhaps that's a little bit why she chose me, for the company, just to have someone there. Someone to see the cave walls, touch them, learn the story, feel the presences. Well, for once in her life Nanny had made a mistake. I wasn't the right one, she should have chosen Whetu. The cave would have suited Whetu a whole lot better than me. Perhaps it wasn't too late? I sighed. Whetu. Something else to sort out.

Why had Emere kept me inside her? There were some things she could have done but she chose not to. Then she had me and let Nanny take me. Had they arranged it between them? Had it got too much for my mother? Did I look like that man who cut Nanny's tongue off?

On the skyline there were sharp black skeletons of trees. They looked forbidding in the gloom outside but they were ordinary old willows really. They'd just lost their summer clothes and as soon as the light changed they'd be glossy brown. To the left a ribbon of light threaded between the trunks like a light piece of harakeke woven between them – water – of course. The river.

I wouldn't get Nanny out at Waipawa, tinpot little place, better wait till Waipukurau to take her to the lavatory. She'd just have to wait. The refreshment rooms at Waipukurau were supposed to be the best. Gus could get us a cup. Or perhaps I wouldn't ask. If Nanny had taken against him, I better get the tea.

What was Gus thinking? What was he really seeing when he stared out the window? In spite of my ultimatum, he'd put a bottle of whisky in his overcoat pocket. I'd seen the top sticking out when he climbed into the driver's seat of the van. But even he knows better than to court trouble on the train. Only needs a whiff and the guard will put him off.

'We'll stop soon,' I said to Nanny. 'Hear that, Gus? When we get to Waipukurau Nanny needs to go. I'll take her and you get some tea.'

Gus nodded.

Everybody's a bloody talker, I thought. That's what I am. I should just shut up and let them get on with it.

When we came out Gus was waiting with the tea. Nanny accepted a cup, if not with grace, at least with resignation. She made no bones about taking the sandwich he held out but I shook my head when he offered one to me. I remembered you told me there was only one woman who was allowed to slice the ham. She had to get so many slices to the roll. They still charged more for those thin slivers than they did for the other sandwiches though. When I held out some money to Gus, he just snorted and walked off, so I put it back in my purse. His loss, my gain. Hey, I told myself, at least allow the man a generous impulse, he's not all bad. I remembered how he'd helped us after the quake, how he'd milked the cows single-handedly, got the cans out to the gate, all by himself after Dolly died.

'She's your mother too,' I said. 'I'll manage the cows.'

He shook his head. 'C-c-cam w-was her f-favour-ite,' he said.

Hug and Lynda were the same. It was like the laws of the Medes and Persians. You were the best-loved and that was that. You accepted it too. As though you had a right to be the best-loved.

On our way back to the carriage Nanny went on past our carriage to the group of old women I'd seen on the way in. A mixture of young and old, most of them with the moko. They were sitting on the platform wrapped in blankets, smoking, waiting. While they smoked they played cards. There was a constant stream of talk, raucous chuckles when someone said something particularly smart or funny, often about someone walking past them. If there wasn't a railway station, they gathered at a bus station, or in a sunny spot on a street. Strangers avoid them but if they have to pass them they walk around in a big arc. The inexperienced silly buggers look at them with contemptuous or amused eyes, but when their eyes meet the fierce black coals in the old wrinkled faces sending their contempt right back to them, they quickly turn their heads away as if scorched. Occasionally one of them spits in the gutter. Most of them have a cough. Too much smoking. Or maybe the coughing sickness. Or both.

When they saw me beside Nanny they got ready for

some fun. 'Ko wai tou ingoa?' asked one of the older ones, eyeing me with real malice.

She already knew the answer, old bitch. 'Ruby,' I said sullenly like I was in front of Sister Augustine again.

'Ko wai tou ingoa,' she said again. Old bitch.

Yes, it's me all right, I was tempted to say, I'm the one who ran off with a Pākehā, and never went back. Left Nanny without a talker. Yes, I'm that one. But all I said was, 'Ruby Hineawa Porohiwi Caird.'

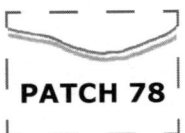

PATCH 78

I was invited to speak at the fiftieth anniversary of the 1951 waterfront lockout, in Wellington, February 2001. This is an extract from the talk I gave called 'Pass It On'.

February 1951. Hot Hawke's Bay days, picnics, babies, the start of the bottling season. Alec Guinness in *Kind Hearts and Coronets* or Orson Welles in *The Third Man*. The pubs close at 6pm, church on Sundays is still more observed than not and children march into school to the strains of 'Colonel Bogey'. At a party one Saturday night, Lillian, Val and I sing 'Goodnight Irene' and my uncle Cliff doesn't join in. My auntie Glad says there's going to be trouble on the wharf.

I remember that party, when in 1986 I decide to write a play about the women's role in the '51 lockout. While the roles of Barnes and Walsh; the Communist, Labour and National Parties; the Federation of Labour and Trade Union Congress have been thoroughly analysed and discussed, I can't find any discussion or analysis of the role of women. There are references to women. Oh yes, everyone says, the women were marvellous. So what's new?

In 1951 I hadn't fully understood what the struggle was about. My uncle Cliff wasn't good at explaining. Apart from our personalities, which made it impossible for us both to be in the same room for more than five minutes without arguing, he had a formidable stutter. He used swear words as stutter-breakers. I remember taking some stewing chops to Auntie Glad and scoffing at the idea that I was breaking the law.

In 1985 the first woman I approached said, 'Oh I didn't do anything. It was the other women, they were marvellous.' I spoke to two unionists in the foyer at Theatre Corporate. 'Good idea,' they said, 'the women were marvellous, absolutely marvellous.'

When I pressed for details, they said, 'Oh they were really marvellous. We couldn't have managed without them.' 'Yes, but what did they *do?*' I said. The bell went for us to go into the theatre and they moved quickly, gratefully, away.

I rang Rona Bailey and had a moan. She said, 'I was mainly involved with the bulletins, you'd be better off asking some of the others. I'll see what I can do.'

I spoke to Elsie Scott. She said, 'Oh no, I didn't do much.' But she invited me round for a cup of tea and after some talk, Elsie said, 'Well I suppose I could tell you a few things we did. It was the other women mainly, they were marvellous.'

I got a letter from Joan Noon, who said that the Women's Committee kept people informed of day-to-day progress. They spread the word when vegetables, groceries, wood, coal, meat, clothing and shoes were available at the depots. They organised sewing groups to make clothes for children. The Women's Committee visited wives who didn't understand the issues and these wives often then became active members. All because someone took the trouble to explain. I suppose their husbands were too busy at meetings to explain to their nearest and dearest.

The Women's Committee cadged donations from people in factories and in shops and raffled them to raise money to pay for social evenings. Accommodation was provided for seamen stranded in Wellington, babysitters were organised so women could attend meetings and work groups. The Women's Committee arranged for wood to be chopped, vegetables to be sorted and pamphlets to be handed out. 'They really were marvellous,' said Joan.

Mary Heppinstall wrote of getting women involved in handing out pamphlets in a hit and run through McKenzies store on Friday night, late-night shopping night. Not all those approached were game. But a few were. The main committees were opposed to these kind of activities. It was unladylike. When a handful of women turned up for a demonstration up Cuba Street, they were put right to the back of the march.

As a seaman's wife, Mary said she should have been invited to debate the issues. She added, 'This would not happen today.' She knew women in Auckland were marching because Freda Barnes had been knocked about by police.

Noeline Harvey wrote of the fear of delivering or handing out illegal leaflets, and doing it anyway. She remembered personal attacks by other women on those who were prepared to be involved. Women were not invited to 'men's meetings'. If you went you invited yourself.

I got a note from my old friend Mary Thomas from Hawke's Bay Women Writers, along with a copy of Dick

Scott's Book. Mary's partner was Cliff Davey. Her note said, 'Cliff is sending you his dearly loved copy of *151 Days*. He was in the lockout in the Carpenters' Union as organiser and used to collect the money. There was a split, and then huge bitterness against Walsh and Butler who supported the Tories to smash the watersiders. Please return the book when you've finished the play.'

From these and women like my auntie Glad I learned about the hardship, the debts that piled up, the years it took to square things and what this did to marriages, families and friendships. I was told of the remarkable compassion and patience of some shopkeepers and farmers, and the intolerance and prejudice of some neighbours and school teachers.

Pass It On, the title of my play, echoes the slogan on the back of the bulletins. My aim was to tell the other side, the women's side. I wanted to show how women's involvement in political struggle is always being interrupted. Babies need clean nappies, there are worries over bills, you have to tell a son he can't have that new cricket bat. A child needs help to cope with bullying, a daughter gets her first period, a mother is anxious and needs reassurance. Meals are a constant interruption. Food has to be queued for, prepared, cooked, put on the table. Children and husbands get sick and need looking after. Police raid your home one night and you hold your breath as they burst into the baby's bedroom. Luckily they don't look under the mattress. A cleaning job at night brings in much needed money so you can't possibly stop doing it.

In between times you help out at the depot, weighing up sugar and flour. And there you have a cup of tea and a laugh with your mates who are going through exactly the same things.

In spite of all this, or perhaps because of it, and while still making time for their priority, which was to get their story out to the public, these women dressed up in hats and gloves to have their photo taken. I liked that.

So I wrote the play and dedicated it to Rona Bailey, who lived the other side of the story. And today I think of all the women who stood loyal through 151 days and I tell you these women were not just marvellous, they were walking bloody miracles.

Pass it on.

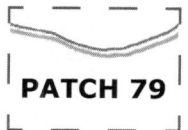
PATCH 79

On 11 January 1993 Bernadette got a call from her boss who offered her a job in Hamilton. They would pay transfer costs including legal fees for selling the house. She was to ring the next day with an answer, and the time frame would hopefully be settled then. We decided to go.

On the next page of my diary that year, there's a list of names under the heading 'OESM research group': Margaret, Tania, Elizabeth, Bernadette, Renée. When I read it, I cannot remember what those letters mean. Am I finally losing it I wonder? It's not that long ago. Twenty-four years. Perhaps, I think, I've already lost it and everyone is being kind and not saying anything? Then I remember. Of course. Otago Early Settlers Museum. Tania's the one who found Emmanuel, my great-grand-father, and we were researching Otago women's history because I was writing *Heroines, Hussies and High, High Flyers* for the suffrage centenary celebrations happening that year.

The idea was the committee and I would research the background and context of women who'd marched for the vote, believed in it but couldn't do anything because of their situation, or didn't want a bar of it because a) they couldn't read, b) they were too busy, or c) they thought the women who wanted it were mad. There were other priorities. Like what were their kids going to eat tonight? Most revolutions are started by middle-class women or men. It's been mainly the middle-class, educated women who've effected change. They have the money and the time. Working-class women are too busy working.

This play would be set in Dunedin so it would include women who were Māori, Chinese, Lebanese, Irish, English, Scottish, Dutch, Jewish and lots of others. I had two images in my mind: the figure of a tall Māori woman standing with a shovel in her hand and a Chinese woman dressed as a man bending over a pan of stones looking for gold. I had other images, lots of ideas, but these were the two main ones. I would wait on the research findings. Something would happen.

That year also saw the publication of my novel *Daisy and Lily* by Penguin, and *Song of the Shirt* by John McIndoe – a collection of three plays for young actors by Paula Boock (*Song of the Shirt*), Fiona Farrell (*Airwaves*) and me (*Form*). *Wednesday To Come* had a successful season in Melbourne. And Bernadette and I moved to Hamilton. I hadn't realised how action-packed 1993 was, but there it is. So I've decided to tackle this year in two patches, and in this one talk about the magic thing that happens when I get an idea for a play, a book, a story.

How do you think of these things? This is a question that comes up at every exchange between writers and an audience, or at a party, in a class, between friends. Often writers say they don't know because they don't. Some things happen because you start writing. You start trusting that they will. For me it's usually a line or an image. Never the plot or the story. That has to be dug up, dusted, buried, dug up again, and is an extremely irritating, exhilarating and sometimes dull process. James Lee Burke describes these processes as 'incremental discoveries'.

Whether you start the actual writing with a detailed plan including character rundowns, plot and storylines and their journeys, both external and internal, or whether you simply start and find out along the way what the hell happens, the book gets written. Some writers are planners, some just start writing. I'm in the latter category. Whether we're planners or pantsers (flying by the seat of our pants) it seems we all finish around the same time. The planners spend time planning before they start – three months, six months, whatever – while the pantsers take time along the way as they find out what really happened to this or that character. There is no one right way. There is only your way.

In *Daisy and Lily* the character Auntie Uncle was the one I thought of first. I was pleased with her name because it seemed exactly the kind of solution a young girl might think of when she was wondering what to call this uncle who'd become an auntie. I chose the names Daisy and Lily because of Edith Sitwell's poem 'Waltz':

Daisy and Lily,
Lazy and silly,
Walk by the shore of the wan grassy sea –

There was something about these lines that I fell in love with and I still love the way they just laze along; it probably took Edith twelve months or more and many,

many drafts to achieve this. So, I had three characters – Uncle Auntie, Daisy and Lily. Just about there, really. I knew nothing about them. I had no story.

Whichever way you look at this, however kind you are, you have to say this is an exceedingly slack way to start a novel. So it's no wonder people look unsatisfied when they ask me how I get ideas and I tell them something like this. Some suspect I'm not telling the secret, because if I did they would all be able to write stories

Leaving aside the fact that Oscar Wilde said the truth is rarely pure and never simple – what did he know? – the truth is that writing is simply putting one word in front of the other. That's all. Okay?

PATCH 80

We got into gear and did all the things you have to do when you move house. In 1993 there are lists after endless lists. Some detail the costs and some say who's doing what.

> Mike $210 (R), Paint $39.95 (R), Anthony (B), Hirequip ladder $30, Weedeater $57.80, Louise $40, Ladder $30, Garage sale $265 ...

And on the lists go ... various meetings of the Otago Early Settlers Museum group ... things like jam, rubbish, bags, cabbages. 'First SITW for the year,' says one entry. I have no idea what this means. Then this: 'Decided on *Under Milk Wood* for the playreading. Rang Play Bureau – $30 for reading copies.' I've drawn a little unhappy face beside this entry:

> **1 February.** Charlie put down.

It's an interesting expression. Putting down. To put down. Put down. I loved Pekinese dogs and had loved Charlie, but over the years, as all dog owners do, I had learned when to be kind to an old or sick pet, and that is before they get to the desperate stage. Willy, a younger Pekinese, and Burns, our black cat, eyed our moving preparations with some anxiety. 'It's okay, you're coming too,' we said, but they still looked at us like, 'Yeah right. So where's Charlie?'

2 February. Chris arrived, stayed for breakfast, then left for Queenstown. Hope the weather's good. Lousy here.

And so on until one day, packing, animal arrangements, goodbye dinners, play reading at the Globe, keys and Globe production sheets to Lisa Warrington were as organised as they were going to be, and I was leaving Dunedin and on my way to Hamilton to a motel, then a rental house on Sandwich Road organised by Bernadette.

Our furniture arrived and we had a Hamilton phone number (yes, those were the days). I was in the middle of unpacking and progressing well, when I got a call from a friend whose lover had left her for someone else, so I invited her for the weekend, then remembered one of the great laws of moving house – *it only gets worse*. But, what can you do? This put a little more speed into the unpacking, and by the time she arrived on Saturday, 7 March, the house was reasonably comfortable. We had one bedroom, she had one, and the door was closed on the other.

Monday I resumed work on *Heroines, Hussies and High, High Flyers*. Bernadette went to Dunedin for work and came back with Burns the cat. After seeing the heartbroken friend off, I had a call from the lover who'd left, could she come next weekend? She had to explain. Her heart was broken too, apparently. Have you noticed how many lovers who leave are heartbroken at what they've done? You'd think it might stop us from doing it? I've been the leaver and I've been the left. It was easier to be the leaver. However, it seemed easier to say okay to the visit — I had to get it over sooner or later, might as well be sooner. George, my brother-in-law, rang. Visit tomorrow. Lunch. 'Great,' I said.

A member of the writing group from SPAN, where I worked in Dunedin, rang to say their work would arrive in the post the next day or the one after. These were the memoirs I'd nagged them into writing. 'Doesn't have to be flash, just something in an exercise book will do,' I'd said, 'as long as there's some sort of record of your life.'

At that stage I wasn't as driven about getting people to write their life stories as I've become, but I was always curious, and I was very curious to know what had made these women so hospitable and friendly, and so willing to give a lesbian feminist a go when she started work at SPAN House in North East Valley. Sure some of them had been daunted and discouraged by life, there are always regrets and heartache, but there was courage and a sense of humour, too, and a real willingness to give something new a go.

Bernadette was doing some study and her first assignment was on industrial relations. I concentrated on writing and getting on top of how the computer worked. I'd bought my first computer, an Amstrad the size of a small house, in 1989, and had not yet come to grips with it. One thing I knew: computers weren't going to go away, so get on with it. Age Concern or Greypower, I can't remember which, offered free lessons, but at the first one I went to, a guy stood up the front and spent half an hour telling us how to turn the damn thing on. So I crossed that off. I tried reading the manual but it was written in a language I didn't understand even though it said 'English Version' at the top. I read an article that was written for women who were struggling with this new technology and the best and most memorable thing it said was, 'Take it easy. You understand and knit Fair Isle patterns? Okay, you're there.'

I finally learned that only repetition did the trick. Learn one thing, do it a lot, then move on to another, and gradually a comfortable sort of relationship with the computer develops. You accept you're never going to know everything. Or even very much. That all you care about is getting the words down in some coherent order. If or when something goes wrong and you can't fix it, accept it as a signal that you'd better get help. Yes, I'm the one you see walking the same route each day for a year, then something happens and I have to find a new route, so the steps are slow and stumbly with lots of swearing at first. Then it becomes familiar and I'm striding out until the next stone in the shoe.

I made one of my best gardens in Hamilton, and I also made the best female gnomes in the entire world there. I had the idea one day when we were walking around yet another garden centre. I said, 'Why are there only male gnomes?'

'Pass,' said Bernadette.

'Why are there no female gnomes?' I asked the woman at the garden centre counter, who wished she was out the back lugging heavy bags of compost and lifting them one-handed onto a truck.

'Because there are only male ones,' she said finally.

'No female ones?'

'None.'

'None at all?'

'That's what none means,' she said, no doubt channelling her mother's words and tone.

I wrote about making gnomes in *Yin & Tonic*, published by Random House in 1998. Learning to deal with wet cement, the vibrating table, the painting, the popularity of the female gnomes took time. I hired a university student to help paint them, but even with that help it got too much so I stopped. Naomi still has her Molly, who seems content enough to stay guarding their place, although the one I gave Bernadette's sister at Little River liked to wander and could be found on one day in the paddock next door and another day visiting the neighbours. She's probably down a ravine somewhere after the big quakes. I didn't have a gnome for a long time, because the two I kept at each side of the garage were stolen. Someone walked up the drive and ran off with my Molly 1 and Molly 2. I rushed around the neighbourhood and asked if people had seen anyone carrying female gnomes. 'No,' was the politest reply, and, 'I'm ringing the police *now*,' the least friendly.

I rang the police and they took down descriptions. 'One a musician and the other a gardener, madam? I've got that right?' They were noncommittal about the likelihood of finding them. A nice female police officer rang me a week later to say there had been no sightings of the gnomes, sorry.

'You *rang* the *police* about two missing *gnomes?*' said a friend.

'They're meant to find lost or stolen things, aren't they?'

'Yes, but valuable things.'

'Well, my gnomes are valuable to me and if I ever find out who stole them they will be not be allegedly sorry, they will be really, genuinely, down-on-their-knees, begging-for-mercy sorry. Okay?'

And, I thought a year or two later, when my desire to hang, draw and quarter the thief or thieves had subsided a little, it gave the cops a story to tell at their Christmas function, or down the police private local.

On 6 July I quote Naomi Wolfe in my diary. Gloria Steinem quoted it in *Revolution From Within*:

> A woman wins by giving herself and other women permission: to eat, to be sexual, to age, to wear a boiler suit or a paste tiara or a Balenciaga gown or a secondhand opera cloak or combat boots, to cover up or go practically naked, to do whatever she chooses in following – or ignoring – her own aesthetic.

And make her own female gnomes, I thought, so some arse can steal them.

'Countrywide won't lend money for a house because my income is irregular and because my age makes a twenty-five-year term unlikely to work,' is one diary entry. 'And because you're both female,' is what they didn't say. Well, sucks to be them because we got the house. I can't remember with which bank, though. I had a good dollop in the bank from the Melbourne performance of *Wednesday To Come* to use as deposit, Bernadette had her job, I had an irregular but reasonably reliable income, we could both finance the repayments.

All of this, and with *Daisy and Lily* out and two plays on the go, a garden to make and granddaughters coming for a visit, the 1993 diary pages are full to overflowing. So much to do, so little time. More things to write, more gardens to make. It was a *good year* and I fell in love with Hamilton and its people (except for the ones who stole my gnomes), and I became besotted with its public and private gardens.

And in the middle of a whole lot of engagements and visits to garden centres, there was a Pride picnic where Willy won the Most Disruptive Dog award. I think they made that category up after he took on a German Shepherd in the grand march and the German Shepherd reared back and tried to climb up its booted, jean-clad, stud-belted, black-singlet-clad owner's arms and made everyone laugh. I was told she was the partner of one of the judges. Hmm. However, I must be fair. Willy also mucked up the handbag-throwing contest by running off with one of the handbags, so this may have been a factor. Or possibly our entrance at the park carrying fold-up seats (whaddarya – what's wrong with the ground?) or our lunch in a hamper with its bottle of cheap bubbles and two stemmed wine glasses (what's wrong with the bottle?) and me wearing a butterfly dress and a large hat might not have helped. Simply following my own aesthetic, darlings.

And if I ever find the sods who took my Mollies then they'll know exactly what that means.

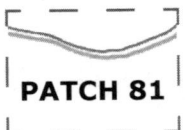

PATCH 81

I hadn't watched TV for a year. I kept it for another year just to test whether I really didn't watch it or whether it was that I was bored by what was on offer at the time. It became clear that the only time my TV set got any attention was when it was dusted, so I gave it away. I don't blame the programmers – they choose what they choose on the basis of research, audience figures and what's available. The fact that it doesn't suit me is a minor bit of fallout, and anyway it might be because I go to bed and read before the good stuff comes on. Or it might be the ads. They drive me crazy.

There's been a wee bit of a hooha recently about the fact that New Zealand books do not sell as well, are not read as much, are not judged as readable by a majority of readers or book-buyers. The reasons given for not liking New Zealand writing, I've read, are fairly uniform – too grim, too mundane, too slow. Well, this is true of some of our books and it's true of some overseas books. This made me start to think about my own reading habits and tastes.

Sometimes when I'm researching something, reading can become dreary, but there's a purpose to the tedium so I tolerate it on the grounds that somewhere in the dull sea is the pearl I'm looking for. I avoid any book that is described by putting the two words 'literary' and 'fiction' together. I never read a preface, a prologue or an introduction.

Recently when I emailed a friend and said I'd bought a new book on Shakespeare, he emailed back and said, 'If you read the preface, introduction and prologue, you won't need to read the book.' I knew exactly what he meant. Academic writers have a preface, a prologue and an introduction because the book first saw life as a PhD thesis, but why, why, why don't they delete these three when it's released to the general public? Maybe some do? Maybe I've just been unlucky? I have no interest in why someone writes a book. It's pure self-indulgence on the writer's part to tell me. Sure, sometimes at writers festivals people in the audience ask you why you wrote the book, so you're forced into a corner and have to tell yet another lie.

How do I choose books? I'm mostly immune to reviews, but not always. A friend might recommend a book, or I might read a poem online or in a paper and buy the collection. I can be swayed by a title. Recently I bought a book for a present, simply because it was called *Doug the Bug that went Boing!* (It was by Sue Hendra.) I read a lot of crime novels and non-fiction. I avoid anything that has 'bestseller' blazoned across the cover. I read book lists, look up any book I think I might like, check out writers that sound interesting, take a punt on an unknown because I like the description of the book. When I find a writer I like, I read everything they've written. I gobble them up like a hungry mower. And I re-read them. At least half the books on my shelves or on my iPad are books I've read before I bought them. I've got more women writers on my iPad at the moment than I have male writers, but if I look in another six months that might have evened out. Reading doesn't bore me – it amuses, teaches, appals, reveals, restores me.

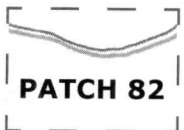

PATCH 82

Teaching is one of the most fascinating, frightening, fully engaging things I do. Preparation and performance are the keys. I have often thought about why I like teaching so much. There's an attraction about being in charge of this course, this class, this group of strangers (if it's a first class), but there is also a deep-rooted unease – perhaps this time what I offer won't work? These people are relying on me to help them, and what's more, they have paid for this assistance and agreed to write the obligatory ten pages a week to attend *Your Life, Your Story* (if they don't agree they don't come on the course). I am there to help them steer their small kayak through the choppy waters, the sharp rocks, the sudden surprising waterfalls that writing a book about their life entails. I am there to tell them that writing is hard work but worth every minute you put into it.

What makes me keep on doing it? Because I get asked when the next course will be? Because someone contacts me and wants me to mentor them? Because someone's mum and dad have not left any real details of their life and they don't want that to happen to their own kids? It takes most of us until we're in our forties before we become remotely interested in what went on before our important lives began, so it's often people this age and older who contact me wanting to write their life stories.

I think we should all have a go at writing our life story even if all we do is list events and dates like an elongated grocery list. This not only does some good things for the person writing it but also becomes a source of interest and pleasure for their descendants – those they know, those yet unborn, two or three generations on when the world has changed. Those who live in the new time read these memories and get a much more illuminating and personal account of everyday life than historians can give. And as I say in my book *Your Life, Your Story*, don't forget the sex, drugs and rock'n'roll.

Look at how the 1950s are described. A grey decade, we're told. A decade waiting for the sixties to happen. A mere blip between the more exciting times of war and the advent of TV, *Hair*, the pill, protests about the Vietnam War, the seventies, feminism, the land march, Ngā Tamatoa, the eighties, political protests and so on.

Apart from the 1951 waterfront lockout and its aftermath of anguish, anger and acrimony (but not boredom), there was Elvis. Elvis Aaron Presley. How could any decade be dull with him in it? Elvis Presley was the end of civilisation as we knew it. Then there was rock'n'roll, Bill Haley and His Comets, Johnny Devlin, Ella and Louis and Sarah Vaughan, all weaving their magic.

For us the 1950s meant the happiness of having our own home, and then – like they wanted to end the decade with a bang – there were the novels. *Spinster* by Sylvia Ashton-Warner, *The God Boy* by Ian Cross, *The Race* by Ruth France, *Owls Do Cry* by Janet Frame. My elation after reading these books was as high as if Louis

Armstrong had suddenly led a jazz band down Emerson Street. I was happy, excited and, as one followed another, incredulous. Something very exciting was happening in New Zealand writing. These weren't the names that were held up as epitomising the best of writing in Aotearoa – there was only one male author in that list for a start. These were strong voices, all different, all memorable. They spoke of lives not far removed from me and those around me. And to add to my excitement, I wrote an article, then another and another, which were all accepted for publication. Yes, the fifties were exciting but maybe you had to be there instead of looking back from another generation.

There's a certain challenge about creating teaching notes. They chart the outline of the session – where I want it to go, what new things will be introduced and what will be reinforced. How do you put some flesh around the bones? Include your own ideas? Find or create examples, stories, writers, poets, lyricists to illustrate what you're talking about? Well, first you stare into the distance a lot. You realise as you prepare your teaching notes that this is an act of faith in yourself and in the class.

Then there's the performance aspect – that edge, which from the start of a class to the end, is like being onstage. Most times what you prepare works. Other times the notes and ideas that sounded so great when you thought of them now seem dull. You're faced with the reality of expectancy, hope and uncertainty, and realise you're on the wrong track. That quote you thought so good is perhaps not as illustrative of the topic as you'd hoped – but are you stuck with what's in front of you? Of course not. You dredge up something. Fear does that. In this situation fear is a great driver. The adrenalin rush, the brain responding, the words starting to flow. Then as you swerve back to the notes you link in the quote via an example you only just thought of ... and it works. Light breaks.

So that's teaching. Preparation, performance, pleasure. Yes, pleasure. Because yet again, you've steered that little kayak around the rocks – the quiet and riotous times, the happy and hideous times – and arrived safely at the shore, the end of that class, and you're already looking forward to the next one.

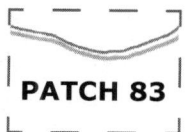
PATCH 83

My brother died on 23 June 2016. He was a year and two weeks younger than me and would have been eighty-six on 2 August.

I always think of him as Jimmy, the name we called him till he got old enough to tell us he wanted to be called Russell. I've written about how he thought his name was Jimmy until he started school at Greenmeadows Primary and then was told his name was Russell. For a few years, he stuck with Jimmy because his mates and everyone else called him that, but then he decided to go with Russell and has been so ever since. Although he didn't mind me forgetting sometimes and calling him Jimmy.

He was a skinny, small, quiet boy to everyone else, but when he was with his mates he was irreverent, always ready for fun and a great joker. I've told this story before but here it is again for those of you who haven't heard it. He, Val and I were all sitting in the long fescue, smoking old tea leaves wrapped in cigarette papers of Rose's that Jimmy had stolen. The tea leaves were horrible, so we progressed to the dry stalks of the fescue that grew liberally around our place at that time. We used to have competitions for 'blowing off', and this time Jimmy let off a big fart and said, 'The next train down that track'll be the goods.' Then he rolled around laughing at his own joke. I was helpless with laughter and Val fell back in the fescue and laughed so much she wet her pants. Val was prone to do this when she laughed too much, but it didn't matter when it was 'just us'.

When Jimmy got a bit older he used to bike to rugby practice at Taradale Park on a one-wheeler, with his rugby boots tied together by their laces and hanging around his neck. At some stage he decided to join the Port Ahuriri Caledonian Pipe Band and learned to play the bagpipes. He practised on the chanter in the woodshed because Rose wouldn't have the noise inside. I don't blame her. It was pretty awful.

He looked very handsome in his green tartan kilt and jacket as he marched along on a street march playing the pipes. Lots of girls fancied him but he was a bit shy. Although he joined in the learners' dances that the Labour Party organised, he really learned to dance in our kitchen with either Val or me and the radio, our old Zenith, providing the music, while Rose pretended to be reading. He still has that radio.

Jimmy married Lillian, whom we all loved, and they had Howard and Lynda. We spent some school holidays together, along with Val and George and their kids – Steve, Robin, Peter, Vonny and James.

One day last year when he visited me, we had a hug and then went inside and Jimmy sat down on the couch and said, 'I thought it was normal.'

'What?' I said.

'The way we lived when we were kids. I didn't realise till I got a bit older and saw how other people lived that it wasn't. Normal.'

When Jimmy was a little boy, Rose took him with her to the coroner's inquest on Stan's suicide, which was held in Wellington. She sat him on her knee all through the inquest. There was a very special relationship between her and Jimmy, and he loved her and she loved him, always. When he talked about Rose, he usually ended by saying, 'She was so little,' which seemed to him to make the things that happened to her so much worse.

As a boy he worked after school at the butcher's shop, which he hated, and then when Rose found him an apprenticeship, he left and went to learn to be a boot repairer. Rose was a fervent believer in doing an apprenticeship because it meant he would 'have a job for life'. After she died he kept on till he finished the apprenticeship because that was what she would have wanted, and then he took off, worked in butter and cheese factories, bought a motorcycle, studied for his boilerman's tickets, passed the exams all the while doing a full day's work, and made a life in that business, which saw him eventually become a highly thought of manager.

Lillian's death knocked him badly. He got a little morose, a little more inclined to lay down the law. He kept a big garden, restored an old Armstrong Siddeley. Then some time later he met Jill and they've been happily together for the last twenty-one years.

I remember Jimmy for lots of things: his sense of humour, his fairly conservative outlook, his work on the Rotary welfare committee to help solo mothers buy shoes for their kids, his insistence on daily walks. He was a good gardener and we only ever competed over those stupid Potato Toms, which flashed on the gardener's world scene for one season.

Jimmy was sometimes irritable, short-tempered and sharp-tongued, just like his sister, and always generous, kind and funny. He liked his meals on time, which meant lunch at midday, even at Christmas, and only grinned and said, 'Midday *is* lunchtime,' when anyone teased him.

We laughed at the same things. Whenever we asked our brother-in-law, George, how he was, he'd say, 'I'm on the way out,' and sigh heavily. He said this for about fifteen years before he died earlier this year. Jimmy rang me and said, 'Well, he might have taken a while to get there but he's finally out,' and we both laughed affectionately.

I think, no, I *know* there were times in our lives when my brother wished I'd shut up and stay home quietly and knit, but whatever I did and however my life went, I was always welcome at his place.

About a fortnight ago he rang me. 'Russell here,' he said as he always did, 'how are you?' I told him about the play I was working on and the plans for it, and although I'm certain that privately he thought I was crazy, he laughed and said, 'Have a happy time.'

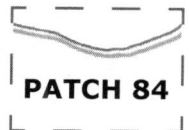

PATCH 84

Massey and Auckland universities were completely different experiences for me. At Massey I was an extramural student, allowed in to the campus on sufferance during the holidays. I enjoyed the work, although my marks were erratic because they depended on how much time I had to study. I always passed but only occasionally got above a B. Mainly C+. The courses I liked best were Greek literature and one about Louis XIV, the Sun King, who, along with his contemporaries, believed fervently in the divine right of kings. Why wouldn't you if you were born into that family? I knew nothing about him before that year apart from an occasional mention of him and his court in a novel.

The Victorian literature paper I did was okay but I was a little bored – I'd already read the Brontës, George Eliot, all of Dickens' novels and had loved the strong passions and anger of *Villette* by Charlotte Brontë. I had also already read all I could about the Brontë family. I still have this image of Emily refusing to lie down for death – Dylan Thomas 'do not go gentle into that good night' kind of stuff. I think Emily had to lie down right near the end though.

In 1972 when I was studying Greek literature, I went along to the internal part of the course and found I was to be billeted in a two-bed room. I wasn't pleased.

However, my room-sharer turned out to be a young woman called Rachel McAlpine, future poet, playwright, novelist, non-fiction writer, and dancer in the Crows Feet Dance Collective directed by Jan Bolwell. We became friends then and are friends still. She'd already achieved illustrious university degrees and diplomas and, from memory, was doing some sort of education paper. She was such fun. Totally different life experience from me and at least ten years younger; I was forty-three and, if I've worked it out properly, she was in her early thirties, but we talked and laughed like we were old friends.

I remember this particular extramural course with huge pleasure, partly because of Rachel and partly because the Greek literature class party was the best of any other course party I'd been to. I hadn't enjoyed other course parties I'd attended so I decided not to go, but a couple of students prevailed on me. I can't remember their names but whoever you were, thank you. Rachel asked if I'd mind sleeping in another room on the Saturday night because she wanted to have a party for her group in the bedroom. I was happy to do that. I forgot to ask her if it was a good party. I usually see Rachel once a year at Jamie Bull's whitebait party so I must remember to ask.

In 1979 being an internal student for a year at the University of Auckland was like stepping onto another planet. I felt there was no way I could measure up to those students who had already completed two years of internal study. A lot of them knew each other and were friends, and all of them knew the ropes. I was going to turn fifty in July and everyone else looked about eighteen. They were insiders and I was, or felt like I was, an outsider.

I enrolled in Russian history and Victorian literature because the professor said I should, and when I thought about it later I realised this was because he needed the numbers. Someone else taught us about the Great Vowel Shift. This was the one who set an essay around the use and non-use of the verb 'do' in any one scene from *Macbeth*, for which I got a 'D'. At the top he wrote, 'I don't think you understood the question.' A man of perception.

The third paper was called *20th Century Women's Literature*. It was taught by the wonderful Aorewa McLeod. She opened a door and ushered me into a room full of rich treasures and I was free to take what I wanted. I just loved that course. Even the thought of it now brings me pleasure. There were lots of American writers I'd never read before: Kate Millett, Jill Johnston. I knew about Gloria Steinem – I'd been buying *Broadsheet* since 1972. I'd read the English writers like Rebecca West and Vera Brittain, Dorothy L Sayers et al. I'd read a few of the modern UK feminist writers and their feminist magazine *Spare Rib*. I'd read Germaine Greer, the Australian feminist who was arrested here in Auckland for saying 'bullshit' in public. I knew Gertrude Stein's work, first because she was mentioned by Ernest Hemingway and second because I'd tracked her down and read about her, then I read her *Autobiography of Alice B Toklas*. I'd read Virginia Woolf's novels quite a few years before, but I'd never read the poetry of Adrienne Rich and she and her work became one of the stars for me. 'Diving into the Wreck' – 'The words are purposes. / The words are maps' – is, for me, the best poem ever written about writing.

And I love this quote from *Sources*:

That's why I want to speak to you now. To say: no person, trying to take responsibility for her or his identity, should have to be alone. *There must be those among whom we can sit down and weep and still be counted as warriors.* [My emphasis.]

The exam paper asked us to write an essay comparing three writers. I chose Gertrude Stein, Virginia Woolf and Jill Johnston. With a kind of mad desperation I wrote the essay, proving, at least to my satisfaction, that there were similarities between Virginia (1882–1941), Gertrude (1874–1946) and Jill (1929–2010). They all broke new barriers, all had an individual style, all shocked their contemporaries with ideas and behaviours that didn't conform to the mores of the time and all of them wrote works that lasted, although Jill Johnston's *Lesbian Nation* is possibly not read much these days except by feminist historians, and Stein's *Autobiography of Alice B Toklas* is probably read more than any of her other works. Woolf's works still sell in the thousands, and her life and death have recently been retold in the film *The Hours*, from the novel by Michael Cunningham, and there is a series available on Lightbox and Netflix called *Life in Squares*.

I got a good mark for this essay – a B+, I think – but whenever I see Aorewa, usually at a funeral these days, she says, 'I should have given you an A.' Rubbish, Aorewa, I was amazed/relieved/happy with my mark.

I left a cleaning job at Theatre Corporate to work part-time in the university bookshop. A perfect job. Other members of staff were friendly, helpful, sharp and funny. Gil Hanly (wonderful photographer) was one, and Kitty Wishart (the manager) was another. I remember the damn till in that shop too because it seemed to always run out of paper during the busiest time of day and always on my watch. I used to get very sweaty changing the roll while the queue of customers began to trail out the door, some patient, some not.

I got to know Auckland Art Gallery and some of the walks around the university. I walked along K Road and Dominion Road as well. And then there was graduation, which seemed like a miracle for someone who didn't get past primary school. To make it even better, I had been offered a job teaching English and drama at Long Bay College. The teacher who'd taught social studies when I taught English at Wairoa College – the one who had nearly killed himself shifting huge and heavy pot plants onstage for the garden scene in *Charley's Aunt*, and who drove me home after the last-night party with us both singing 'Guide Me, Oh Thou Great Jehovah' as the car wove slowly around the roads trying to find home – mentioned me to the principal. So I had a job to go to.

PATCH 85

From *Jeannie Once*, (Victoria University Press 1991), first performed at the Fortune Theatre, Dunedin, on 15 June 1990, with the following cast:

    Jeannie Brannigan … Julie Edwards
    Margaret May O'Connor … Billie Atkinson
    Honoria Wishart … Hilary Norris
    Martha Lewis … Sima Urale
    Mary O'Malley… Bernadette Doolan
    Barney … Sean Allen
    Alec McPherson … Martin Inwood-Phelan
    Geroge Lamont … Barry Dorking
    Bessie Marchmont … Molly Anderson

The play is set in Dunedin in 1879.

SCENE SIX

MARY'S kitchen. Wednesday lunchtime.

BARNEY is seated at the table. MARY approaches with a pot of stew. She serves some to BARNEY. On the table is bread, a pot of tea and a jug of milk.

MARY: Alec's late.

BARNEY: He's off seeing Larnach's foreman again.

MARY: He's a very frustrated man.

BARNEY: He's not on his own.

MARY: Do you not think so?

BARNEY: We gather at the Golden Nugget all the time.

MARY: Not Alec McPherson, I'll be bound.

BARNEY: Oh no, Alec's not a frequenter of saloons … Dens of iniquity.

MARY: He might have a point.

BARNEY: I thought you enjoyed the billiards.

MARY: I do. Wasn't it your father himself who introduced me to the game?

BARNEY: It is billiards we're talking about?

MARY: You're not too old to have your mouth washed out.

BARNEY: I beg your pardon. I'll go and get the soap if you like.

MARY: Don't forget you're meeting with Mr Mowat this afternoon. Four o'clock. Mind you're neat and tidy.

BARNEY: The fact is, Mary, darling, I've got another appointment.

MARY: Then you'll just have to cancel it. James Mowat is expecting us.

BARNEY: I can't break this appointment.

MARY: What sort of appointment can take over

from one that might settle your future?

BARNEY: I've got an audition.

MARY: Don't talk soft. Who'd give you an audition?

BARNEY: Mr Lamont, that's who.

MARY: *(this is a real shock)* Oh Barney.

BARNEY: Don't stir yourself into a tizzy, he doesn't know who I am. Mary, I haven't always shown it but I hope you know I do appreciate the way you've looked out for me and I'm very grateful. But I have to decide this for myself.

MARY: You owe me nothing. I did what Diccon thought was best.

BARNEY: It's a pity he didn't think about that before.

MARY: And it's a pity you don't take some responsibility for your own part in the affair before making judgements about others.

BARNEY: It was an accident.

MARY: I'm not saying anything else. But it's stupid to blame your father for what happened.

BARNEY: I don't blame him.

MARY: No. It's very clear who you blame, Barney, so let's hear no more rubbish about being grateful.

BARNEY: I want to go on the stage and if Mr Lamont says I've got what it takes, then that's what I'll be doing. I can't help it, Mary, I have tried, honest to God, I've tried to settle on being a tailor but I wouldn't suit.

MARY: Very funny. So it's George who's to have the say. How does he look?

BARNEY: The crowd last night loved him.

MARY: I'm not asking what the dregs of Dunedin think.

BARNEY: There were some very respectable people there.

MARY: At Music Hall?

BARNEY: We're talking high class, Mary. Even in Dunedin they've heard of George Lamont and Bessie Marchmont. He did Polly Perkins and they clapped and cheered as if it was the first time they'd heard it.

MARY: He is good, is George. How's Bessie?

BARNEY: She's having trouble with her throat.

MARY: Probably a judgement. She's the biggest gossip in the business.

BARNEY: Mr Lamont wanted to know if we'd met before.

MARY: Damn. What did I tell you?

BARNEY: Can I help it if the theatre's in my blood?

MARY: You're growing into the spitting image, in more ways than one. Diccon always liked his own way. And the risk is all for nothing. George won't give you a job.

BARNEY: He will if you'll help me.

MARY: Oh you're a real joker, aren't you.

BARNEY: Please, Mary, just a little of your time.

MARY: Are you admitting there are some things I can do better than you?

BARNEY: I never had any doubts about your ability on the stage.

MARY: Suppose I might be able to quote that sometime.

BARNEY: Thank you. You won't regret it. I knew I could rely on you.

JEANNIE enters.

MARY: I had some hope that you might see sense. I need my head examined.

BARNEY: Now there's an admission. What do you think, Jeannie?

JEANNIE: Leave me out of it.

MARY pours her some tea. ALEC enters

ALEC: Good news, Jeannie, love. I saw Walter Riddell again and Mrs Larnach wants a married couple all right *and* she wants the wife for a seamstress.

JEANNIE: Darning and mending, Alec.

ALEC: With the possibility of some sewing for Mrs L and her daughters.

JEANNIE: Darning and mending.

MARY: (*gesturing to ALEC*) Some tea?

ALEC: Walter says if she takes a fancy to us we could count on being permanent.

MARY: Or some stew? It's nice and hot.

JEANNIE: If Mrs Larnach and her daughters want new gowns they don't go to the woman who patches their sheets.

MARY serves stew anyway.

ALEC: There's a cottage on the estate. Small, Walter says, but it could be ours.

JEANNIE: You're the one saying *ours*, not me. I've been straight with you, Alec, you've taken yourself down this path.

MARY: Your tea, Alec.

BARNEY: I don't think he's interested, Mary.

ALEC: This job could mean security.

JEANNIE: I didn't come here to curtsey my life away with yes ma'ams and no ma'ams. I could've done that at home.

BARNEY: But just think, Jeannie, you'd be married to Alec.

JEANNIE: Do you ever shut that smart little gob of yours?

ALEC: If you're looking for trouble, Barney O'Malley, you've come to the right place.

BARNEY: It's my big mouth, Alec. It just opens wide and out the words pop.

ALEC: *(To JEANNIE)* You'd be a seamstress. I thought that's what you wanted.

JEANNIE: I'd be a sewing woman. There's a difference. I'd rather stick with old Pengelly. Miserable sod though he is, he doesn't expect me to kiss his feet every time I pick up a box of shirts. It's not fair for you carrying on like this.

ALEC: Fair? What's fair? I'm going mad for want of work. I don't want to spend the rest of my life bowing and scraping to actors for tips.

JEANNIE: But it's all right for me to grovel to Mrs Larnach? No and no and no.

PATCH 86

Presents

Freddie gives me a card.
To Renée on the back
next to a house with flowers.
Inside another house
with windows and flowers.
I hope you have. A good time.
I made this. Card especially.
For you.

Tui brings me a painting.
Red and purple slashes,
'don't mess with me' stuff.
She brings me a painting.
I give her a banana.
She gives me daffodils.
Where is this going?

Jasper, Keeper of the Jewels,
gives me a smile.
It's a little bit cheeky.
He's started walking.
I think he'll go far.

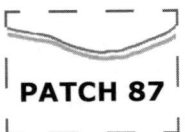

PATCH 87

In February 2008 I'd arrived back home at my apartment in Wellington after working at the Robert Lord cottage on Titan Street, Dunedin, for two months. While I was there I'd visited my cousin Adrienne, whose cancer was getting progressively worse. She died in April. I didn't know Adrienne very well but we enjoyed each other's company, and she liked that I brought along poems about gardens to read to her. I mucked around in the little garden at Titan Street. Walked around Dunedin.

Back in Wellington, I was to continue teaching on the Whitireia creative writing course at their Porirua campus. I liked going there because there was always parking available. I prepared class notes for scriptwriting and contextual studies and checked out the room I'd be teaching in.

On 6 February, Chris, Naomi and Abbie came to play five hundred and at my request brought poems to read. 'Finger food', I noted. I must have been more interested in playing cards than providing a proper dinner.

I went to plays at Downstage and Circa. This was easy to do because they were both within reasonable walking distance. I liked living in the city. I liked walking around it. Up Molesworth, up Hill Street, onto Tinakori Road and back down Bowen, then along The Terrace to home. A friend of a friend took me on walks around the hills.

She slowed her pace and did shorter walks of only two hours when she was with me. I joined in Around the Bays walks and once walked from Wellington city to Miramar to prove to myself I could do it.

I'd met Sarah Delahunty at a Playmarket conference the year previously, when she'd been delegated to drive me to and from the conference. We both knew of each other but had never met, although during one of our conversations it turned out I had written Sarah a letter about my admiration of her very successful play *Stretchmarks*. We both liked talking about writing and decided we should do it on a regular basis, and also decided to think about what we'd like to work on when we were together, so something constructive would come out of our meetings. As a result Sarah wrote *2b or nt 2b*, with characters from famous plays living as teenagers now. Hamlet, Helena, Antigone, Hedda, Irena and Masha – all of them up to date with technology and filled with angst – eventually meet, after various byways, on a bridge in Lower Hutt.

Described as a 'comic gem' by the reviewer in the *Dominion Post*, the play was a standout right from its exciting first night at Downstage on 18 February. The quality of this play is due entirely to Sarah's imagination and hard work, but I felt pleased that it came into being because we agreed to talk about writing on a regular basis. Sarah ends her introduction to the book of the play with a description of what's at the heart of her characters:

> Like the heroes and heroines they are, they discover that the answers to their questions and their unhappiness lay in each other. The only answer there is.

This was a good year for another reason – I realised that I wanted (needed) a garden. That pots on the patio weren't enough. I wouldn't have been without the experience of living in Wellington city – I loved my time there – but eventually, inevitably, necessarily, I had to have a garden.

I wanted to see Donna Banicevich Gera's play *Anton's Women* when it was performed in Auckland and to see some old friends while I was there. Donna had written a draft of it while a student in my class. Amelia Batisich was the first writer to show us what growing up in the Dalmatian community was like and I was glad Donna was carrying the torch. I enjoyed the play … and then there in the audience was an old friend. We both screeched hello at each other and managed to forge our way to hug – unexpected and lovely.

I made numerous trips to Ōtaki before I shifted in April 2008, bringing bits and pieces out with me to save packing them. I met with blinds and curtains people, sorted New Zealand Post and their botched re-direction. On 6 April I emailed Elizabeth Smither my new email address. Elizabeth was my mentor when I did the poetry course and at the time I noted:

> How does one collect 60 good poems? Lots of people do collect 60 poems but they're very rarely all good – Elizabeth is the exception. Hers are all good at first reading and even better a few readings on.

And this:

> I am so over all this dismantling and packing – I hate it – it's like childbirth, you forget the horror and then once it starts again you think oh yes, oh God yes …

Nearly every page of this diary has a note, a reference, a list or a memory of gardening. With exceptions:

> My neighbour has an I LOVE JESUS T-shirt.
> Went to Arrowtown to do a weekend workshop.
> Chris brought largesse – cakes plus bread for Pam.

Then back to business:

> Pam and Ian brought back my worm farm, which they've been looking after since I moved from the Hutt.

In November 2008 Barack Obama was elected president of the United States, and the next day I drove to Whanganui and bought a little yellow car. A Hyundai Baby Getz. I loved it from the moment I first saw it and still do. The thing about a yellow car is you never lose it in car parks. Tim came for the weekend and we went looking for a new kettle. I bought a purple one.

> **21 June.** Saw the doco by Clare O'Leary on JC Sturm. Loved it, bought the DVD, played it many times.
>
> **21 July.** Told Pip I was thinking of resigning as a tutor at the end of the year. We talked. She was very nice. Agreed to mull it over. 'Turning eighty,' she said, 'is no reason.'
>
> **30 July.** Power went off late afternoon and stayed off. Had candles, matches and good torch. Thought of food in freezer. Power off for two days. A friend drove up from Raumati with two hot-water bottles and they were still warm when she got here.

14 August. John Vakidis [writer of that lovely play *Tzigane*] is going to mow my lawns.

17 August. Sent Naomi a text for her birthday – it wasn't her birthday but Abbie's. Naomi's is the day after. I do this every time. Next year I'll get it right. [I didn't. I got it right *this* year following a quick text to Naomi to ask.] Chris is going to China, sooner rather than later. He and Zuzu are talking, discussing and planning. She lives in Guangzhou. Tim will happily take Chris's stuff and is glad of it. I'll look after his books.

8 September. Sharon rang. Yesterday Naomi fell through the skylight when she was on the roof terrace of the flat she shares. Badly bruised but no broken bones.

11 September. Had email from Fiona Samuel. Her screenplay based on my novel *Does This Make Sense To You?* has got the nod. She's been so staunch and her script is so good. Hope all goes smoothly.

I flew down to Dunedin for the Robert Burns Fellowship reunion and stayed with Anna at Warrington. On Saturday I note: 'The session went well.' I think that must be the one Witi, Rawiri, Keri and I did. Keri was late, she'd mistaken the time. Rawiri had to go as soon as it was over because he was catching a plane to Berlin.

28 November. Abbie and Saskia had a housewarming at their place in Mt Cook but I couldn't go.

29 November. Naomi and I went to Auckland to the wrap party for the film of *Does This Make Sense To You?* called *Piece of the Heart*. Party was held on Sunday 30th. It was lovely to see Fiona again and to meet the cast …

Keisha Castle-Hughes, Annie Whittle – who was in the first production of *Setting the Table*, Rena Owen – who asked where could she get a copy of the novel, and Emily Barclay. Home again to the garden ...

11 December. Worked in garden most of the day. Cleaning, taking out veges that have served their time. Then went to Watson's to buy plants. Lettuces, silver beet, parsley, asters, zinnias, pansies, a swan plant, a bay tree [still going], a Ted's red tamarillo [not].

I got the tamarillo to spur on the other one I had but both of them remained sulky, so out they went. And that is only half of what happened in 2008. A year, I have decided, that was no more significant than any other year but probably representative of most. If you think I'm a bit carried away with gardening, here are some definitions I live by:

Spade: Something to lean on while you muse about life.
Secateurs: Implement with a hidden agenda – be afraid.
Weeds: All Blacks of the plant world – they never lose.
Fork: A pronged implement you stick through your foot.
Old pots: Five-star motels of the slug world.
Garden stakes: Long sticks that fall over.
Pruning roses: Existentialism among the pricks.

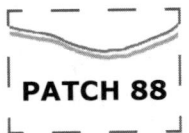

PATCH 88

In 2019 I was diagnosed with macular degeneration, and Sue Wootton of the website *Corpus*, a forum for conversations about medicine and life, commissioned me to write about it.

L et there be warriors ...

> *There must be those among whom we can sit down*
> *and weep and still be regarded as warriors.*
> —Adrienne Rich

I was taught to read before I was five by my mother, Rose. I read stories, then long books, then joined the library, changed both Rose's and my books, read both, went out to work at the woollen mill when I was twelve and read my way around libraries wherever I worked. I worked at all sorts of jobs, then when I was forty, I began studying for an extramural BA degree. I taught in my forties, and at fifty I began writing plays. Since then I have read and written (worked) every day.

Now I am ninety. I've just finished teaching a course on writing memoir, and The Cuba Press has just published my first crime novel, *The Wild Card*.

Two years ago I was told I had macular degeneration. This is a desolate and unhappy place to be. Being labelled 'vision impaired' doesn't go anywhere near describing the impact of it on my life. As a reader and a working writer it is the worst thing that has ever happened to me.

Yes, I now have a large screen and large type; yes, I now read only ebooks and get all my news online. Technology rules, okay? And I am grateful for it. But it's the same old grey gauze curtain I'm peering through and it's thickening all the time.

What annoys me, out of all proportion, is that everything I've done to help myself has had to be explored/discovered/instigated by … me. A couple of friends have passed on information. Blind and Low Vision NZ (formerly the Blind Foundation) has been helpful but needs to drag itself into 2019. When you join you still have to choose between Māori and Pākehā. My mother was Māori, my father Pākehā, so I want to include both. But I had to choose one, so I chose my mother.

The ophthamologists, the eye specialists, have done no more than pronounce the verdict: 'macular degeneration'. 'You will always be able to find your way around,' one said, as if he was reading the weather forecast. 'You will be able to see shapes.'

None of them, not one, has offered any help, suggestions or advice on how to deal with it. No information about possible aids, not even the information that white light is better than yellow. They were happy to accept the large fee though.

I have a white stick and at first I used it all the time. But I discovered that people treated me differently from when I walked with the yellow-and-black hi-vis stick I'd bought in Dunedin. When I use the white stick no one says, 'Kia ora Renée.' In fact they edge around me, trying to look as though they haven't seen me. When I use the yellow stick they say, 'Kia ora Renée, how're you doing?' So that's the stick I've been using.

I sound angry and I am. This is huge for me. I have had cancer twice, and the second time, I had a bilateral mastectomy. I've had heartaches and happiness and I know, because every damn medical person tells me, that I'm old. Like it's something I might not have noticed? Old age is to blame for everything. But my old age doesn't make the medical professionals so uncaring or dismissive – they do that all by themselves.

Just because I'm ninety and have macular degeneration does not mean I stop thinking, working, feeling, living, peeling potatoes (with great care), peering at the first spring iris. Just because I'm ninety doesn't mean I lose the power to feel, to experience, to know when I'm being patronised.

It's a constant struggle to be recognised as a living, breathing, intelligent female human being anyway. I still have to correct some of the medical people from calling me Mrs. And others have to be stopped ticking the 'retired' box without asking me first. Hello? I go to work every day, mate. The fact that I'm ninety does not change that. And if one more person, most likely male, tells me that exercise and walking will bring me joy and love, so help me, I'll do something drastic.

I am not alone. There are still people who read books, garden, laugh, sing, smell roses. There are still people who hold out a hand when I'm coming down steps. And there are still those among whom I can sit down and weep and still be regarded as a warrior.

PATCH 89

From *The Wild Card* (The Cuba Press 2019)

Ruby stopped by the path over the large culvert, ignored the stream glaring palely through the gloom and stared at the back of the house. The door on the side opened into a room that used to be the laundry, and the door in the middle opened onto a passage that led to the main corridor, passing the kitchen on the way. There was a rickety fire-escape ladder from the top floor to the lower one. It stopped a good human-length from the ground so you'd have to let yourself fall the last metre or so. God help you if you had a broken leg or were old and frail.

Well. This wasn't too bad. No ghosts of Matron or the balaclava man. No drowned Betty lying on the path. Why had she built up such a fear of the place? It was nothing but a sad old house that had outlived its time. It wasn't responsible for what human beings had done inside its walls. She took hold of the window frame and shook it. The house grumbled in protest. The window was secured by little levers each side – not really burglar-proof. If she slid her knife up the side, where age had warped the wood, it shouldn't be too difficult. The old back door was a bit creaky but held firm. Same thing. If she pushed the knife between the lock and the frame surely it would give enough to force the tongue?

She leaned on the door and the house moaned like a ghost was walking the old passage. Human footsteps? Ruby listened intently.

Shivery possibilities trembled in the air.

Okay. Time to go. She'd come back.

She turned and stared at the shed. The door hung open a little bit so she pushed it, clicked on her phone torch and had a look inside. A mess of cans and bottles, some Kentucky Fried packets, Big Mac burger bags, even a used condom. Yucko. Must have been really drunk or really desperate.

Ruby started down the other side. Her arm caught the end of a wet branch and water splashed her jeans. Cold needle tips on warm skin. This light had exactly the right feel for a Swedish noir movie. The dark shapes of the bushes and trees, misty air and the sound of water dripping. Any minute someone called Arne would step out of the bushes, throw away his cigarette and say in a thick accent, 'Okay, Ruby, time to talk.'

The lower she went, the more she became aware of the change in light. It hadn't exactly been well lit further up, but down here it was really dark. The clinging moisture embraced her in its damp grey arms, made her want to be home, warm and alone, sipping a glass of red, listening to one of those old songs that Kate had liked and she liked too. Sam Cooke, she thought, 'A Change is Gonna Come'.

Change has already come and I hate it.

One of the bushes moved.

She stopped thinking, breathed quickly, heart beating like a snare-drum tattoo. An illusion caused by the wind? Hardly. This was a breeze by Porohiwi standards.

First rule. *Don't muck around.*

She swerved away, and now it was definite. The shadow moved too. *Shit.*

She was three quarters of the way down the slope. Too late to go back. What to do? *Take cover? Take off? Take them on?* The old mantra.

Not much choice.

She felt in her pocket, yes, okay, phone. Turned. Took up the stance. The shadow moved faster now, unworried about noise as it crashed through the bushes. *Fuck.*

He came out of the dark, a running black ghost. Black balaclava, black trousers, black top. He was not quite as tall as Ruby but bigger. She yelled and kicked out.

Got the top of his leg, which must have hurt but not as much as if she'd connected with his balls.

Momentum carried him on. Anger helped. She ducked but he was too quick. A closed heavy fist thudded on her cheek, another sharp slap around her left eye. Blood slid down her face and throat. He hit her on the arm and she staggered.

Her heart was pounding, serious pain a second or two away. Don't fall, she told herself, *don't fall*, but when he hit her again she fell. Her face hit the ground. As she skewed around she yelled again.

Make as much noise as you can.

She kept yelling, grabbed at a bush and hung on.

Then voices from the street. Someone laughed.

She screamed. A moan was all that came out.

He grabbed at her jeans, found the phone, got it out, threw it. Felt in the other pocket. Car key. Threw it.

A final kick and he was gone.

And so was she.

That was the start of my first crime novel, *The Wild Card*, published by new publishing house, The Cuba Press. After it came out Steve Braunias, books editor at online news site *Newsroom*, asked me to write him something about the background to the novel, so I did, and here it is.

If it hadn't been for my mother, Rose, I'd have been a state ward. When my father shot himself he knew she was living in a house that went with the job. He knew if he wasn't there doing the job she'd be evicted. He knew she had no money. He knew she was Māori. His mother had said to him, 'If you marry that Māori girl, I'll never see you again.' She died a couple of years before he did, but two of his brothers ignored their mother's racism and were generally around on their days off. One of them supplied wood and they both stole fruit for us. But no good going over old ground, right?

Wrong.

I had to go over this old ground when I decided to write my crime novel, *The Wild Card*. No escape. No flinching. Full-on stare, okay? I had been one of the lucky ones. Who did I think I was to turn away?

So Rose made the hard choice. She was twenty-seven. Three kids. No money. Was she tempted to put us in a Home as she was advised to do? I only heard her talk about it once and that was to Daisy, a British immigrant who let Rose a room in an old villa and whose husband was in jail. She must have asked Rose why she didn't stick us in a Home. Rose said, 'If I put them in a Home, they'll be separated.'

Then she said what became something of a mantra. 'Renée will be all right, Jimmy will be all right, but Val is soft, she needs them to look after her.' By soft she meant tender-hearted. And it was true. Val was much more inclined to believe the sad stories, while Jimmy and I would think, 'Look, mate, you've got a bed, you know where your next meal is coming from, you're okay.'

Now I think, no I know, that the three of us would have been sexually and physically abused, starved, wrecked. Jimmy and I would probably have survived, Val probably would not.

> *We are, I am, you are*
> *by cowardice or courage*
> *the ones who find our way*
> *back to this scene*
> *carrying a knife, a camera*
> *a book of myths*
> *in which*
> *our names do not appear.*
>   —from 'Diving into the Wreck' by Adrienne Rich

I thought of this poem all the time when I researched, read, talked, wrote and worked on *The Wild Card*. The thing was that I wanted to write this crime novel in a style that was easy to access, funny, triumphant. I wanted to write a hero whose lips don't fucking quiver, who doesn't turn to the nearest male to fight on her behalf, who has doubts, fear, memories that sometimes overwhelm her but that also arm her, protect her, inspire her. I didn't want it to be a 'literary' novel. I wanted it to be a novel that people who live near the wreck would read and have a laugh and a cry over.

Obviously the wreck in this case is the New Zealand state care system, and even more obviously I had to dive down and talk to people about things both of us would rather not talk about.

But we look into each other's eyes and we know. We know those eyes.

This Royal Commission of Inquiry into Abuse in Care? You have to ask if anything will ever be done. Will those who abused the kids ever be brought to justice? You've got more chance of winning the Melbourne Cup on a donkey.

So I dived. I faced the wreck. I came back with *The Wild Card*.

PATCH 90

At ninety, I went into social isolation early to keep safe from Covid-19. When lockdown began on 25 March 2020, I was asked by *The Spinoff* to contribute to their Lockdown Letters series. Here I have combined two of the letters, published in March and April of that year.

Yes, a few cyclists out and about today. I remember my first bike, bought from Farmers around 1942, five shillings a week, all up nineteen pounds. Oh the freedom, the independence. Before then I had to cadge rides with my brother and sit on that horrible crossbar that boys' bikes had. I don't see many people being doubled now.

The other day when I was out for a walk I was stopped by a cop in a big red car. 'Where you from?' he shouted.

Now I'm short, skinny, grey-haired, and I use a yellow-and-black hi-vis stick, so for a moment I wanted to tell him to piss off. Instead I waved vaguely. 'Down there,' I said.

'Okay you can cross over,' he said.

Maybe he thought I was an escapee from the retirement home down at the beach? I wish I'd given a more coherent answer, but I'm not used to having my movements questioned.

Yesterday I walked up to the medical centre to get the flu vaccine, the furthest I've walked since I went into self-isolation.

It was strange walking past silent shops on a practically silent street. A teenage boy, a woman and a black dog passed me, and as we observed our social distance, I felt an almost overwhelming desire to explain why I was walking up empty Main Street. There were three people waiting outside the pharmacy, so I crossed over and walked on to the medical centre.

They've set up a tent, with a few chairs, on the marae lawn – in case it rains, I suppose. Someone shouted my name and I said yes, and a cheerful guy did the deed, and then I sat on the porch in the sun for the obligatory five minutes and watched cars pull up and go, pull up and go. I walked back home feeling something like Hillary must have done after he reached the summit of Everest.

Full of self-congratulations, I decided to climb the next peak and clean out the store cupboard.

I went into self-isolation a week before the country-wide lockdown. There had been plenty of publicity around the fact that old people, especially those with underlying health problems, were at risk. But hey, it wasn't the thought of getting sick and dying that drove me, it was the thought of being called stupid – yeah, nah. I know, very shallow.

I am so, so sick of hearing people – radio hosts, online writers, commentators – using the term 'the elderly'. It's such a grey ghost of a term. It makes us 'the other' and reveals, in some cases, a deep irritation that we need to be considered at all, a suggestion that it's probably a good thing if we're all knocked off, because we're such a drain on the community's purse and time.

Prime Minister Jacinda Ardern calls us 'older New Zealanders', which means she sees us as part of the general population and not a group of outliers huddled on the edge somewhere. I like the word old, but a lot of my contemporaries aren't so keen. I think they see being described as old as meaning they've joined a cohort they've always dreaded, whereas I see the word 'old' as a stronger and more accurate (maybe more vigorous?) term than 'elderly'.

I've lived longer than any other female in my whānau ever, so have entered new territory. This is a place that has its ups and downs and is very interesting, if sometimes irritating. The thing is, I know the eventual destination, but I don't have a map so I'm sort of making it up as I go along ... with a lot of help from my friends ...

Once upon a time there was a little girl who went to the Greenmeadows Methodist Sunday school, where she was told that every good deed she did was another gold star in her crown and when she died and went to heaven and met Jesus, he would hold the crown, sparkly with good deeds, and say: 'Well done, Renée.' (Or Reeny, as they called me.)

All I can say is that a good few of my friends will have gold stars in their crowns when this is over.

Seven strawberries in the garden today.

PATCH 91

Naomi comes to cook

She brings the salad (green beans, red peppers, garlic, pine nuts), we drink red wine, talk about how what is given – land, a heart – is forever, this year, next year, sometime, never, how one falls in love and why, what was it really that changed my world.

There were days when I thought if I explained the position clearly it would all be okay – now I know better. I fell in love with a principle, I say.

But – she's my moko after all – so I say it began, it began … the laughter, the tears, one day, one moment, one beat, I looked out – all these kids playing in my backyard – and *whammo* it occurred to me that if we lived *there* my kids would be classed as coloured, there would be none of this here business, cowboys and Indians and a Chinese sheriff, a Māori good guy (he had the hat), Pākehā/Māori Indians behind bushes or round the corner or up the woodshed roof chucking plums, sometimes just the stones, and yelling gotcha …

I hope you don't mind me asking? She places the lightly fried haloumi on top of the salad.

Everything starts with a moment and that moment leads to a letterbox with Fuck off Bitch on it and that leads to Fowlds Park and *Patu!* and who cleans the toilet and why don't we say anything when he hits her – and why why why and then why not why not? Simple.

One moment leads to another moment to this moment when she leans back on the couch, we sip wine and she does not ask was it worth it, Nanny?

So – so – I say – it's the salad, the mix of chemistry and context, the after-taste of moments, some bitter as rocket, heady as mint or wry as chives – your choice, my choice – dressings of oil, vinegar, rue or rosemary.

I regret nothing, I say. Nothing? Nothing.

Tonight

the fence of brown plaited wood
the line of hills the sky glowing over

this particular day when the sods
give way to the fork and for a moment

all the hands that ever dug
are in the sweat rolling lazy on your skin

and there it is again
the feeling of being part of a story

ACKNOWLEDGEMENTS

To everyone who nagged me into writing this memoir – you see what it led to?

To my whānau, who have helped me with facts, dates, feedback, encouragement, food and poems.

To Jan Hughes, for your work on Porohiwi's story.

To Mary McCallum of Mākaro Press, who got in touch with me two seconds after I announced on Facebook that I was writing a memoir and said she'd like to publish it. This was a supreme act of faith. I hadn't even put a word on the screen at that stage. I also want to thank Mary for her intelligent reading of the manuscript, and her care and attention to the details and infelicities that had passed me by.

To Paul Stewart, for all the work you've done to make *These Two Hands* look so good and for your awe-inspiring work on the index.

To Sucheta Raj, for your hard work and good questions.

To Penny Howard and Doug Lilly, for the lovely images on the cover.

And to all of you who appear in *These Two Hands*, thanks for the memories.

Renée

We acknowledge the following publishers and editors, who kindly gave us permission to include extracts from Renée's work:

'Change of Life'. *Broadsheet* 111 (Nov 1983).

'Dear Publisher'. In *Yin & Tonic*. Auckland: Random House, 1988.

Daisy and Lily. Auckland: Penguin Books NZ, 1993.

Does This Make Sense To You? Auckland: Penguin Books, 1995.

Finding Ruth. Auckland: Heinemann, 1987.

Jeannie Once. Wellington: Victoria University Press, 1991.

Kissing Shadows. Wellington: Huia, 2005.

'Let There be Light: macular degeneration and me'. *Corpus: Conversations about Medicine and Life*, 4 November 2019.

'Lockdown Letters' adapted from #3 and #8. *The Spinoff*, 29 March and 3 April 2020.

'Novelist faces the wreck of life in state care'. *Newsroom*, 20 November 2019.

Pass It On. Wellington: Victoria University Press, 1986.

Secrets. The Theatrescript Series, edited by David Carnegie. Wellington: Playmarket, 1982.

Setting The Table. The Theatrescript Series, edited by David Carnegie. Wellington: Playmarket, 1982.

The Skeleton Woman. Wellington: Huia, 2002.

The Snowball Waltz. Auckland: Penguin Books, 1997.

Tiggy Tiggy Touch Wood. In *Playlunch: Five Short New Zealand Plays*, edited by Christine Prentice and Lisa Warrington. Dunedin: University of Otago Press, 1996.

Wednesday To Come. Wellington: Victoria University Press, 1985.

The Wild Card. Wellington: The Cuba Press, 2019.

Willy Nilly. Auckland: Penguin Books, 1990.

Other work by Renée mentioned in the book:

Asking For It, 1983.

Born to Clean, 1987.

Form. In *Song of the Shirt: three one act plays for young actors*. Dunedin: McIndoe, 1993.

Heroines, Hussies and High, High Flyers, 1993.

Te Pouaka Karāhe (The Glass Box), 1992.

The MCP Show, 1983.

Touch of the Sun, 1990.

What Did You Do in the War, Mummy? 1982.

For more of Renée's writing, go to **WednesdayBusk.com** or **playmarket.org.nz/playmarket/renée**

And we acknowledge work by the following authors quoted in *These Two Hands*:

Bollinger, Nick. *How to Listen to Pop Music*. Wellington: Awa Press, 2004. Used with permission.

Davies, William Henry. *Leisure. In Songs Of Joy and Others*. A C Fifield, 1911.

Dickens, Charles. *Hard Times*. Bradbury & Evans, 1854.

Goldman, Emma. *Anarchism and Other Essays*. Mother Earth Publishing Association, 1910.

Hardy, Thomas. 'After the Last Breath'. *The Collected Poems of Thomas Hardy*. Wordsworth Editions, 2002.

Henderson, Jim. *The Exiles Of Asbestos Cottage*. Hodder & Stoughton, 1981.

James, P D. *Time to Be in Earnest: A Fragment of Autobiography*. Ballantine Books, 2001.

Noyes, Alfred. 'The Highwayman'. In *Forty Singing Seamen and Other Poems*. W. Blackwood and Sons, 1907.

NZ Truth. An unnamed article, 1934.

Oakenstar, Jess Hawk. 'Dear Gertrude Stein'. In *Leave a Little Light Behind*. Used with permission.

Picasso, Pablo. Posthumous publications, 1990s.

Reuben, David (Dr). *Everything You Always Wanted to Know About Sex (But Were to Afraid to Ask)*. McKay, 1969.

Rich, Adrienne. *Diving into the Wreck: Poems 1971–1972*. WW Norton & Company, 1973.

Rich, Adrienne. *Sources*. Heyeck Press, 1983.

Sitwell, Edith. 'Waltz'. In *Façade and Other Poems 1920–1935*. Gerald Duckworth & Company Limited, 1930.

Steinem, Gloria. *Revolution from Within: A Book of Self-Esteem*. Little, Brown and Company, 1993.

Wairoa Free Press. An advertisement, 2 June, 1877.

Wolfe, Naomi. *The Beauty Myth: How Images of Beauty Are Used Against Women*. Chatto & Windus, 1990.

INDEX

2b or not 2b 401
4th Floor 142

Allen Hall Theatre 297
Allen, Sean 392
Amey, Sunny 268, 272, 331, 340–41, 347
'And as we gather' (poem) **151**
Anderson, Molly 392
Angelou, Maya 14
'Anzac Day' (poem) **78**
Ardern, Jacinda 417
Armstrong, Dave 347
Artists Against Apartheid 41
Asbestos Cottage 338–41
Ashton-Warner, Sylvia 380
Asking For It (revue) 217
Atkinson, Billie 392
Auckland: 25, 37, 39, 41, 72, 80, 109, 111, 114, 224–26, 236, 256, 271, 332, 362, 389, 402, 404; University 387–88

Bailey, Rona 249, 332, 348, 361, 364
Barclay, Emily 405
Bargh, Brian 244
Barrett, Mick 156
Batisich, Amelia 402
Baxter, James K 288, 347
Belvoir Street Theatre 217
Billing, Roy 109
Bland, Peter 347
Bludgers on the Dole (play) 130–31

Bollinger, Nick 311
Bolton, Heather 109
Bolwell, Jan 166, 272, 287, 331, 340–42, 388
Bone People, The (Keri Hulme) 221
Boock, Paula 366
Born to Clean (revue) 217–19
Braunias, Steve 412
Bridger, Bub 155
Brittain, Vera 134, 137, 389
Broadsheet 125, 127, 131, 137, 211, 224–26, 228, 293–95, 389
Burns (cat) 316, 330, 369–70
Byrne, Pip 346, 403

Cameron, Anna 297
Cancer Society 101–02, 144, 148–49
Cape Verde 120
Carey: Rosalie and Patric 288
Carnegie, David 109, 256
Carpenters' Union 363
Castle-Hughes, Keisha 405
Chapman, Ann 309, 318, 335–36
Charley's Aunt (Brandon Thomas) 267, 318, 391
Charlie (dog) 369
Child, Shirley 230
Chilvers, David 109
Christchurch 176, 229, 274, 293
Circa Theatre 247–48, 400
Civic Theatre 270

Cockrem, Marilyn 201, 348
Colquhoun, Glenn 336
Corpus 406
Cross, Ian 380
Crows Feet Dance Collective 287, 388

Daisy and Lily (novel) **39–41**, 349, 366–68, 375
'Dance, The' (poem) **21**
Davey, Cliff 363
Davies, Sonja 311
'Dear Grandmother' (poem) **353**
Delahunty, Sarah 146, 272, 291, 335–36, 401
Does This Make Sense To You? (novel) **171–73**, 223, 404
Doolan, Bernadette 48, 100–03, 125, 127, 129, 137–38, 220, 222–23, 227–30, 234–36, 240–43, 248–50, 252, 255–56, 262, 293, 295, 314, 316, 345, 349, 365–66, 370–72, 374, 392
Dorking, Barry 392
Downstage Theatre 60, 293, 335, 347, 400–01
'Dowsing' (poem) **279**
Dudding, Ruth 60
Duncan, Lee-Anne 297
Dunedin: 48, 72, 76, 103, 123, 208, 224, 229–30, 248–50, 263, 270, 288, 292, 296, 314, 366, 370–71, 392, 395, 400, 404, 407; Feminist Collective 229

Eccles, Marylin 227
Edmond, Frances 109
Edwards, Julie 392

Farrell, Fiona 366
Federation of Labour and Trade Union Congress 360
Feminist Arts Festival 256
Finding Ruth (novel) **97–99**
First International Women Playwrights Conference 220, 234
Frame, Janet 81, 380
France, Anna Kay 221
France, Ruth 380

George (cat) 54–59
Gera, Donna Banicevich 402
Gibson, Judith 25
Gilchrist, Alec 270
Give Us a Kiss and I'll Tell You (William Dart) 228
Glenroy Auditorium 252
Globe Theatre 48, 248, 251, 270, 288–89, 370
Gore 11, 22, 56, 72, 119–20
Grace, Patricia 234
Grace-Smith, Briar 348
Grant-Sutherland, Donald 26
Greenmeadows: Methodist Sunday school 417; School 30
Greer, Germaine 389

Hall, Roger 220
Hamilton 126, 327, 329,

365–66, 370, 372, 375
Hamilton, Bill 90–91, 93–94
Hamilton, Carol 90, 93–94
Hamilton, Joy 91
Hanly, Gil 390
Harcourt, Kate 60
Harris, Jocelyn 229, 316
Harvey, Noeline 362
Havelock North 179
Hawke's Bay: 55, 88, 104, 117, 161, 167, 179, 360; Women Writers 362
Haynes, Lois 227
Hemingway, Ernest 91, 245–46, 389
Henare, George 109
Henderson, Jim 338, 342
Heppinstall, Mary 362
Heroines, Hussies and High, High Flyers (play) 365, 370
Hill, Kim 189
Holst, Alison 183
Homewood, Tim 60
Homosexual Law Reform Bill 240
Hood, Kate 109
Hotere, Ralph 288
House, Richard 297
House To Let, A (play) 334
Hughes, Jan 166
Hulme, Keri 221, 404
Huria, John 244
Hurst, Michael 25
Hutchison, Caroline 26

Ihimaera, Witi 404
Invercargill 22, 24, 72, 121
Inwood-Phelan, Martin 392
IRIS theatre group 248

Jansen, Adrienne 336
Jeannie Once (play) **392–98**
John O'London's Weekly 67–70
Johnston, Jill 224, 389–90
Joy, Heather 142

Kanawa, Phil 348
Kāpiti Writers' Retreat (Kahini) 142
Katene, Merania 250
Kightley, Oscar 347
King, Hilary 218–19, 228, 230
King, Michael 347
Kissing Shadows (novel) 122, 217, 346–47, **355–59**

Labour Party: 30, 88, 90, 92, 94, 244, 360, 384; Ōtaki Women's Branch 244
Lane, Amanda 109
Le Harivel, Kirsten 142
Leafy greens: a fairy tale (story) **191–94**
Lees, Nathaniel 109
Leuthart, Michelle 60
Little, Andrew 336
Long Bay College 391
Lord, Robert 246, 248, 400

Macdonald, May 106, 107
Mailer, Norman 224
Man Alone (John Mulgan) 342

Maniapoto, Moana 307, 308, 311
Mansbridge, Frances and Albert 231
Maraetōtara School 104
Maraetōtara/Waimārama Country Women's Institute 104
Marsich, Anna 230, 316, 340, 346–48, 404
Massey: High School 271; University 80, 387
Mayo, Andrew 26
McAllister, Ralph 331
McAlpine, Rachel 287, 388
McDowell, Pam 152, 403
McGee, Greg 75, 219–20
McGill, Roger 26
McGuire, Michaela 142
McIntyre, Peter 26
McKay, John 109
McKinnon, Kingi 349
McLean, Donald 167–68
McLeod, Aorewa 389–90
MCP Show, The (revue) 217
McRae, Elizabeth 109, 256
McTavish, Terry 248
Mead, Margaret 138
Mercury Theatre 109
Metekingi, Merle 335
Miller, Nola 290
Millett, Kate 389
Milligan, Christina 227
Ministry: of Foreign Affairs 222, 234; of Women's Affairs 229
Missy (dog) 330
Montgomery, LM 17, 31

Mooney, Kay 104–07
Morrissey, Michael 26
'Mum and the bull' (poem) **285**

Napier: 11, 20, 34, 67, 76, 104, 106–07, 117, 119, 121, 132–34, 156, 163, 245, 259, 260, 274, 288–89, 327–28; Intermediate 34; Repertory Theatre 272
National Poetry Day 337
New Zealand: Festival of the Arts 220; Women Writers' Society 104, 161
Niu Sila (Oscar Kightly and Dave Armstrong) 347
Noon, Joan 361
Norris, Hilary 48, 248–49, 251, 392
Norris, Richard 249

Oakenstar, Jess Hawk 218, 228
Obama, Barack 403
O'Leary, Clare 403
'Old people are' (poem) **324–26**
'Old songs' (poem) **333**
Oliver, Bill 347
'Once upon a time' (poem) **96**
'Open home' (poem) **344**
Orchid Society 251
O'Regan: Mary 229; Pauline 229
O'Sullivan, Aileen 109

Otago: Early Settlers Museum 365, 369; University 117, 222, 249, 296–97
Ōtaki: 142–44, 147, 200, 244, 258, 266–67, 269–72, 283, 288–89, 291, 317, 337, 402; College 335; Players 270, 288–89; *O Temperance!* (Mervyn Thompson) 106, 319, 348
Owen, Rena 405

Paekākāriki 268, 272, 291, 331
Palmerston North 71, 117, 143–44, 146, 258–59
Paratene, Rawiri 404
Parr, Larry 221
Parry, Marion 26
Pass It On (play) **25–28**, 334, 363
'Pass It On' (speech) **360–64**
Pitts, Priscilla 256
Playmarket 109, 125, 127, 131, 249, 256, 296, 401
Prast, Simon 26
Prentice, Christine 297
Presbyterian Support Services 248, 251
'Presents' (poem) **399**
Prince Tui Teka 307

'Rain' (poem) **174**
Randell Cottage writers' residency 260
'Red moon time' (poem) **354**
Rich, Adrienne 389, 406, 413

Richardson, Miriam 141
Robert Burns Fellowship 103, 117–18, 123, 222, 288, 292, 314, 404
Robert (cat) 316
Rosier, Pat 347

St Joseph's School 13
Samuel, Fiona 404
Samways, Anna 297
Sandys, Elspeth 347
Saphira, Miriam 143, 229
Savage, Michael Joseph 30, 244, 336
Sayers, Dorothy L 65, 69, 134, 137, 389
Scott, Elsie 361
Secrets (play) 109, **256–57**
Setting the Table (play) **109–13**, 127, 256, 293–94, 405
Shand, Brett 250–52
Sheehan, Lucy 60
Simpson, Tony 270
Skeleton Woman, The (novel) 121, **195–98**
Smither, Elizabeth 402
Snowball Waltz, The (novel) **176–78**
SPAN community group 248, 250, 252, 371
Spare Rib 211, 389
Springbok Tour 1981 240
Stapp, Ann-Marie 336
Stein, Gertrude 121, 218, 245, 259, 390
Steinem, Gloria 374, 389
Stopes, Marie 135–36

Sturm, Jacquie (*also* Baxter) 347, 403

Taki Rua 249
'Tall woman in a frame' (poem) **139**
Taradale School 29–31, 353
Taylor, Miles 26
Te Mānuka Trust 221
Te Waka Toi 287
Te Wānanga o Raukawa 269
Theatre Corporate 25, 361, 390
Theatre Federation 267
Theatrescript 109, 256
Thomas, Mary 362
Thompson, Mervyn 106, 221, 293–95, 319, 348
'Tiger Country' (poem) **265**
Tiggy Tiggy Touch Wood (play) **297–306**
Touch of the Sun (play) **48–53**, 248, 255

United Women's Convention 137–38
Urale, Sima 392

Vakidis, John 404
Venables, Ivo 64
Venables Willis 63–64, 134
Victoria University Press 25, 60, 312, 392
Villa Maria College 229

Waddell, Jane 60
Wairoa: 13, 72–73, 80, 106, 125, 138, 155–59, 162–64, 167, 169, 220, 246, 266–67, 307, 309–10, 315, 318, 320, 328, 346, 348, 391; College 159, 289, 309, 318, 346, 391; Little Theatre 105, 137, 155, 157, 158, 246, 267, 319, 320, 348; Museum 267
Walker, Geoff 222
Wall, Alison 26
Ward-Lealand, Jennifer 25
Warrington, Lisa 297
Waru, Ray 221
waterfront lockout 1951 25, 360, 380
Watson, John 25
Webby, George 221, 296
Wednesday To Come (play) **60–61**, 126, 131, 223, 251, 253, 270, 272, 296, **312–13**, 334–35, 366, 374
Wellington 42, 60, 103, 117, 137–38, 142, 144, 146, 174, 221, 249, 260, 263, 268, 288, 290, 293, 342, 360, 362, 385, 400–02
Whaanga, Mere 348
Whānau: **Abbie Marie** 76, 126, 129, 142, 156, 181, 220, 268, 309–10, 328, 400, 404; **Adrienne** 400; **Alitalyia** 349; **Charles (Harmer)** 13, 157–59, 162–65, 351; **Christopher (Taylor)** 22, 42–44, 47, 73, 125, 128, 130, 142–47, 149, 156, 179–80, 186, 203, 222, 234, 259, 273–74, 308–09, 332,

346, 348, 351, 370, 400, 403–04; **Cliff** 11, 121, 158, 216–17, 360–61; **David (Taylor)** 73, 82, 109, 142, 156–57, 159, 211–12, 220–21, 225–26, 256, 259, 267, 274, 309, 319, 328–29, 346, 349, 351–52; **Emmanuel (Jonis,** *also* **Jones)** 119–21, 199, 365; **Freddie Renée** 42–43, 46, 77, 149, 399; **Frederick** 274; **George (West)** 56–59, 253–55, 371, 384; **Gertrude (Jones née Knowles)** 119, 121, 327–28; **Glad** 361, 363; **Grace (Brown née Harmer)** 13, 351–52; **Hoot** (*also* Peepi) 220, 328–29; **Howard** 384; **Jimmy** (*also* Russell) 11, 14–15, 18, 33–34, 71, 89, 94, 135, 216–17, 253–54, 285, 353, 383–86, 413; **Joseph (Jones)** 119, 121; **Kokotui (Lambert)** 349; **Kokotui (Lewis)** 13, 166; **Laurie (Taylor)** 72, 104–07, 126, 133, 135–37, 155, 158, 179–80, 183–85, 225, 253, 267, 273–77, 319; **Lillian** 217, 253–54, 360, 384–85; **Lynda** 254, 358, 384; **Mick** 36, 38; **Naomi** 42–45, 76, 126, 128–29, 142, 156, 220, 269, 310, 328, 349, 373, 400, 404, 418; **Olive** 32, 120–21; **Ormond** 30, 119–20, 135, 158, 217, 338; **Porohiwi (Lewis)** 13, 166, 168–69; **Puti Mary (Harmer née Lewis)** 13, 36, 158, 162–64, 166, 199, 351; **Rose (Jones née Brown)** 11–20, 30, 32–37, 54–56, 64–66, 68–69, 71, 90–94, 118, 121, 123, 125–26, 129, 131, 133–34, 136, 155–56, 158, 160–61, 163–64, 217, 244, 260, 273–74, 327–28, 340, 347, 351, 383–85, 406–07, 412; **Rubina (Taylor née Barr)** 273–75, 277; **Saskia (Booiman)** 142, 268, 309, 404; **Sharon** 125–26, 128–29, 142, 156, 220, 268–69, 309, 328–29, 404; **Stanley (Jones)** 14–15, 20, 22, 68, 117–19, 120–22, 260, 327, 347, 384; **Sula** 329–31; **Timothy (Taylor)** 60, 73–74, 82, 105, 142, 157, 212, 225–26, 258–59, 268, 309, 328, 346, 349, 351, 403–04; **Valerie** 11–12, 14, 18–19, 29, 33–34, 89–91, 94, 133, 216–17, 223, 251–55, 273, 285, 351–52, 360, 383–84, 412–13; **Vonny** 102–03, 254–55, 384; **Walter** 13, 143, 351–53; **William (Brown)** 13; **Zuzu** (*now* **Susana**) 42–47, 144, 404

What Did You Do in the War, Mummy? (revue) 217, 224, 227–28, 316
White, Helen 127, 296, 316
White, Jenny 128, 130
Whitehouse, Davina 60
Whitireia Polytechnic 142, 346, 400
Whittle, Annie 109, 405
Wild Card, The (novel) 406, **409–11**, 412–14
Willis, Norman 64
Willy (dog) 204, 221, 329–30, 369, 375
Willy Nilly (novel) **204–10** 221
Wishart, Jude 229
Wishart, Kitty 390
Wolfe, Naomi 374
Women's Committee 361–62
Wood, Cliff 60
Woolf, Virginia 389–90
Wootton, Sue 406
Workers' Educational Association (WEA) 131, 231
Working Title Theatre 294

Yin & Tonic (anthology) 100–02, **321–23**, 373
Your Life, Your Story: book 380; workshop 142, 379